Management for Professionals

For further volumes:
http://www.springer.com/series/10101

Michael Missbach • Josef Stelzel •
Cameron Gardiner • George Anderson •
Mark Tempes

SAP on the Cloud

Michael Missbach
SAP Competence Center
Cisco Systems
Walldorf
Germany

Cameron Gardiner
Tokyo
Japan

Mark Tempes
Carnegie
Australia

Josef Stelzel
Leimen
Germany

George Anderson
Cypress
USA

ISSN 2192-8096 ISSN 2192-810X (electronic)
ISBN 978-3-642-43604-8 ISBN 978-3-642-31211-3 (eBook)
DOI 10.1007/978-3-642-31211-3
Springer Heidelberg New York Dordrecht London

© Springer-Verlag Berlin Heidelberg 2013
Softcover reprint of the hardcover 1st edition 2013
This work is subject to copyright. All rights are reserved by the Publisher, whether the whole or part of the material is concerned, specifically the rights of translation, reprinting, reuse of illustrations, recitation, broadcasting, reproduction on microfilms or in any other physical way, and transmission or information storage and retrieval, electronic adaptation, computer software, or by similar or dissimilar methodology now known or hereafter developed. Exempted from this legal reservation are brief excerpts in connection with reviews or scholarly analysis or material supplied specifically for the purpose of being entered and executed on a computer system, for exclusive use by the purchaser of the work. Duplication of this publication or parts thereof is permitted only under the provisions of the Copyright Law of the Publisher's location, in its current version, and permission for use must always be obtained from Springer. Permissions for use may be obtained through RightsLink at the Copyright Clearance Center. Violations are liable to prosecution under the respective Copyright Law.
The use of general descriptive names, registered names, trademarks, service marks, etc. in this publication does not imply, even in the absence of a specific statement, that such names are exempt from the relevant protective laws and regulations and therefore free for general use.
While the advice and information in this book are believed to be true and accurate at the date of publication, neither the authors nor the editors nor the publisher can accept any legal responsibility for any errors or omissions that may be made. The publisher makes no warranty, express or implied, with respect to the material contained herein.

Printed on acid-free paper

Springer is part of Springer Science+Business Media (www.springer.com)

I think the Internet was the last big change. The Internet is maturing. They don't call it the Internet anymore. They call it cloud computing

Larry Ellison

Preface

Since the turn of the millennium, the IT industry has regularly been besieged by new hype. Derived from the word *hyperbole*, hype denotes a phenomenon whereby the media devotes such a high level of attention to something that it appears to be more important than it really is. One of today's most hyped terms is cloud.

What started with adaptive infrastructures and was later called grid and utility computing has now condensed to metaphoric clouds.

"Real clouds" in the sky have an interesting property: You can't see what's inside them, a sometimes-disastrous result for planes cruising at low altitude without the benefit of radar. In the case of cloud computing, the mantra is that you don't really have to know exactly what's inside a cloud as long as the price for the requested cloud service is acceptably low enough.

This may be sufficient to store your personal pictures and host a web page. But what about mission-critical applications and the sensitive data they contain? And what to do with application architectures established decades ago that simply are not "cloudable?"

SAP systems and solutions are among the most mission-critical applications within enterprises, tasked with maintaining highly sensitive data and business-critical processes. The majority of these systems are based on an SAP Basis architecture which was developed literally a century ago. Moving these systems and solutions to the cloud is not necessarily straightforward if even warranted. Even the most careful of system migrations may suffer from hiccups, obstacles, and other challenges despite the generally undisputed benefits of cloud computing.

In numerous conversations with our own SAP customers around the globe, we have learned that there is a need for a concise overview about the technologies, architectural concepts, and proven practices necessary to avoid such obstacles and challenges and successfully run SAP system landscapes atop various cloud infrastructures. This book is in response to those conversations. Our hope is SAP on the Cloud helps provide our readers with the necessary instrumentation to safely lift off and sail through the clouds, bypassing obstacles and circumventing most of these challenges on the way to quickly realizing the cloud's benefits.

Contents of This Book

This book provides an overview of the various facets of building and operating SAP applications on cloud infrastructures. It describes and discusses the latest developments, challenges, and suitable solutions, and also outlines future trends where plausible or possible.

To ensure that this book is also useful to readers who do not consider themselves to be "gurus" in this area, this book explains in detail the backgrounds of several possible cloud solutions in the context of various SAP applications and components. Examples are provided throughout this book in order to make the reader aware of essential but perhaps less-obvious points. However, keep in mind that this book concentrates exclusively on the setup and operation of the SAP infrastructure; it does not give details related to installing and customizing the SAP software itself, nor does it deal with the much more complex tasks involved in business process implementation and reengineering.

Chapter 1, *A Little History of Cloud Computing*, describes how the development of IT has culminated in the concept of cloud computing. In preparation for the topics dealt later in this book, it describes the different flavors of cloud computing and their relevance as a possible SAP platform.

Chapter 2, *From R/3 to HANA*, deals with the technical characteristics of the most commonly used SAP solutions from ECC to HANA and discuses how well they fit into the various cloud concepts described in the first chapter. This chapter gives you a good understanding of the very specific requirements of SAP systems and why not any cloud offering is a good fit for SAP.

Chapter 3, *Service Levels for SAP on Clouds*, takes you through the definition of appropriate service levels for SAP systems in cloud environments. It focuses on the prediction of the necessary resources to fulfill the SLA and how to measure and bill their actual consumption. Additional topics include service guarantees and availability as well as innovative billing tools for SAP systems.

Chapter 4, *Security Aspects for SAP Systems*, deals with one of the key topics for the decision between public and private cloud computing. The chapter provides a detailed description of the risks of cloud computing as well as hints how to harden the x86 operating systems typical for clouds.

Chapter 5, *Change and Configuration Management*, discusses the topic of lifecycle management of ever-changing business processes in cloud environments. It focuses on cloud-specific constructs such as resource pools, failure domains, scale units, health models, stateless computing, service profiles, and more, in the context of SAP.

Chapter 6, *How Public and Private Clouds Work*, assesses the technical concepts of cloud computing. Amazon AWS and Microsoft Azure are described as examples for the technologies used in public cloud; VMware vCloud and Microsoft Private Cloud as examples for software solutions used in private clouds.

Chapter 7, *From Traditional IT to Public Cloud Computing*, discusses the controversial topics of governance, control, and security of highly shared, multi-tenant computing environments. This chapter also provides an overview on a current cloud infrastructure offering for SAP and eventually presents an outlook on new developments.

Chapter 8, *Private Cloud Infrastructures for SAP*, demonstrates how companies that prefer to retain their mission-critical SAP systems and sensitive data in-house or in their own premises can benefit from infrastructures boasting cloud attributes. This chapter introduces new developments as well, including lossless Ethernet, converged networks, and unified computing.

Chapter 9, *Stateless Computing*, describes how innovative concepts like unified computing and service profiles enable full flexibility for SAP on public and private cloud implementations and how these influence the organizational structure of SAP operations. Within the chapter containerized datacenters as well as block and pod based datacenter concepts are discussed. The chapter closes with a discussion on how green clouds can be.

Chapter 10, *Economic and Legal aspects of Cloud Computing*, explores which of the numerous promises of cloud computing may actually be realized for different organizations. This chapter indicates how business applications in the future will offer enterprises a competitive edge by enabling them to "fail fast." In doing so, cloud-enabled organizations will benefit from their ability to pilot and change their business processes faster than their traditionally hosted counterparts.

Prerequisites

The solutions presented in this book generally refer to the latest versions of the relevant SAP products at the time of writing. While new hardware and software solutions are developed increasingly quickly, the underlying technologies and architectures change more slowly. Therefore, the cloud solutions or techniques described in this book will likely prove useful for future SAP releases. Also, many of the technical solutions and techniques presented here should be suitable for other enterprise-critical software systems, both off the shelf and custom developed.

This book has intentionally taken a neutral stance in terms of products. However, because most of the authors and contributors are employees of Cisco, Microsoft, HP, and Realtech, much of their expertise draws on the concepts and best practices developed in these companies through their partnerships with SAP and customers. For this reason, Cisco solutions are used as best practise examples of technologies that proved their worth in thousands of installations. Where the name of a specific product is mentioned, this is intended only as an example of a class of solutions and does not represent a value judgment of that product.

Acknowledgments

This book is the product of voluntary work done in our free time over many nights and weekends. We therefore dedicate this work to our wives and children, who have had to spend more time than usual without our full attention.

We would also like to thank all of our customers and colleagues who selflessly provided much help in the form of tips, contributions, reviews, and constructive criticism. Without their support, we would not have been able to write this book. In particular, we would like to call out the following people: Oliver Widhölzl from Egger Holz, Austria; Mike Bieley from Glencore International, Swiss; Nick de Groof from Maersk, Denmark; Otto Bruggeman from Intel, Deutschland, Tobias Brandl from Gopa-it; Heike Brendemuehl from Unisys; Wolfgang Neumar from Voest Alpine; Peter Klewinghaus from Amazon; Derek Kaufman retired from LS&Co; Weber Michael from Munich-Re; and Dr. Walter Dey, Peter Sladeczek, Klaus Aker, Anver Vanker, Yves Fauser, Andreas Wentland, Josephine Bruggeman and Ulrich Kleidon from Cisco.

Special thanks are also due to Robert-Andreas Riemann from Porsche, whose detailed comments influenced the content of several chapters.

The practical experience of all our advisors greatly added to the value of this book, and their support was a great source of encouragement.

A special mention, however, must also go to Christian Rauscher, our editor at Springer Heidelberg, for his involvement in the production of this book. It is due to his expert feedback that only unavoidable errors remain in this book. Mr. Rauscher has been a constant and much-welcomed partner and supporter in this regard.

Wolkenschlösser werden von Visionären gebaut,
Träumer bewohnen sie und Psychiater kassieren die Miete[1]

---

[1] Castles in the clouds are build by visionaries, they give home to dreamers, but psychiatrist cash in the rental fee – German proverb.

Foreword by Nick De Groof

Today's business demands agility, availability, and faster speed of execution to meet tighter SLAs. This is provided by the office of the CIO, which has the mission to provide more capabilities, but with less human and infrastructure resources. Clearly, traditional architectures are no longer sufficient and thus new forms for deployment and management are necessary. These new Cloud architectures should not only be designed for the infrastructure but should also include whole ready-made solutions for the enterprise.

SAP solutions continue to be the most mission- and business-critical applications for an enterprise, with new SAP technologies and solutions that can integrate into an existing SAP environment, the operational and management complexity can increase dramatically. SAP on the Cloud will allow your enterprise to do more with less and effectively meet increasing business demands at a lower operational cost.

While many have just begun their adventure and are stumbling through the "mist"-eries and hype around cloud computing, the authors will guide you through the crucial initial stages and beyond in this book. As the storm rolls in, they help clear the fog and provide guidance for your enterprise to navigate through the shallow waters and underwater obstacles on your journey to running SAP on the cloud. All aspects will pass the revue, from the basics of the infrastructure requirements to host complete SAP-based solutions, to the service-level management processes and functions to best support these environments. With proper planning and navigation, the final destination of SAP on the Cloud will deliver the requirements of your enterprise, with a manageable and agile distributed architecture.

So enjoy reading and be guided...

Nick De Groof
SAP Technical Architect
Maersk Line IT, Copenhagen, Denmark

Foreword by Robert-Andreas Riemann

Today "the Cloud" is everywhere – analysts urge you to investigate in cloud technology and TV spots call to move all your private data to the cloud.
And the buzzwords sound great for your IT department – always enough resources on hand and a lot of money to save.
The reality may be a far cry from slogans like "Put all of our services into the cloud and you will get rid of all problems."
As a manager in an enterprise IT you have to consider topics like Security, Governance, Validations, release management and SLA and legal issues. You also have to consider which of your IT services fit to what type of the numerous cloud flavors – if they fit at all?
Going cloud will also have an impact on the organization of your IT that breaks up established silos – organizational "kingdoms" have to be conquered to build a new federated union of collaborating teams.
This book is about SAP in the cloud. SAP solutions are among the most mission-critical applications of any company. Performance and stability of such systems often have priority over cost; nevertheless, costs are always a major issue. But to impair the business to save some money is not an option.
On the other side, the classical SAP architecture is "cloud friendly" and fits well to IaaS concepts because most SAP environments are very well standardized. However this is not true for all SAP solutions, BWA and HANA are examples of individual services that do not fit the cloud paradigm yet.
Knowing such nifty details and the technologies to overcome the obstacles offer a good chance to launch a successful SAP-on-cloud-project.
This book shows you how to move SAP into the cloud without ending up in fog.

    Robert-Andreas Riemann
    General Manager
    IT Platformservice
    Dr. Ing. H.c. F. Porsche AG

Contents

1	**A Short History of Cloud Computing**		1
	1.1 From Big Iron to Commodity		1
	1.2 The Internet Area		3
	1.3 Performance and Address Space		4
	1.4 Virtualization Is Back Again		4
	1.5 The Flavors of Cloud Computing		6
		1.5.1 Public Cloud	6
	1.6 Anything as a Service		7
		1.6.1 Public Cloud Platforms for SAP	8
	1.7 Cloud Applications		9
	1.8 Private Clouds		10
	1.9 Summary		12
2	**From R/3 to HANA**		15
	2.1 SAP Business Suite		18
		2.1.1 SAP ERP/SAP ECC	19
		2.1.2 SAP CRM	20
		2.1.3 SAP SCM	20
		2.1.4 SAP SRM	21
		2.1.5 SAP PLM	22
		2.1.6 SAP CPM	22
		2.1.7 SAP GRC	23
		2.1.8 SAP Solution Manager	23
	2.2 SAP NetWeaver		24
		2.2.1 SAP NetWeaver BW	24
		2.2.2 SAP NetWeaver Portal	25
		2.2.3 SAP Knowledge Warehouse	26
		2.2.4 SAP NetWeaver Mobile	27
		2.2.5 SAP NetWeaver Master Data Management	27
		2.2.6 SAP NetWeaver Process Integration	27
	2.3 Business Objects		28
	2.4 SAP Solutions for Small and Medium Companies		28
		2.4.1 SAP All-in-One	28

		2.4.2	SAP Business One	28
		2.4.3	SAP Business ByDesign	29
	2.5	SAP Appliances		29
		2.5.1	Duet and Alloy	29
		2.5.2	SAP Business Warehouse Accelerator	30
		2.5.3	SAP High Performance Analytical Appliance	31
	2.6	Summary		37
3	**Service Levels for SAP on Cloud**			39
	3.1	IT Service Management Reference Model		41
	3.2	Service Level Management		42
	3.3	Performance Management		43
		3.3.1	Response Time	43
	3.4	Units of Measure for SAP Applications		47
		3.4.1	Predicting the System Load	48
		3.4.2	Can the Performance Be Guaranteed?	51
		3.4.3	Measurement Based Sizing	52
		3.4.4	SAPS-Meter	54
	3.5	Load Profiles		58
		3.5.1	Load Profiles of Transactional Solutions	58
		3.5.2	Load Profiles of Analytical Systems	60
		3.5.3	Load Profiles of Other SAP-Solutions	60
	3.6	Availability Management		61
		3.6.1	How to Define Availability?	62
		3.6.2	How Many Resources Are Needed in Case of a Disaster?	63
		3.6.3	How Much Stability Is Required?	64
	3.7	Summary		64
4	**Security Aspects for SAP on Cloud**			65
	4.1	The Threat Landscape		66
		4.1.1	External Threats	67
		4.1.2	Internal Threats	68
		4.1.3	Technical Attacks: Viruses, Worms, Trojan Horses, etc.	69
		4.1.4	Non-Technical Threats	70
	4.2	Legal Aspects		70
	4.3	Classical IT Security and the Cloud		71
	4.4	Security on Public Clouds: Who Is Responsible?		73
		4.4.1	Security Concept of Amazon AWS	73
	4.5	Public Cloud Security Automation and Management		75
		4.5.1	Hardening Red Hat Linux as Guest Operating System	75
		4.5.2	Hardening Windows as Guest OS	76
		4.5.3	Hardening the Hypervisors	81
	4.6	SAP on Private Cloud: A Practical Example		81
	4.7	Summary		82

5 Change and Configuration Management ... 83
- 5.1 Introduction to Change and Configuration Management ... 84
  - 5.1.1 Elements of the CCMS ... 84
  - 5.1.2 Change and Configuration Data Types ... 85
  - 5.1.3 Integrating Change and Configuration Management with SAP ... 85
- 5.2 Managing SAP Business Changes ... 86
  - 5.2.1 Change Management Drives the Business and IT Lifecycle ... 87
  - 5.2.2 IT and Business Accountability and Alignment ... 87
- 5.3 Managing Technology Changes ... 87
  - 5.3.1 Understand the Configuration Management Process ... 88
  - 5.3.2 Manage Service Templates and Profiles ... 89
  - 5.3.3 Use a Technical Sandbox ... 90
  - 5.3.4 Protect the Development System ... 90
  - 5.3.5 Review the SAP Technology Stack and Tools ... 91
  - 5.3.6 Leverage Regression Testing Tools and Capabilities ... 91
  - 5.3.7 Maintain Technical Change and Configuration Management Rigor ... 91
- 5.4 Managing Organizational Change ... 92
  - 5.4.1 Understand the Four Technology Perspectives ... 94
  - 5.4.2 Minimize Human Involvement ... 95
  - 5.4.3 Optimize Organizational Change Processes ... 96
  - 5.4.4 Plan for SAP Staffing Backup Before Disaster Strikes ... 96
  - 5.4.5 Leverage Help Desk and Operations Support Teams ... 97
  - 5.4.6 Thoughtfully Outsource and Augment ... 98
  - 5.4.7 Mitigate Risk by Open Exchange of Real Life Experience ... 98
  - 5.4.8 Increase IT's Process Discipline ... 99
- 5.5 Summary ... 100

6 How Private and Public Clouds Work ... 101
- 6.1 Cloud Services Principles ... 101
- 6.2 Technologies for Public Clouds ... 103
- 6.3 Windows Azure Cloud Fabric ... 103
  - 6.3.1 Provisioning a New Node in Azure ... 105
  - 6.3.2 Deploying a Service into Windows Azure ... 106
  - 6.3.3 Roles and Instances in Azure ... 107
  - 6.3.4 Fault Domains and Upgrade Domains ... 107
  - 6.3.5 Azure Storage ... 108
- 6.4 Amazon Web Services ... 110
  - 6.4.1 Amazon EC2 Availability ... 111
  - 6.4.2 Storage in AWS ... 111
- 6.5 Technologies for Private Clouds ... 113
- 6.6 Microsoft Private Cloud ... 114

	6.7	VMware vCloud	115
	6.8	Summary	116
7	**SAP Solutions on Public Clouds**		117
	7.1	Public Clouds: A Short Overview	118
		7.1.1 Cloud Standards	119
		7.1.2 Cloud APIs	121
	7.2	Can Public Clouds Meet SAP Application Requirements?	122
	7.3	Amazon Web Service for SAP	125
		7.3.1 Instance Types for SAP (Server Building Blocks)	126
		7.3.2 AWS Storage for SAP	127
		7.3.3 Network: Amazon Virtual Private Cloud	128
		7.3.4 Backup/Restore of SAP Applications on EC2 Instances	129
		7.3.5 SAP High-Availability in AWS	130
		7.3.6 Monitoring with Amazon CloudWatch	131
		7.3.7 Other Aspects of SAP on AWS	131
		7.3.8 AWS Service Levels	132
	7.4	Outlook: Public Clouds and SAP	132
		7.4.1 Beyond the Physical Boundaries	133
		7.4.2 SAP NetWeaver Cloud	134
		7.4.3 Project Titanium	135
	7.5	Summary	136
8	**Private Cloud Infrastructures for SAP**		137
	8.1	SAP Landscapes	138
		8.1.1 SAP System Architecture	139
		8.1.2 2-tier versus 3-tier	140
	8.2	Server Architectures: Nifty Details?	141
		8.2.1 Multi-core and Multi-thread	142
		8.2.2 Inter Core Communication and Access to Main Memory	144
		8.2.3 Scale-up Versus Scale-out	146
		8.2.4 Rack Mount Versus Blade	146
		8.2.5 Memory: Fast but Volatile	148
	8.3	Storage: Hard and Other Disks	149
		8.3.1 Sizing for Throughput	149
		8.3.2 The Disk Is Dead: But Is SSD Already King?	152
	8.4	Network	153
		8.4.1 User Network	153
		8.4.2 Server Network	156
		8.4.3 Storage Network	156
		8.4.4 Fibre Channel over Ethernet (FCoE)	157
		8.4.5 iSCSI	159

	8.5	Unified Computing	160
		8.5.1 Converged Network Adapters	161
		8.5.2 Port Extenders	162
		8.5.3 Fabric Extender	162
		8.5.4 Fabric Interconnects	163
		8.5.5 Unification and Virtualization	163
		8.5.6 Software Based Fabric Extender	164
		8.5.7 Hardware Based Fabric Extender	165
	8.6	Summary	165
9	**Stateless Computing**		**167**
	9.1	Service Profile Definition	169
		9.1.1 Unified Computing and VMware's vCenter	171
	9.2	Cloud Operation with Stateless Computing	173
		9.2.1 IDPools	173
		9.2.2 Server Pools	175
		9.2.3 Administrative Organization for SAP on Cloud	176
	9.3	Cloud Data Center Facilities	177
		9.3.1 How Green Clouds Can Be?	178
	9.4	Summary	180
10	**Economic and Legal Aspects of Cloud Computing**		**181**
	10.1	Trial and Error-Fast and Cheap	182
		10.1.1 Economic Risks and Other Considerations	182
		10.1.2 Legal Implications	183
	10.2	Economic Myths, Realities, and Other Observations	183
		10.2.1 Innovative Cloud Platforms Do Not Necessarily Cost Less	184
		10.2.2 Volume Discounts Rarely Drive Economies of Scale	184
		10.2.3 The Cloud May Not Yield Greener IT for Some Time	185
		10.2.4 Cloud Software Licensing Models Remain Unchanged	185
		10.2.5 CapEx Versus OpEx May Myths	186
	10.3	Business Economics of the Cloud for SAP	186
		10.3.1 Macroeconomics and Other Market Drivers	187
		10.3.2 Business Risks, Functionality, Data Sensitivity, and Role	188
		10.3.3 Developing Cloud Business Cases for SAP	189
	10.4	Technology Economics and Considerations	190
		10.4.1 Demand, Supply, and the Buying Hierarchy	190
		10.4.2 Technology Attributes and Challenges	191
		10.4.3 Public Cloud Opportunities and Challenges	191

		10.4.4	Private Cloud Opportunities and Challenges	192
		10.4.5	Hybrid Cloud Opportunities and Challenges	192
	10.5	Organizational Economics and Considerations	193
		10.5.1	The Business End-User Community	193
		10.5.2	Reinventing the Internal SAP IT Organization	194
		10.5.3	Organizational Process Discipline or Hardening	194
		10.5.4	Cloud Service Providers and Hosters	195
		10.5.5	Evaluating Organizational Readiness for Change	195
		10.5.6	An Effective Model for SAP IT Organizational Change	196
		10.5.7	Organizational Skills and Staffing	197
	10.6	The Legal Landscape for SAP Cloud Computing	198
		10.6.1	Governance, Risk, Compliance, and Geographic Constraints	198
		10.6.2	Internal GRC Considerations	199
		10.6.3	Data and Security Considerations	199
		10.6.4	People Considerations	200
		10.6.5	Developing a Legally-Informed Cloud Economics Plan	201
	10.7	Summary	201

About the Authors 203

Index 207

A Short History of Cloud Computing

Cloud Computing is the latest buzzword in the IT. This chapter helps to understand why Clouds have become so prominent in the IT world, what benefits are expected to be achieved by cloud computing and in which flavors computing clouds are available.

Hardly any other word in IT in recent years has been used as frequently as Cloud Computing. The difficulty here is that the term Cloud Computing does not refer to an individual and isolated subject, but rather that it is an umbrella term for a variety of services and solutions.

▶ *A clear view into the cloud*

In order to provide a sound basis for considering the form in which Cloud Computing can be used for SAP applications, we will first deal with the question of how Cloud Computing has developed in detail and from what components it is composed.

1.1 From Big Iron to Commodity

Let us first go back about 20 years in IT history. Around 1990, major changes occurred in the IT landscape of many companies. While companies were committed for decades to mainframes as a platform for business applications like SAP R/2, a small revolution became apparent: the client/server technology enabled by the UNIX operating system and SAP R/3 as a complete business solution. As in real life, IT revolutions never happen without reason.

▶ *From dinosaur into the stone age*

Mainframes were quite powerful, but expensive machines. Because memory was extreme limited, their processors had been optimized over decades to perform complex tasks with as little machine code as possible. Due to their complex commands, they were called Complex Instruction Set Computers (CISC).

In contrast, the then new developed processors utilized in UNIX systems had relatively few simple commands that could be processed very quickly. More complex tasks were modeled in the compiler as a series of simple commands. With the Reduced Instruction Set Computer (RISC), UNIX system outperformed the CISC based mainframes by far at much lower costs.

Under these conditions the competition between mainframes and RISC systems resembles soon as the race between the tortoise and the hare. The evolution took its course and many businesses decided in favor of the combination of UNIX systems and SAP applications.

In the following years, the RISC systems became larger and boasted a steady increase in processing power. This development was initially triggered by the Symmetric Multi-Processor (SMP) architecture which supported typically up to eight processors running in parallel in a server to run in.

A few years later the Non Uniform Memory Access (NUMA) enabled servers with up to 128 processors and 64-bit architecture provided the necessary large memory configurations. Such servers that have been referred to as scale-up solutions.

By the use of partitioning they could in turn be divided into smaller logical units. This enables mainframe like consolidation, the pooling of as many applications as possible. The UNIX servers however have become also quite expensive this way. Thus a new form of mainframe was resurrected at the end of the '90s.

A relatively unspectacular development occurred about 1993; the support of servers based on processors from Intel and AMD for SAP applications with Windows and later Linux as operating systems. Although these systems were not comparable with the scalability of the big UNIX systems, they established an entry level segment for SAP systems.

▶ *Early settlements and agriculture*

The first published benchmark of an SAP system on Windows reached about 100 SD users with 4 CPUs of the Pentium-Pro family, a value which was then exceeded by even small UNIX servers easily.

The biggest advantage of these servers was their low cost, which enabled SAP to win a large number of medium-sized companies for their applications on the "Wintel" platform. Because of their low costs, plenty of these servers are been used in data centers – resulting in the so called "server sprawl".

New and interesting developments such as High-Performance Compute Cluster (HPCC) used such low cost computers in large quantities in parallel. Because of the more distributed character of their usage, the term Scale-Out computing soon established itself for this class of computers.

1.2 The Internet Area

Around the year 1995 there was a very different revolution: the Internet became commercially viable. According to an estimate, the usage of the Internet for global data exchange in 1993 was only about 1 %. However, by 2000 the Internet was already the main telecommunications network with 51 % of the worldwide traffic. By 2007, the utilization of the Internet for all data transfers was at 97 % and since than has approached the 100 % mark.

▶ *Coal and iron establish industrialization*

The Internet was one of the most important technical developments at the end of last century and in the end dominated all areas of communication.

Hand in hand with the ever-increasing acceptance and the range of available content, telecommunications companies made huge investments in network expansion and bandwidth as they realized that the Internet promised to be the largest gold mine since the invention of the microprocessor.

In spite of the huge investment, the price of internet services dropped dramatically driven by the worldwide competition in the telecom market. Data transfer with superior performance at a practically negligible price became a matter of fact.

One of the biggest challenges to companies wanting to use this publicly accessible medium for their sensitive data was the aspect of security. This consisted of the potential for data theft, spying and the manipulation of the data.

With new technologies such as encryption and Virtual Private Networks (VPN) communication over internet became secure enough for business systems. IT infrastructures were operated with firewalls and gateway servers located in so-called De-Militarized Zones (DMZ) in order to isolate the crucial server environments from the public Internet. An entire industry and new IT architectures was developed around the issue of security to become the essential foundation for the commercial use of the Internet today.

The result of extremely high bandwidth at a reasonable cost and security level was the foundation for new business models for IT operations on the Internet. Hosting providers and outsourcers adopted this business model and delivered IT operations as a "commodity" at lower cost than would have been possible with traditional IT operations. The foundation of this business model is maximum automation and standardization in the data centers of the hosting providers.

The principle of economies of scale benefited the big players and led to the fact that a few large companies such as EDS (later acquired by HP), IBM and T-Systems dominate the market.

The worldwide availability of affordable network connectivity through the Internet was the most important enabling technology for cloud computing.

1.3 Performance and Address Space

Let us now step back in time and consider the development of the industry standard server with Intel or AMD processors. Till the turn of the century, these platforms were only available with 32-bit architecture which results in a relative small addressable memory of only 2 GB. In spite to this limitation which restricted such servers to relatively small SAP systems, they enjoyed a widespread acceptance as SAP application servers in mixed environments.

▶ *Economy of scale*

The economy of scale keep costs low and the ever-increasing power of these processors helped to win an ever increasing number of customers. However, the address space requirements needed for large SAP systems, particularly those using Unicode dictated the use of high-end RISC machines with 64-bit processors at least for the database.

While Intel 64-bit processors were initially offered only in the Itanium family, AMD K8 processor introduced in 2002 extended the 32-bit CPU registers of the traditional x86 architecture[1] to 64-bit, thus making 64-bit computing available with standard servers.

Linux supported this capability already in 2002, Windows followed 2005. The 64-bit processors with the "enhanced" x86 architecture were a spectacular success for AMD and forced Intel to offer a 64-bit extension of its Xeon product line as well. This competition between the chip giants led to a quantum leap in performance gains for industry standard servers.

Successive generations of CPU chips increased the computing power of its predecessor by orders of magnitude. When the physical limits made it impossible to further increase clock frequencies of the processors, technology evolved by adding more cores on a chip die (multi-core concept).

The excellent performance of x86 processors makes x86 processors the second most important enabling technology for cloud computing.

1.4 Virtualization Is Back Again

Increased computing power and 64-bit address space enabled the utilization of industry standard servers for large, resource-hungry applications. But due to the fact that not all applications are so hungry all the time, most Windows and Linux servers were typically utilized between 5 % and 25 % on average.

---

[1] Named after Intel's 286, 386 and 486 CPUs who laid the foundation for the PC, sometimes also called x64 in the Windows world and x86_64 in the Linux universe.

1.4 Virtualization Is Back Again

▶ **Abstraction and pooling of resources**

The solution for efficient utilization of the additional processing turned out to be – almost an irony – the technology that had been developed in 1960 for mainframes: virtualization.

What was implemented once completely in hardware on the mainframe was adapted to industry standard processors using software based hypervisors from 2002 onwards – after a number of problems were solved with the underlying IA32 architecture. One of the first commercially successful solutions was VMware's vSphere followed by XEN, Microsoft Hyper-V and recently Linux KVM.

Virtualization offers the opportunity to completely isolate multiple guest operating systems on a shared server infrastructure and thus get the server utilization to above 90 %.

The first virtual machines provided a relatively low performance. This was due to factors such as complete emulation of I/O components in software, poor support for hypervisor capabilities in the processor hardware and no enhancements in the operating system to take advantage of virtualization- factors which improved significantly over time.

Current hypervisors support up to 32 logical processors in a VM and work with I/O concepts which enable the mapping of physical I/O devices directly into virtual machines to enable almost physical I/O performance in VMs. Additionally, modern processors now support many functions of a hypervisor directly in the processor hardware. With the right interface card it's possible to operate even relatively large and powerful SAP systems in a virtual machine without any performance restriction.

In addition, there were completely new benefits associated with virtualization which were not possible with physical servers. For example a VM can be relocated easily from one physical server to a server with more or less resources – without disrupting the application.

Also a VM can be generated within a few minutes using a template and deployed with pre-installed operating system, patches and application components.

Maintaining the Service Level Agreements (SLA) became a lot easier with VMs. High availability solutions, disaster recovery configurations and even server replication configurations are now standard technologies.

All the topics above are no really new – they have been developed under the terms Adaptive Infrastructures and Utility Computing already over the last decade however not deployed often for mission critical applications besides a few pioneers.

▶ **The next evolutional step of IT services**

As of today, the broad adoption of Cloud Computing – both Private and Public Clouds – indicate that this will become the new standard infrastructure for enterprise IT.

1.5 The Flavors of Cloud Computing

Cloud computing or cloud services are terms used for many things. In the most general sense, it means that an application, a service, a resource or a platform can be used via the Internet where users subscribes to a set of service definitions rather than the details of the service implementation.

▶ *Service orientation in IT*

According to the IT Lab of the National Institute of Standards and Technology (NIST),[2] cloud computing is characterized by:
- **Ubiquitous network access** – Capabilities are available over the network and accessed through standard mechanisms.
- **Location independent resource pooling** – computing resources are pooled to serve all consumers using a multi-tenant model. The customer generally has no control or knowledge over the exact location of the provided resources.
- **Rapid elasticity** – Capabilities can be rapidly and elastically provisioned to quickly scale up and rapidly released to quickly scale down.
- **Measured Service** – automatically control and optimize resource use by leveraging a metering. Resource usage can be monitored, controlled and reported, providing transparency for both the provider and consumer of the utilized service.

The European Telecommunications Standards Institute (ETSI)[3] emphasize of the need of Interoperability between the offerings of different cloud providers. Cisco coined the term "Intercloud" in analogy to the Internet for the ability to build solutions which orchestrated from software and data hosted in more than one cloud infrastructure. For this purpose cloud specific APIs and SLAs have to be defined.

The ESTI report mentions also that "Software licensing is a major inhibitor of the adoption of flexible computing models, including cloud infrastructure services. Cost savings in hardware, IT infrastructure management and energy can be negated by the need to purchase in advance, sufficient licenses to cover the maximum size of an application deployment."

The first distinction to be drawn in cloud computing is the difference between *public cloud* and *private cloud*.

1.5.1 Public Cloud

A public cloud is always operated by a service provider and is available to many users – businesses or individuals. Public clouds are typically based on highly

---

[2] http://www.nist.gov/itl/cloud.cfm.
[3] http://www.etsi.org/website/document/tr_102997v010101p.pdf.

integrated data centers with thousands of computers and massive storage pools. The operation of this data center is automated to a degree that is simply not possible in typical enterprise data centers.

Cloud Fabric controllers are software components in these cloud infrastructures which maintain the life cycle of services – from the creation to deletion – and monitoring performance, availability and compliance with the SLAs.

Typical providers of large public clouds include Amazon, Google and Microsoft with gigantic data centers widely distributed geographically.

Important distinctions from the classic offerings of hosting providers and outsourcers are the principles of pay-per-use and the fact that resources can be requested and released literally at any time.

This on-demand and pay-per-use approach offers significant advantages for service consumers, who doesn't need to incur the capital cost of investing in new servers and can react flexible, to respond to changing business conditions.[4]

By massive automation, the use of pools of compute, storage and network resources and economies of scale, public cloud providers can offer their services for extreme low prices. Windows Azure for example offers at its introduction in 2010:

- A single logical CPU for $0.12/h; 4 CPUs in a VM for $0.96/h
- Storage of a GB for $0,15 per month in so called blob storage
- $0.01 for each 10.000 access operations to a VM.
- Network bandwidth adds $0.10 for each incoming GB and $0.15 for each outgoing GB to the bill.
- A relational database of 10 GB – SQL Azure – comes for $99 per month
However SAP is not supported on Azure at the time of writing.

Besides "full service" clouds there are cloud providers like Apple's iCloud or Dropbox who focus on convenient storage space only. It is expected that the range of cloud services will increase in the future by new vendors offering specific cloud resources for specific target markets.

1.6 Anything as a Service

Two ways to utilize public clouds are popular but often confused: Infrastructure as a Service (IaaS) and Platform as a Service (PaaS).

▶ *IaaS example: Amazon Web Services (AWS)*

Amazon Web Services (AWS) is a typical example for IaaS. AWS provide server, network and storage resources and give the customer the choice of Windows or Linux as operating system.

---

[4] Actually pay per use is nothing new, already 40 years ago mainframe capacity could be utilized remotely for a dollar per minute over telephone lines.

The virtual environments available through AWS behave exactly like a local infrastructure, so customers configure the infrastructure according to the demand of any specific application.

Such access to the configuration is a mandatory demand for the installation of SAP NetWeaver solutions and the SAP Business suite. However the customer is also responsible for all admin tasks like patching or configuring the Operating System.

A typical example for PaaS is Windows Azure. In such a setup, the customers have not to deal with admin tasks like patching or configuring the Operating System which are maintained by the cloud fabric controller.

▶ *PaaS example: Windows Azure*

The fabric controller monitors also the utilization of the VM resources and maintains the agreed service level. In case of failure the fabric controller even provide a backup VM.

The advantage of this model is less effort required for the administration of the cloud platform. The disadvantage is that a customer has no control over the operating system in a VM, as this part has been delegated to the cloud fabric controller.

While applications like web servers deal well with this model, many applications – especially those heavyweights like SAP NetWeaver – do require control over the operating system during installation and operation.

As a consequence, applications that are scheduled to be run in the PaaS model need to be developed and adapted for this environment. Microsoft offers tools, support and integration with Visual Studio for this task. However, the probability that SAP will reworks the technical basis for their Business Suite based on the SAP NetWeaver stack for this model is highly unlikely.

▶ *No SAP on PaaS !*

In the 2012 Microsoft expanded Windows Azure from a pure PaaS model and made IaaS an option. Also Linux is since 2012 a supported Operating System in Windows.

1.6.1 Public Cloud Platforms for SAP

The use of a public cloud platform for the installation of an SAP application is currently only supported with Amazon AWS. As discussed the reason is that AWS is offered an infrastructure as a service solution that enables the administration and configuration of a virtual machine by a customer.

As discussed in Chap. 2 SAP applications based on the SAP NetWeaver stack have a variety of interfaces to the operating system and even the hardware and need to have deep control over the operating system. Details of Amazon's AWS as platform for SAP installations are described in detail in Chap. 7 of this book.

SAP has also put a stake into the cloud management with the Landscape and Virtualization Manager (LVM), capable to communicate with the controllers of a private cloud solution, but also to request and manage resources from a public cloud provider.

1.7 Cloud Applications

Applications which are exclusively made available by the vendor over the internet are referred to as Software as a Service (SaaS). Customers of SaaS don't have to care neither how the application is installed and maintained nor how the data is stored or anything in regards of the operating system or the underlying hardware.

▶ *Tailored service offerings*

All they need is to trust the SaaS vendor that their sensitive data like the core financial situation of their company, the credit card numbers of their customers or the salaries of their workforce is kept save in the datacenter of the SaaS vendor and the mission critical application is always available.

This category existed already long before the term cloud was coined. A somewhat unknown example is DATEV[5] who offer since several decades ERP and HR applications for small and medium businesses in Germany.

A more prominent example is Salesforce.com who offers the usage of their CRM solution exclusive as a Service.

Another example is Google who offer a SaaS based alternative to Microsoft Office as Google Applications. As an reaction Microsoft now offers Office 360, Exchange Online, SharePoint Online and Microsoft Dynamics CRM as SaaS solutions to snatch a share of this market.

SAP announced Sales OnDemand (CRM) as their first SaaS type solution already in 2006. The ERP solutions SAP Business byDesign (ByD) became available 2010 as the first solution from SAP developed from the ground up as a cloud application, followed by Carbon Impact OnDemand (sustainability), Sourcing OnDemand, and Travel OnDemand (expense reporting).

▶ *SaaS from SAP*

One of the biggest benefits of ByD is that it can be used with very little customization, enabling extreme fast implementation. However this is also the

---

[5] www.datev.com, actually a cooperative of tax consultants, auditors and lawyers who turned itself into a software company and IT service provider as well for their clients.

biggest drawback, because it also didn't allow customizing of the solution according to customer demands.

The analogy of a hand-tailored suit versus a machine-made garment reflects not only the different price categories and the time before a company can utilize a solution, but also the degree of fit that can be expected.

In 2011 SAP acquired talent management solution provider SuccessFactor. Besides a well-adopted SaaS platform for performance and talent management SuccessFactors offer also a learning management system (formerly Plateau) workforce planning and analytics (formerly Inform) and social collaboration (formerly CubeTree).

A special category are hybrid solutions like SAP x-Apps which can be composed of SaaS application and application residing on premises using the web services paradigm.

The co-existence of best-of-breed talent management solutions (typically SaaS) alongside core HR (typically on-premises) is also quite common.

1.8 Private Clouds

Private Clouds as opposed to public clouds are cloud infrastructure provided exclusively for the uses of a specific organization. In many cases, the private cloud is hosted in the company's owned data center and operated by their own IT organization.

▶ *On premise clouds*

This way, sensitive data can be kept within the company and control of the data and processes is secured. Consequently, legal or security aspects of handling such data do not need to be considered and audited, representing the major advantage of the private cloud.

But private clouds are not limited to on-premises operations in a company. Ironically private clouds can be also provided as a service from a public cloud provider, however exclusively for a specific customer.

▶ *Off premise clouds*

In this case the infrastructure is not set up as a multi-tenant architecture but as single-tenant architecture to minimize the risk of "intra-cloud" attacks.

In order to build private cloud solutions, building blocks for hardware and software can be combined in a modular fashion. Hardware vendors such as Cisco in partnership with VMware and EMC or NetApp for example, offer pre-configured and SAP-certified building blocks with carefully optimized combinations of server, virtualization and storage infrastructures "ready to run" for private clouds (Vblock or Flexpod). This infrastructure can be combined with cloud-controllers and automation software, for example SAP LVM.

1.8 Private Clouds

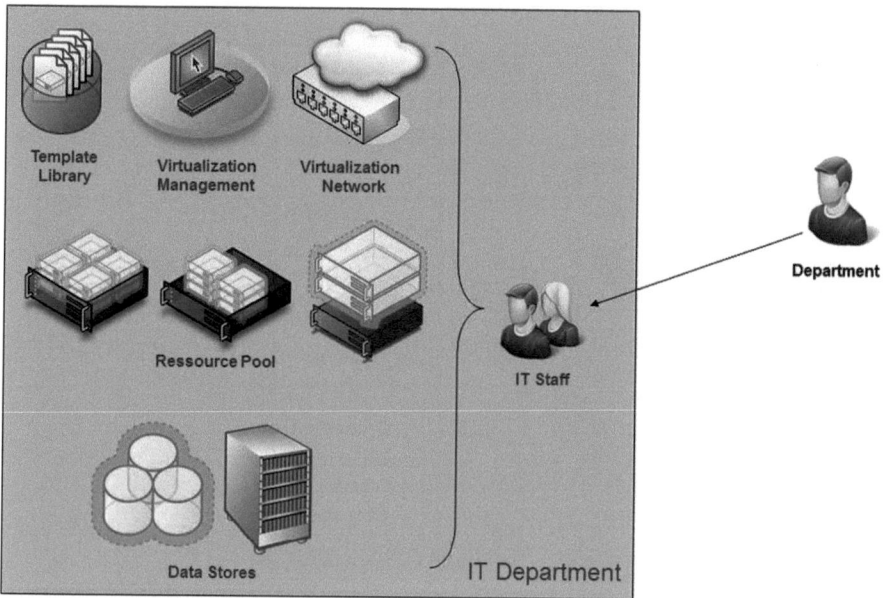

Fig. 1.1 Traditional IT service delivery

You may ask how do private clouds distinguish from traditional data center and hosting or outsourcing concepts when both are based on virtualized servers, storage and networks on standardized and pooled resources with highly automated installation and provisioning of applications?

▶ *Private cloud versus classic outsourcing*

Just compare the Figs. 1.1 and 1.2 – in boot cases all resources are virtualized, standardized and pooled. Also the users can access all applications via the Internet. In the traditional approach however any user demand on utilizing a specific service has to be routed through the IT personnel to be enabled by assigning the necessary access rights, providing credentials and bill the occurring costs against a cost center number.

In the private cloud delivery model the user can select the necessary services through a self-service portal and the consumed resources are billed automatically to the cost center number.

This way the users get what they need immediately and the IT experts can focus on orchestrating, monitoring and management instead of endless discussions what solutions should be delivered on what platform with what budget.

With the metering of resource consumption as described in Chap. 3 and pay per use-concept to costs of providing the services can be assigned to the correct cost centers consuming the services. This makes an end to the endless discussions about budgeting additional resources when demand is rising.

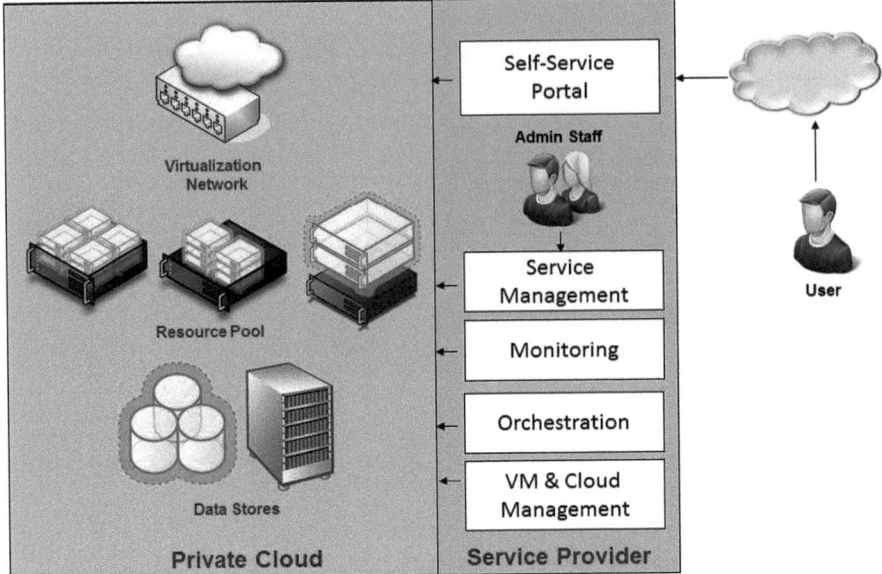

Fig. 1.2 Private cloud service delivery

Summing up the characteristics of Private Clouds in comparison to outsourcing we can conclude:
- Private Clouds provide Self-Service access
- The orchestration and deployment of solution is automated
- Private Clouds provide metered use of resources

1.9 Summary

There are three mainstream technologies which lead to cloud computing:
- The Internet as ubiquitous communication platform,
- High-performance low-cost x64 processors
- Virtualization for granular resource sharing.

Besides the traditional strategies of standardization, automation and consolidation cloud architecture made massive use of resource pooling and sharing to minimize TCO.

Cloud computing comes in three different usage models:
- Infrastructure as a service (IAAS)
- Platform as a Service (PAAS)
- Software as a Service (SAAS)

The "classic" SAP business suite and NetWeaver solutions fit to the IAAS model. SAP solutions like Business by Design and SuccessFactor are exclusively available through the SaaS model.

The decision between private and public clouds depends mainly on the demand of security, governance and control an enterprise need on their mission critical applications and sensitive data.

A common denominator for public clouds is the non-exclusive service offering. Private clouds are dedicated to their respective users and can be on-premises or hosted. As cloud computing evolves, the basic characteristics of private and public clouds are getting more and more harmonized.

From R/3 to HANA 2

> *Within the last 40 years SAP developed a large portfolio of business solutions deploying different technologies. Because most of the solutions are developed before the proliferation of virtualization and cloud concepts there is not always an ideal fit. This chapter briefly introduces the functionality and the technical characteristics of the most used SAP solutions from ECC to HANA and discuses how well they fit into the various cloud concepts.*

SAP business processes are provided by the SAP Business Suite, NetWeaver, and appliances like BWA and HANA. But even for experts it is difficult to cope with the somewhat overwhelming number of components based on different technologies which pose different demands and restrictions to be considered when building a cloud infrastructure.

To best understand the future requires knowledge of the past; this section gives insight into the SAP roadmap to the real real-time business solutions

▶ **The founders of SAP**

In 1972, Hasso Plattner, Dietmar Hopp, Hans-Werner Hector, Klaus Tschira, and Claus Wellenreuther founded a company called *Systems, Applications, Products in Data Processing*, or SAP for short. Their vision was to develop standard software for business processes. Based on the leading edge technology of the time the first versions materialized on then thousands of punch cards. During the next 20 years SAP developed into the leading provider of ERP solutions for large enterprises.

▶ **"R" stands for real-time**

In 1991 Hasso Plattner initiated "Project Heidelberg" aimed at developing an integrated business system for mid market companies, christened in 1992 as SAP R/3. Similar to its mainframe-based ancestors R/1 and R/2, the "R" stood for "real-time,"

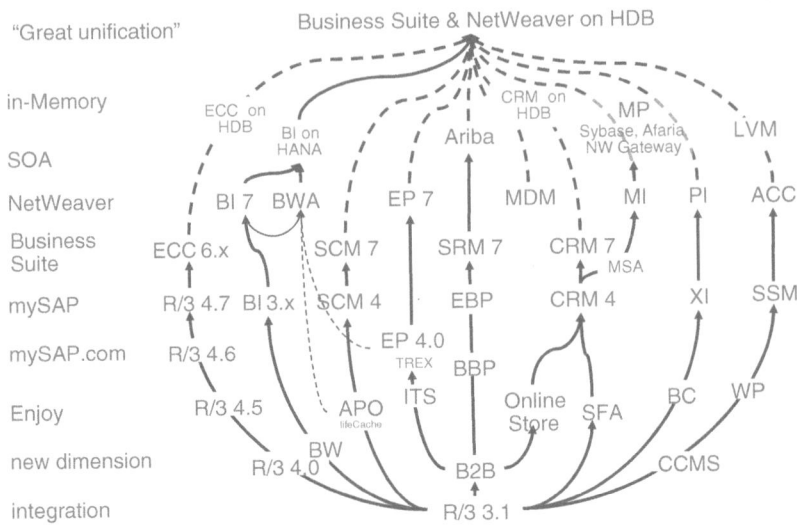

Fig. 2.1 Development of SAP applications from legacy R/3 to contemporary in-memory solutions

a significant innovation at a time when punch cards and needle printers were the common user interface.

Covering the basic business processes of a whole company in one monolithic application with a single database had the tremendous advantage that the result of any transaction would become available for all other users and reports at literally the same moment, hence the "R" in realtime. For example, every movement of capital and goods in and out of the company could be reflected real-time in the company's bookkeeping, a feature largely unparalleled by previous business applications. And that was only the beginning.

▶ *New dimension*

Since the early days of the first R/3 system, the SAP solution portfolio has been undergoing continuous development and extension (see Fig. 2.1). With its "new dimensions" initiative, SAP complemented R/3 with standalone solutions for data analysis (*SAP Business Information Warehouse*, BW), production planning (*Advanced Planner and Optimizer*, APO), sales management (*Sales Force Automation*, SFA), and system administration (*Computing Center Management System*, CCMS).

Dedicated solutions for data analysis became necessary because the performance of early platforms didn't allow running transactions and reports the same time on the same system. While these solutions optimized for specific business processes became a great success, the concept of the integrated real-time system was broken since each of this solutions demand their own database instances to grant performance. Data generated in the different systems had to be replicated and consolidated. Because the extraction would have a negative effect on the response time of the transaction systems, the replication is usually done at night, with the effect that all reports reflect the "truth of yesterday" only.

▶ **Enjoy SAP**

With the "enjoy SAP" initiative, the user interface was given a complete overhaul. Further, an Internet gateway (the *Internet Transaction Server*, ITS), a central user administration (*Workplace, WP*), and solutions for Internet-based purchasing (*Business to Business*, B2B) and sales (*Online-Store*) were added to the SAP portfolio.

▶ *mySAP.com*

During the "mySAP.com" era, the purchasing solution was enhanced as *Business to Business Procurement* (BBP) and Internet-based communication with third-party systems enabled by *Business Connector* (BC).

With the burst of the "dot com bubble", SAP dropped the ".com" in its product names and continued to develop the business functions of its solutions even further. SFA was developed into *Customer Relationship Management* (CRM), APO became *Supply Chain Management* (SCM), BBP evolved into *Enterprise Buyer Professional* (EBP) and later *Supplier Relationship Management* (SRM), BC into *Exchange Infrastructure* (XI), and WP into *Enterprise Portal* and SAP *Solution Manager* (SSM).

▶ **NetWeaver**

With SAP NetWeaver, SAP extended its portfolio with the *SAP Enterprise Portal* (EP), *Mobile Infrastructure* (MI), *Master Data Management* (MDM) and *NetWeaver Administrator* (NWA). XI was renamed to *Process Integration* (PI), and the Business Warehouse moved to the NetWeaver portfolio whereas the other solutions were grouped into the business suite. Finally, SAP's traditional ERP product R/3 Enterprise was renamed into *Enterprise Core Component* (ECC).

▶ *accelerated reporting*

With the introduction of *service-oriented architecture* (SOA), SAP didn't offer an additional software system, but enabled the functionality of the existing solutions to be re-used in so called composite applications. Also, functionality provided from other vendors as web services can be easily integrated.[1]

To accelerate business analysis in Business Warehouse, SAP combined in-memory technologies already developed for APO (the MaxDB based Live-Cache) and EP (TREX) and developed them further into the BW accelerator (BWA). In a kind of "side car" approach, the BWA enables analysis of segments

---

[1] Within a project at the SAP Co-Innovation Lab, the telephony and tele-presence functionality of Cisco Unified Communication was made available for SAP business processes as an example.

of BW data in seconds. However users still need to know what data they want to analyze to have the data indexed and modeled.

▶ **One database to serve them all**

Further development and scientific studies at the Hasso Plattner Institute of the University of Potsdam resulted in the High performance ANalytical Appliance (HANA), a technology SAP envisions will one day replace the traditional databases for all of their business applications.

During the announcement of HANA at Sapphire 2010, Hasso Plattner presented his vision of SAP HANA becoming a common database for SAP's entire enterprise software portfolio. Within this concept, the different software solutions will stay independent, but share one single "HDB".

As a consequence all data will become again available to all applications and users at the same moment. Omitting the need for data replication between different databases, and SAP applications. This vision would see SAP solutions circle back to the real-time business processes covering the demands of a complete enterprise as it began more than 40 years ago.

2.1 SAP Business Suite

This section provides a highly condensed overview of the SAP solution portfolio and their underlying technologies as a basis for the discussion how the individual components fit into the different cloud concepts.

Because of the novelty of SAP HANA however, we granted some extra pages for an extended explanation of the principles of the new hybrid column/raw oriented in-memory technology.

Be aware that the solutions named and their descriptions are far from being complete.[2] Readers which familiar with the different SAP solutions can skip the beginning of the sections describing the functionality and technology in condensed form and go directly to the marginal "...*on the cloud*" to see how well the specific solution fit to cloud environment.

▶ **"Office for enterprises"**

The *SAP Business Suite* provides literally thousands of "ready to run" business processes for any department in an enterprise – in this regard the SAP Business Suite can be seen as an "office package for enterprises" providing the business processes to run the various departments of a company.

---

[2] http://help.sap.com/saphelp_glossary/en/index.htm provides an overview of SAP acronyms.

2.1.1 SAP ERP/SAP ECC

Given its longevity, Enterprise Resource Planning (ERP) is for obvious reasons still the most deployed SAP solution. ERP deals with the fundamental business processes in every enterprise: financial accounting, production, and human resources. In other words, among other functions SAP ERP ensures that orders can be accepted, fulfilled, tracked, and paid for.

SAP ERP is a bundle and consists of SAP ECC and SAP NetWeaver. Technically, ECC represents the newest incarnation of the famous SAP R/3. In contrast to SAP R/3, the business process logic is split into Enterprise Core and Extension Sets to make updates less intrusive.

The main components of SAP ECC are SAP Financials (FI), Sales and Distribution (SD), Production Planning (PP), Quality Management (QM) Warehouse Management (WM), Logistics Execution System (LES), Project Management (PS), and Plant Maintenance (PM). Human Resources (HR) and Human Capital Management (HCM) provide functions for payroll, time management, gratuities, incentives, statutory reporting, and cost planning. Depending on their roles, users can directly access HCM functions using Employee Self-Services (ESS) and Manager Self-Services (MSS). SAP HCM also provides solutions for e-recruitment and e-learning.

▶ *Industry solutions*

SAP offers also a wide range of industry-specific solutions (*Industry Solutions*, or IS) for more than 25 industries, from IS-Apparel & Footwear, down to IS-Waste. These industry solutions consist of modified and extended ECC standard components.

▶ *ECC on cloud*

In general SAP ECC is a good fit for IaaS cloud services because of the excellent horizontal scaling and stability of ABAP[3] and the relatively predictable load patterns (see Chap. 3). Knowing the resource demands ahead of time is an ideal fit to the adaptive concepts of the cloud.

However you have to be careful with the IO demands of industry solutions which many public cloud offerings will have difficulties to cope with. IS-Retail is a good example, the typical industry-specific business processes is the analysis of the daily sales data collected by the Point-of-Sales (POS) systems in order to replenish the warehouse stock of the individual shops.

As a result of an optimization run, the picking orders are placed and the delivery notes for the trucks are printed in accordance with the route plan. These processes are very CPU-intensive and also generate high IO loads. Same is true for monthly billing runs in IS-Telecommunication and IS-Utility.

---

[3] Advanced Business Application Programming, SAP's process programming language.

2.1.2 SAP CRM

Customer Relationship Management (CRM) is also found in many customer installations. CRM provides processes for interactions with customers such as marketing, sales, service, and support transactions. Technically an offspring of R/3, the SAP CRM core is coded in ABAP; however there are also several JAVA based components.

▶ *Call center*

SAP CRM can become quite complex. For example the call center solution Customer Interaction Center (CIC) requires a telephony gateway, a telephony server, and a corresponding interface to the PBX. Low response times are critical for CIC implementations because long wait times easily drive customers away.

▶ *Web-shop*

Even more complex are Web shops. In addition to the basic SAP CRM system, the SAP Internet Sales scenario also consists of SAP *Internet Pricing and Configurator* (IPC), SAP *Biller Direct*, a catalog system, SAP Knowledge Provider (KPro), permanent shopping basket, etc.

▶ *CRM on cloud*

Like ECC, CRM systems are a good fit to IaaS cloud services because they scale well horizontally and can easily be adapted to rising resource demand by adding additional application servers. However this short overview demonstrates that a SAP CRM cloud implementation can become a quite complex effort because of the high number of JAVA and ABAP components.

Especially Web shops make high demands on the infrastructure because their performance has to be acceptable around the clock, with a practically unpredictable number of users. They must also guarantee a high level of security to protect business and customer data. Therefore SAP Internet Sales is one the most technically demanding business scenarios for cloud implementations.

2.1.3 SAP SCM

SAP supply chain management (SCM) also has also a high number of scenarios, but only a few technical components. However SAP SCM has its own challenge for cloud implementations: SAP's first incarnation of an in-memory database; the APO LiveCache.

SAP Advanced Planner and Optimizer (APO) is the core component of SCM, covering forecasting future requirements on the basis of historical data by Demand Planning (DP), optimization of cross-plant distribution of orders onto the available transport and production capacities by Supply Network Planning (SNP), Production Planning–Detailed Scheduling (PP-DS), Transportation Planning–Vehicle Scheduling (TP-VS) *Vendor Managed Inventory* (VMI), *Availability-to-Promise* (ATP) for example provides a multilevel availability check that can be carried out against material stocks, production, warehouse and transport capacities and costs across plants, etc.

▶ **LiveCache – first SAP in-memory database**

All of these business processes demand complex optimization runs with a high number of characteristic combinations which demand extremely fast access to data, impossible to achieve with hard disks.

For this purpose SAP developed LiveCache, one of the first in-memory databases, based on MaxDB (previously called SAPDB). In combination with special object-oriented technologies, the in-memory concept significantly accelerates the algorithmically highly complex, data-intensive and runtime-intensive functions of APO.

▶ **SCM on cloud**

The main challenge of APO LiveCache in regard to Cloud infrastructures is that it doesn't scale horizontally – all the memory must be available in one single server, a demand which exceeds in many cases the capacity of the standard blades in most public clouds. Also virtualization of LiveCache is not supported.

In future SCM may be used with HANA which will allow the LiveCache to be distributed over multiple nodes.

The optional SAP APO Optimizer poses its special challenge for clouds based on Linux because it is exclusively available on Windows only.

Components which fit much better to the cloud are SAP Event Management (EM), providing functions for managing deviations between planning and reality, and SAP Inventory Collaboration Hub supporting cross-enterprise integration for *Supplier Managed Inventories* (SMI) or *Vendor Managed Inventories* (VMI).

▶ **RFID**

The SAP Auto-ID Infrastructure (AII) to connect RFID scanners however can become a source of high IO load.

2.1.4 SAP SRM

Supplier Relationship Management (SRM) is the SAP component for purchasing and procurement departments, covering the complete process from placing the order to paying the invoice. Flexible approval procedures and tracking functions ensure that spending levels are monitored and controlled.

The core component is SAP Enterprise Buyer Professional (EBP), which is enhanced by a catalog server. Optional components are SAP Content Integrator, SAP Bidding Engine for online auctions, SAP Supplier Self-Services (SUS) and

SAP Live Auction Cockpit Web Presentation Server (LAC WPS) for online auctions (implemented as a Java applet).

▶ **SRM on cloud**

SAP SRM uses SAP ERP for the receipt of delivered goods, inventory management and financial accounting, whereas it uses SAP APO for production planning and SAP BW for reporting. Due to the usually low number of users in procurement, SAP SRM has no challenges to run on IaaS cloud services. With the acquisition of Ariba, SAP added a fully clouded purchasing solution to their portfolio.

2.1.5 SAP PLM

SAP Product Lifecycle Management (PLM) is the SAP solution for product development, plant maintenance, and quality assurance as well as hazardous substance management, industrial hygiene and safety, and environmental protection. Although SAP PLM is a standalone solution, it is not an SAP system of its own. Instead it uses a combination of functions from SAP ERP, SAP CRM, SAP SCM, and other components. Therefore, rather than requiring its own infrastructure, PLM is usually simply installed as an add-on to SAP ECC.

The knowledge warehouse can be used to store and distribute large files like scans, CAD drawings, video files, and so on.

▶ **PLM on cloud**

If the transfer of such large files poses a challenge to a cloud infrastructure, local cache servers at customer premises can be deployed. All these solutions fit well in to IaaS cloud services.

2.1.6 SAP CPM

Corporate Performance Management (CPM) is part of SAP Financial Performance Management and has replaced Strategic Enterprise Management (SEM). It includes SAP Strategy Management through acquisition of Pilot Software, Business Planning and Consolidation (BPC) through acquisition of OutlookSoft and several other components from partners.

▶ **CPM on cloud**

Due to the fact that these solutions are not based on the SAP standard web application server special care is necessary to implement them on public or private cloud infrastructures.

2.1.7 SAP GRC

SAP Government- Risk- Compliance (GRC) is the solution for Sarbanes Oxley Act (SOX) compliance. The *Global Trade System (GTS)* make sure that companies don't export something which is on a black list for certain countries, *Environment, Health & Safety (EH&S)* manage the documents required for industrial hygiene and safety, and environmental protection, such as material safety data sheets, TremCards, and waste manifests.

▶ *GRC on cloud*

The good message in regards of cloud deployment is that all components are based on the standards SAP web application server. Even *Access Control*, (former *Virsa Compliance Calibrator*) a segregation of duties auditing software is coded in ABAP, so it can be implemented on IaaS cloud services.

2.1.8 SAP Solution Manager

SAP Solution Manager (SSM) is the central system management system of SAP. While the legacy Computing Center Management System (CCMS) which is still included in any classic SAP application monitors the individual systems, the SAP Solution Manager controls the entire system landscape. SAP uses SSM as a vehicle to sell their maintenance services. SSM is also instrumental to generate the installation keys necessary to install an SAP instance.

It's comprised of the System Landscape Directory (SLD), SAP Central User Administration (CUA), and the SAP NetWeaver Landscape & Virtualization Management (LVM) solution, each described next.

The System Landscape Directory (SLD) provides a description of the technical parameters of the system landscape.

SAP Central User Administration (CUA) enables automatic distribution of users and roles to the various systems in the landscape. However, passwords are not synchronized in this case between the CUA and Active Directory.

For Java components the SAP User Management Engine (UME) manages roles and permissions. A SAP NetWeaver Administrator (NWA) support the administration of the JAVA based SAP NetWeaver components.

▶ *ACC & LVM*

As part of the SSM, the SAP NetWeaver Landscape & Virtualization Management (LVM) and its predecessor SAP Adaptive computing controller (ACC) enable you to drag and drop SAP systems onto available hardware resources. Technically, it simply connects the LUN where a SAP system is stored to an OS instance and boots the instances.

To save energy unused systems can be send to sleep simply by shutting them down. Also the relocation of SAP instances between physical and virtual machines is supported. LVM provides in addition features like automated system copy or workload balancing by unattended installation of SAP instances when needed.

Like ACC, the LVM depend on agents running on the OS to collect status and performance of a machine and interfaces to virtualization managers and storage arrays to perform its tasks.

▶ *LVM on cloud*

Installation of agents in a cloud based platform requires administrative capabilities and full access to the platform; this is basically only possible on IaaS Services. Other types of cloud services like Platform as a Service (PaaS) do not provide the required level of control over the infrastructure.

2.2 SAP NetWeaver

In some way SAP NetWeaver can be characterized as an "operating system for enterprises." Like Microsoft Windows provides not only a user interface but also ways to store, search and retrieve data, interfaces to the internet etc., the components of SAP NetWeaver unify the user interface to the different core business systems and take care of communications between these systems.

In the same way the SAP Business Suite can be regarded as the "office package for enterprises" providing the enterprise the necessary applications to do the real work of running the business, just as Microsoft's Outlook, Word, Excel and PowerPoint applications provide individuals with the solutions necessary to do their individual work.

2.2.1 SAP NetWeaver BW

As the first sibling of classical R/3, the *SAP Business Information Warehouse* represents (BW) is the most widely-used SAP solution besides ECC. A dedicated "Data Warehouse" became necessary because the performance of early platforms made it cumbersome running transactions and reports at the same time on the same system.

In addition the proliferation of SAP solutions dedicated to the different departments in an enterprise made it mandatory to consolidate the transactional data of all these individual systems for reporting and analysis. However the splitting of the BW from R/3 and its successor ECC generate the need to extract, transform and load (ETL) data from the source system into the BW. This batch process puts such a high load to the source system that it has to be run at night. So any reports derived from BW are always based on the "truth of yesterday".

▶ *InfoCubes*

In contrast to an *online transaction processing system* (OLTP) where all data records are stored in a normalized form for the sake of consistency, BW is an *online analytical processing system* (OLAP), based on special data structures, known as multidimensional InfoCubes.

Roughly speaking, a Dimension in an InfoCube corresponds to a classic report. In addition to the source data it provides also key figures like sums and averages. These figures are calculated directly after the data is loaded and are therefore immediately available when a query is made.

However, the design of multidimensional InfoCubes is quite a time-consuming job and needs specialized skills and experience. It can take weeks for a new type of report to become available to management. To solve this issue SAP developed the In-memory appliances BWA and HANA described in the SAP appliance section.

▶ *BW on cloud*

Based mostly on ABAP code, the NetWeaver BW can be implemented on IaaS services. However the ratio between database and application server of usually 1:2 (compared to 1:4 for ECC and CRM) may result in some cases in a resource demand for the BW database instance that exceed the limits of public cloud offerings. Also the massive IO throughput may cause problems, especially because public cloud providers publish (and charge) only the size but not the IO throughput of their storage devices. Other challenges are the unpredictable, "spiky" load pattern of a BW (see Chap. 3) which made the reservation of peak load resources all the day long necessary.

2.2.2 SAP NetWeaver Portal

The *Enterprise Portal* (*EP*) provides personalized access with Single Sign-On (SSO) to all SAP backend solutions with any Internet-enabled browser.

▶ *Portal on cloud*

Implemented in Java the portal seems to be an ideal fit to IaaS cloud services. However practical experience demonstrated that Java code is not always stable enough for mission critical applications. This is one of the reasons why SAP coded the central services of EP in C+. Because no user can access the SAP backend solutions via a browser when EP is down, the portal infrastructure should be designed fully redundant.

Practical experiences also result in the best practice to keep JAVA application server instances much smaller than ABAP ones. This ends up in a high number of instances for larger user numbers which generate a relative high appetite for memory resources.

Also consumption of CPU resources can be quite high, especially for the connection to directory services like Microsoft Active Directory (AS). To enable single sign on, the directory service must be sized adequately for hundreds of users logging in to the SAP system the same time.

Practical experience also demonstrates that the boot time of EP can become pretty long if the parameters in the storage configuration are not set correctly.[4]

▶ **TREX**

In addition to the Portal platform, SAP also developed a knowledge-management platform composed of a search engine (*Text Retrieval and Information Extraction*, or TREX) and content management. TREX can search documents, from simple text files to Microsoft Word or PowerPoint, and index files that are stored in Lotus Notes, Microsoft Exchange, or Documentum. Besides searching such unstructured data, TREX can also index and aggregate structured business data which made it a key component of Business Intelligence Accelerator (BIA) and the in-Memory database HANA.

▶ **TREX on cloud**

TREX loads all its data into main memory. Indexes for structured data are compressed quite efficiently, but for larger systems, the hunger of TREX for memory chips resembles to a carnivorous T-Rex. Other than LiveCache however, TREX can be distributed horizontally over any number of blades necessary to provide the needed memory. For such a distributed system, the file system must be a clustered or shared file system to present all files to all nodes.

2.2.3 SAP Knowledge Warehouse

SAP Knowledge Warehouse (KW) is used to create, manage, and distribute documents, training materials and manuals, and so on. SAP offers the training materials for SAP courses, including instructor guides as KW content for a fee so customers can do their own SAP trainings.

▶ **KW on the cloud**

Large files can be replicated to local cache servers to improve access speed and to reduce network load over remote connections. This way a local server at customer's premises can accelerate access times of files stored at a SAP KW hosted by a cloud provider.

---

[4] In this case validated designs like the ones of Cisco for Flexpod and vBlocks became handy.

2.2.4 SAP NetWeaver Mobile

SAP Mobile Infrastructure (MI) provided replication mechanisms to mobile devices to access to SAP solutions without a wireless connection. The MI client is executed locally on the Laptop and has its own database and process logic. As a relative heavyweight application it needs a powerful CPU and plenty of memory. After the acquisition of Sybase with its Sybase Unwired Platform (SUP), and Afaria SAP has chosen to drop further development of MI.

2.2.5 SAP NetWeaver Master Data Management

The topic of master-data management (MDM) exists since enterprises have used more than one business application. As the result of mergers and acquisitions, enterprises are faced with the need to eliminate duplicate master records to grant consistent reporting. *SAP NetWeaver Master Data Management* (SAP MDM) is designed to tackle this problem. For example, you can use SAP MDM to compare lists of suppliers by name and address, VAT ID number (in Europe), or Dun & Bradstreet numbers, in order to identify duplicate master data records.

▶ *MDM on cloud*

Usually a small system with only a few users SAP MDM doesn't pose a challenge to a IaaS cloud service. However various components use Windows specific DLLs, and so they must always be installed on a Windows Guest.

2.2.6 SAP NetWeaver Process Integration

The problem of communication between the different applications used in an enterprise (*Enterprise Application Integration*, or EAI) has also existed for as long as companies have used more than one computer. *SAP Process Integration* (PI) provides a central data hub for interconnecting business processes across the boundaries of an enterprise.

▶ *PI on cloud*

SAP PI has no users apart from the connected applications and the administrator only. From a cloud perspective, the biggest challenge with SAP PI implementation is the "digital" load profile, the system is literally idling till XLM packages arrive from a source system. In this case the resource consumption peak to 100 % during the routing mapping and transformation processes, going back to nearly zero again after the packages are delivered to the target. Therefore the sizing is simply a question of throughput so XML packages do not queue up and an acceptable forwarding time can be granted.

2.3 Business Objects

SAP Business Objects (BO) provides a suite of tools specialized in business intelligence like:
- BO Crystal Reports, an application to design and generate reports from a wide range of data sources from spreadsheets to data marts.
- BO Xcelsius, an environment to design highly-interactive, flash-based BI dashboards in NetWeaver Portal, PDF, documents, and presentations
- BO Web Intelligence for self-service reporting and analysis. The solution sits on top of BO Enterprise Universes.

The concept of "universes" as a semantic layer made database structures transparent for "non technical" users. To generate a universe, specialists must translate the database logic into something the user can understand and export the new universe to the central BO XI server.

▶ **BO on the cloud**

All user queries generate load on the BO XI server which in turn generates load on the source databases. This architecture can generate significant network traffic because the display of a few facts in a dashboard may cause the fetching of millions of data from the database which has to be cached on the BO XI server. Therefore high IO load has to be considered for operating SAP BO solutions on cloud infrastructures.

2.4 SAP Solutions for Small and Medium Companies

In addition to the SAP business suite and NetWeaver, SAP developed several solutions for small and medium companies.

2.4.1 SAP All-in-One

Basically a SAP ERP system with some functionality from BI, CRM and SCM delivered with approximately 80 pre-configured, industry-specific solutions from various partners with industry know-how. However, these solutions are reduced to the core processes of each particular industry. SAP All-in-One is based on the proven SAP technology, can be virtualized and scales well, so it fits quite well to IaaS cloud services.

2.4.2 SAP Business One

An out-of-the-box ERP solution acquired 2002 with TopManage Financial Systems that fulfills the demands of small and medium businesses. SAP Business One (B1) can be extended by hundreds of Add-ons, however has no code or architecture common with the classical SAP applications. In principle a Windows Server-based software application; Business One is well-suited for public clouds.[5]

2.4.3 SAP Business ByDesign

Based on a Service-oriented architecture(SOA), SAP Business ByDesign (ByD) is a fully hosted Software as a Service[6] offering with monthly rental prices targeted for customers with around 10–250 employees.

Using SOA principles the functionality can be extended by SAP partners. One example is Cisco Unified Communication (UC) supporting seamless integration of soft phone and video conferencing functionality into SAP business processes.

2.5 SAP Appliances

In the next section, we outline Duet, Alloy, BWA, and especially HANA, the newest addition to the SAP portfolio. What makes these solutions different from the other solutions described above is the relatively restricted delivery model. As described in Chap. 8, the solutions of the SAP business suite and NetWeaver can be installed on a broad range of Hardware platforms, operating systems and databases. SAP appliances however have to run on a strictly defined environment and in case of BWA and HANA have even to be delivered pre-installed by the hardware vendor.

2.5.1 Duet and Alloy

Duet enables Microsoft Office user to access SAP applications directly from their Office applications and MS SharePoint. For example, employees can use Outlook calendar to enter the time they use for projects in the relevant SAP applications. They can also enter leave requests directly in Outlook and transfer them to the SAP system. When the manager approves the request in Outlook the employee receives a notification.

The Duet Architecture consists of an add-on to the Microsoft Office on the user's client machine and the SAP backend system and a dedicated Duet server running .Net components from Microsoft and the NetWeaver components from SAP.

Alloy by IBM und SAP enables literally the same for Lotus Notes Office user. The backend infrastructure consists of an IBM Lotus Notes Alloy Add-On running

---

[5] SingTel for example is hosting SAP B1 for a monthly subscription fee on their PowerOn cloud based on a Vblock infrastructure.

[6] Currently SAP hosts Business ByDesign exclusively on its own data centers in Walldorf, Germany and Newton Square, Pennsylvania.

on an IBM Lotus Domino Server and an SAP Alloy Add-on running on a SAP Java WebAS.

▶ *Duet and alloy on the cloud*

Both appliances pose no special challenge to cloud architectures.

2.5.2 SAP Business Warehouse Accelerator

For faster analytics of specific BW InfoCubes SAP developed the Business Warehouse Accelerator[7] (BWA) as an add-on to SAP BW. For this purpose SAP extended the existing TREX technology to support querying of massive amounts of data distributed over multiple blades.

InfoCubes in the BW system can be marked to be indexed in BWA so that all database-bound queries on this InfoCubes are actually executed in-memory. InfoCubes loaded from SAP BW are compressed and the tables are decomposed into columns stored completely in main memory. This combination of "column orientation" and "in-memory" result in the dramatic acceleration of queries and reports compared to classical BW which gave the add-on its name.

▶ *BO accelerated*

BusinessObjects Explorer (BOE) can be connected directly to the BWA. This version called SAP BOE Accelerated features a simple web-based user interface for less experienced BI users. The combination with SAP BO Data Services enable data loaded into BWA from virtually any data source independent of SAP BW. This combination is called SAP BOE Accelerated Wave 2. To support the additional workload some additional blades have to be added to the basic BWA.

▶ *BWA on the cloud?*

A single BWA can be extended up to 64 blades with excellent scalability, so it sounds like an ideal fit to any cloud architecture. But the facts that each blade has to support up to 96 GB memory with the actual version, no virtualization is allowed, Intel E5 2670 is the only supported CPU and Suse Linux the only supported operation system would make it difficult to fit BWA to most of the public IaaS cloud offerings.

However what makes BWA even more unsuitable to any "classical" cloud concept is the fact that the appliance has to be shipped pre-installed by the server vendor with exactly the server and storage certified – even which cable is plugged into what switch port has to be identical with the reference installation in Walldorf.

---

[7] Formerly SAP NetWeaver Business Intelligence Accelerator.

2.5.3 SAP High Performance Analytical Appliance

Based on the scientific research[8] at the Hasso Plattner Institute (HPI) for IT Systems Engineering,[9] SAP combined the technologies of TREX, MaxDB,[10] liveCache, and Ptime[11] to enable real real-time business with the speed of thought. Some sources claim that the name HANA for the resulting hybrid database stand for "Hasso's new architecture".[12]

▶ *The speed of thought*

The average reaction time for a human to a simple stimulus has been measured to be 220 ms.[13] The average recognition reaction time is 384 ms however, because of the time necessary for understanding and comprehension. The recognition reaction time increases with the complexity of the context up to a range of 550–750 ms which is assumed as the speed of thought. With some exercising the reaction time becomes shorter.

Any time longer than the speed of thought interval will be perceived as waiting time, causing the user's mind to unconsciously deviating to other topics. The further the mind is taken off the task at hand, the longer it takes to focus on the topic again after the waiting period. Such context switching between tasks is extremely tiring for human brains. Response times in the range of the speed of thought allow the users to stay focused on one topic and be more productive and creative by omitting tiresome context switches.

▶ *Most relevant versus complete answers*

Part of the popularity of today's web search engines result from fact that they magically deliver results with the speed of thought. Answers appear on the screen instantly even before the user finished entering the question. Why is such magic not available for enterprise business applications also?

The answer is the difference in the necessary completeness of the result between enterprise applications and web search. The response of a web search displayed on the first page represents only the hits rated most relevant for the query.

---

[8] A Hybrid Row-Column OLTP Database Architecture for Operational Reporting, Jan Schaffner, Anja Bog, Jens Krüger, and Alexander Zeier.
[9] Donated to the University of Potsdam by Hasso Plattner.
[10] Acquired 1997 from Software AG, also known as ADABAS-D and SAPDB.
[11] Acquired 2005.
[12] Manager Magazin 9/2012.
[13] Information Theory of Choice-reaction Times, Laming D.R, Academic Press 1968.

A legal business report however must reflect all relevant data in its result. Whereas a web search just has to shift through an indexed data set, the business application has to scan the complete dataset to guarantee completeness in addition to processing such complex aggregations.

Search engines like Google, Yahoo and Bing can be so astonishingly fast because the result of their searches just has to be "good enough" for the common user.

However no tax authority will accept payment based on anything else than a complete scan through each and every accounting number. Therefore some more advanced technologies than "just in-memory" are necessary to derive the complete answer from a business grade system with the speed of thought.

▶ *In-memory: a no-brainer?*

Given the fact that access to data in a computer's memory is orders of magnitude faster than the ones stored on disk, the concept of in-memory computing seems to be obvious even for the simplest minds. SAP has followed this approach already more than a decade ago with the APO LiveCache, literally a maxDB running completely in main memory.

Thanks to the advances in microchip production technologies large amounts of main memory become affordable nowadays. So simply enlarging the main memory till it can keep the complete dataset of an application seems to be a straightforward strategy.

With the majority of databases used for SAP business applications being in the range of 1–3 TB and considering the advanced compression features of state of the art database systems it should be easy to hold the complete data set in the database memory buffer.

Such an approach however will still not be sufficient to achieve the necessary performance for ad-hoc analysis. To enable business users to distill useful information from raw data within the blink of an eye, a deep understanding is necessary how data is organized not only in the main memory but also in the CPU and intermediate caches.

▶ *Memory is slower than CPU cache*

Even if main memory is several times faster than disk, it's still not as fast as the processor itself. As the time this book is written, typical memory run with clock speeds between 800 and 1,600 MHz, an Intel CPU is rated for up to 3.6 GHz Therefore state of the art CPU designs deploy different levels of caching to decrease the latency for repetitive access to the same piece of data.

To load a value from main memory it has to be copied subsequently through intermediate caches till it reaches a register in the core. Accessing main memory can consume up to 80 times the number of CPU cycles compared an access to the Layer 1 cache.

2.5 SAP Appliances

As lower the cache level the speed increase, but size decrease. Level 3 cache with a capacity of 30 MB run with a little more than half o the CPU clock speed. Level 2 and 1 run at the same clock speed as the core itself but they can only store 256 and 64 KB of data.

In an ideal world, all data requested by the processor would be always available in the cache. In real world however so called "cache misses" happen, when the necessary data is not currently available in a certain cache level. Every cache miss slows down and wastes resources.

Worst case is a "full miss" when requested data has to be loaded from main memory. So even the fastest data transfer is futile if its delivers the wrong data. Therefore data structures have to be optimized to maximize the likelihood that all the data necessary for the next computing step are in the same cache line.

▶ **Row- versus column orientation**

All the facts described above result in the case of the optimal layout of the database tables. Whenever database structures are discussed it's implicitly assumed that data is logically stored in 2-dimensional tables like a spreadsheet. In the physical world however, all the bits and bytes representing the data are stored and transmitted in one single string.

Consequently there are two ways to transform a table into a single string: you can either arrange one row of the table behind the other or you can queue each column after the other. The first option is called row oriented, the second column oriented.

▶ **The case for row-orientation: OLTP**

For good reasons, most databases used for business applications store the data values in a row-oriented fashion. This way much of the data belonging to the same business transaction like an order number, the number of the customer who bought the item, the part number of the item ordered, the number of parts ordered, the price per piece and the total sum are stored in adjacent memory blocks.

Such row-oriented organization of data increase the likelihood that all data belonging to a single business transaction are found in the same cache line, reducing the number of cache misses. The fact that since decades row-oriented databases enabled sub-second response times even with disc based storage demonstrate that this concept fits well to the On-Line Transaction Processing (OLTP) systems.

▶ **The case for column-orientation: OLAP**

Unfortunately Row-oriented storage is not well suited for reporting, where not the complete data set of a single business transaction is of interest, but for example only the part numbers, how much of them are bought on average or the total sum per order.

In contrast to a typical business process, only a small number of attributes in a table is of interest for a particular query in a typical analysis. Loading every row into cache when only a fraction of data is really used is clearly not an optimal way for On-Line Analytical (OLAP) Systems, even if they run completely in-memory.

Organizing the tables in a way that columns are stored in adjacent memory blocks make it possible that only the required columns have to be moved into cache lines while the rest of the table can be ignored.

This way, the cache has to keep only the data needed to process the request, reducing the data traffic from main memory to CPUs, in-between CPU's and down through the whole cache hierarchy significantly. Maximizing the likelihood that data necessary can be found in the level 1 cache will obviously speed up the processing and minimize the response time.

Analysis of database accesses in enterprise warehouse applications as well as practical experience demonstrate that column-oriented solutions like SAP BWA and Sybase IQ are an excellent choice for on-line analytical systems.

The obvious disadvantage of these systems is that their performance with row-based transactions is poor. So what is good for business transactions is bad for reports and vice versa.

For many years the only answer to this dilemma was to deploy two sets of applications optimized either for OLTP or for OLAP, doubling not only the amount of data to be stored and subsequently also the hardware and operation costs, but stipulating also the demand to synchronize the data between the different systems.

▶ **Best of both worlds: two engines under one hood**

To combine the best of both worlds and support analytical as well as transactional workloads in one system, HANA combines the two different types of database systems under one umbrella by means of two dedicated database engines:
- TREX to store data column oriented for analytical operations
- Ptime to store data raw oriented for transactional operations

▶ **SAP HANA database**

For each individual data table the best suited engine has to be selected at the time of creation. To grant optimal performance of a hybrid database, the access pattern has to be known in advance. Therefore typical queries are analyzed with regards to their cache miss behavior. Together with the weight of the query this is used to determine the optimal layout – either row or column. If necessary the layout can be changed at a later time.

Both database engines can be accessed through SQL (JDBC/ODBC), MDX (ODBO), and BICS (SQL DBC) interfaces. HANA provides also a library of business functions and allows the execution of the application logic directly on the database avoiding unnecessary move of data to an external application server. Such commands can be invoked by an HANA-specific SQL script language.

2.5 SAP Appliances

▶ *Compression*

Advanced data compression technologies like dictionaries are implemented to reduce the demand for still precious main memory and minimize the movement of data between memory and caches further. The compression factor depends mostly on the number of attributes in the source data. The higher the numbers of unambiguous attributes, the lower the compression factor with almost no effect on already compressed data. Because the database itself needs also some working memory the sizing rules published by SAP recommend doubling the amount of memory needed for the compressed data.[14]

▶ *Real real-time or the "truth of yesterday"?*

As discussed at the beginning of the chapter one of the obstacles of "traditional" data marts like SAP BW is that the extraction of data from source system has to be done during night shift to avoid negative impact to the operation of the business systems during day time. Therefore even when accelerated by BWA reports reflect only the "truth of yesterday".

SAP HANA therefore supports a trigger-based replication method where ABAP coded "triggers" on the source ERP system detect changes to the source database and replicate these changes real time to the SAP HANA database in a so called "side car" configuration.[15]

The ultimate vision however is to enable one single HANA database to become the single source of truth for all SAP applications of an enterprise. This way the result of any transaction will be available in real time for analysis.

▶ *Volatile and persitent data storage*

Main memory is fast but volatile by nature and loses all its content immediately in case of an electrical power outage (as any book author knows when he has to reboot because his text processor "hangs").

To avoid such "Alzheimer disease", HANA has to make all data persistent on non-volatile storage like SSD, flash or disk drives. For this purpose SAP implemented a MaxDB shadow server providing a persistence layer shared by both database engines.

---

[14] SAPnote 1514966 for HANA replacing a traditional database
SAPnote 1637145 for HANA replacing a traditional SAP BW.

[15] There is also a Log-based replication method that extracts changes in the source system from the transaction logs. This method however is only available for certain versions of DB2 as source and only recommended for customers who have been invited to use it during the ramp up of HANA 1.0.

▶ **Savepoints and logs**

The main memory is divided into pages. Changed pages, are asynchronously written by default every 5 min in savepoints to non-volatile storage. In addition a database log captures synchronously all changes made by the transactions, ensuring that all transactions are permanent.

After a power failure or a maintenance shutdown the database can be restarted like any disk-based database. First the database pages are restored from the savepoints and then the database logs are applied to restore the changes that have happened between savepoints (rolled forward).

▶ **Restore**

To restore the database within a few minutes and guarantee high performance during a savepoint, SAP specified an IO throughput of 100.000 IO per second for T-shirt sized appliances and corresponding numbers for large Scale-Out HANA implementations.

To reach this extraordinary high throughput SSD or Flash devices can be used for small and medium sized HANA appliances. For large scale out solutions we come to the paradox situation that most vendors deploy disk based storage arrays for the persistency layer of the in-memory appliance. This approach allows utilizing proven data replication technologies for HA and DR scenarios.

SAP distinguishes between the HANA in-memory database and the SAP in-Memory Appliance as a combination of hardware and software delivered in a validated configuration by certified SAP hardware partners Cisco, Dell, Fujitsu, Hitachi, HP, IBM, NEC and VCE.

▶ **HANA delivery**

Following the HANA operational concept[16] the hardware partners deliver the SAP HANA appliance software together with corresponding, validated hardware as a pre-packaged solution to the customer site and connect the HANA database to the source systems.

The exact bill of material for hardware components, the operating system, additional software components such as a scalable file system, and the SAP HANA software itself is provided also by the hardware partners, since the hardware partners install and configure the SAP HANA appliance software prior to shipment.

Only the HANA database is running on the HANA appliance hardware.[17] Other parts of the SAP BI solution like BusinessObjects Enterprise or BusinessObjects Explorer must run on separate servers.

---

[16] See SAPnote 0001603671.

[17] Plus a Sybase replication server if the Log-based replication method is used.

In addition to the SAP HANA database the HANA appliance contains also the HANA Studio, a data-modeling and administration tool based on Eclipse and a set of libraries required for other applications to connect to the HANA database. Both the HANA Studio and the client libraries are usually installed on a client PC or server. The software update manager (SUM) for HANA enables an automatic download and installation of software updates from the SAP service marketplace.

Because of the tight optimization of the code to certain Cache structures and sizes described before, SAP HANA is only certified on selected Intel CPU models and Suse Linux as operation system.[18]

▶ *HANA on cloud*

HANA scales well horizontally for analytical applications. Therefore blade based Scale-Out solutions are an excellent fit for HANA deployments. Scale-Out solutions inherit also a higher availability because spare blades can be automatically deployed in case of an hardware failure and a persistency layer outside the server enables HA and DR scenarios.

The demand of CPU resources per user is relative low, however because only 12.8 GB of main memory can be supported per core, only 512 GB of memory is available on a blade with 40 cores which could have 2 terabytes installed.

Just as with BW Accelerator, SAP HANA sound like an ideal fit to any cloud architecture because of his horizontal scalability. However like for BWA, no virtualization is supported and even the IP addresses are fixed ones.

What makes HANA also unsuitable to "classical" cloud concepts is the fact that the appliance has to be shipped pre-installed by the server vendor with setup identical with the reference installation in Walldorf down to the cabling.

Neither storage nor the switching infrastructure interconnecting the blade enclosures of a scale-out HANA can be shared with any other application at writing. This would make it difficult to fit productive HANA implementations to public cloud offerings.

Development systems however are available in Amazon AWE[19] and special agreements with large hosting companies for special HANA on cloud offerings are under discussion at the time of writing.

2.6 Summary

The multitude of SAP business processes are provided by a broad portfolio of solutions bundled into the Business Suite and NetWeaver. In-memory technologies developed over more than a decade have now reached a state that will allow storing

---

[18] See HANA platform availability matrix at http://service.sap.com/pam.
[19] http://scn.sap.com/docs/DOC-28294.

the data of all SAP business solutions into one common hybrid database. This way all data will become again available to all applications and users at the same moment enabling real-time business processes like with R/3 four decades ago.

The different solutions have different characteristics and pose different demands and restrictions on infrastructure which have to be considered when building a cloud infrastructure:

- OLTP solutions like SAP ECC, CRM, SRM and PLM are an ideal fit to private and public IaaS cloud services because of their ideal horizontal scaling and predictive load pattern.
- OLAP solutions like NetWeaver BW and SAP SCM do not fit so well to most public cloud offerings because of their relative large databases, high IO throughput and "spiky", unpredictable load pattern. A special challenge is the APO liveCache in-memory database which has to be run on bare metal.
- Because no user can access the applications of the SAP back-end systems via a browser when the NetWeaver Enterprise Portal is down, the infrastructure should be designed to be fully redundant.
- The SAP solutions for small and medium businesses like All-in-one, and Business One fit well to IaaS cloud services. Business ByDesign is offered exclusively as a SaaS cloud service by SAP.
- Installation of agents necessary for SAP cloud management solutions of NetWeaver Landscape & Virtualization Management (LVM) requires full access and administrative capabilities to the platform. This is basically only possible in Service Platform (IaaS) concepts.
- In spite of excellent horizontal scaling, the SAP in-memory Appliances BWA and HANA are currently somewhat unsuitable to any cloud architecture because the appliance has to be shipped pre-installed by the server vendor as an exact replica of the reference system and due to the fact that neither virtualization nor sharing resources with other applications are supported.
- SAP HANA: One which is offered on Amazon AWS is restricted to 60.5 GB of memory; therefore support roughly 32 GB of compressed data (a single table for analytics of 160–190 GB worth of data). Because HANA is not optimized for the "Sandy Bridge" architecture used for the EC2 Compute Units HANA performance will be sub-optimal (approx 20 % less). Focused on the SMB and entry market, HANA ONE comes with a special EULA that restricts support to a "community" one like for Linux.
- However multi SID implementations are already fully supported by SAP for non-productive environments and multi-tenant configurations on blade architectures like Cisco UCS are a ideal fit for private clouds. Such systems can be considered "cloud ready" for large mission critical systems and can be deployed on a "by use" method. As long as the connectivity and storage access remains in certified ranges, you can deploy a pool of HANA configured appliances and split for example a 16 blade configuration into 8+8 or 4+4+8, etc. So this does allow some "HANA on demand" deployments. As a matter of fact SuccessFactor run already multiple production HANA instances on a shared Cisco UCS infrastructure with a special authorization.

Service Levels for SAP on Cloud

This chapter discusses the definition of appropriate service levels for SAP systems in cloud environments. It focuses on the question how to predict the necessary resources to fulfill the SLA and how to measure and bill their actual consumption. Topics such as service guarantees for SAP systems and availability as well as an innovative billing tool are described in detail.

"The electricity has to be of good quality" – in the early days of electrification when customers didn't have experience with this new technology the city council of a German village wrote this sentence in the contract with a utility company. This is quite similar to the definitions in many service level agreements for SAP solutions on public and private clouds.

▶ *How to define?*

As units of measurement like the Ampere rating define the power necessary to run an electrical appliance, the unit SAPS was developed to define the necessary "horsepower" of a SAP implementation. However a utility company has also to grant that voltage will not drop and phase not shift under high load. With the proliferation of utility-like cloud offerings also a meaningful and mutual agreed unit for the resource consumption like the kilowatt-hour (kWh) becomes necessary for IT.

▶ *How to measure?*

When Thomas Alva Edison established the first commercial power plant in New York, he charged his customers by the number of light bulbs they had installed. As a result the proud owners of an electrical lights had them switched on all day long, because there was no incentive to save energy. Subsequently Edison's power plant always ran at 100 % capacity.

This situation is quite similar to classical outsourcing contracts which count just "number of seats" without considering how much computing resources the ones who sit in the seats consume. So just like today everyone is used to the Watt-meter to grant a fair billing of utilities we need something like a SAPS-meter to grant fair billing in cloud environments.

▶ How to predict?

In theory the resources available in a cloud are infinite. However as practical experience with public grids demonstrate, all resources available have their limits, ending up in blackouts if demand exceeds the capabilities of generation and transport.

It is quite difficult to store electricity in large quantities; with computing power there is simply no way to store.[1] Whatever is consumed at a certain point in time has to be produced at this time. Like public and private utility companies have to predict the total demand of their consumers to size their power stations, public and private cloud providers have to predict the total demand of their consumers to size their cloud data centers.

Both utility grids and cloud infrastructures have to consider worst case scenarios. In both cases however you can also utilize leveraging effects. The bigger the number of small and medium consumers, the more the individual peaks cancel each other out. But like in utility it is critical to predict load peaks of big consumers to ensure that the necessary resources are always available just in time.

▶ How available?

SAP systems are usually among the most mission critical systems of a business. Like modern life depends on the availability of electricity, enterprises are dependent on the availability of their SAP solutions. Therefore a meaningful definition of the necessary level of availability has to be also part of the Service Level Agreement (SLA).

To grant the necessary stability of a business critical system however it is not sufficient to take care for the obvious parts of the infrastructure, such as computers and networks. You also have to include IT services such as data backup, file and print services, directory services for managing users, deployment services for the installation and update of operating systems, and network services like DNS or DHCP.

As in all areas, the weakest link determines the stability of the entire process chain. For example, a SAP transaction can be canceled because a name resolution via the DNS service does not work or because an access to a file system has failed because of the usage of a data volume reach 100 %.

---

[1] The way utilize excess compute power during times of low demand is to "store the request" instead of the power. This is nothing but batch processing.

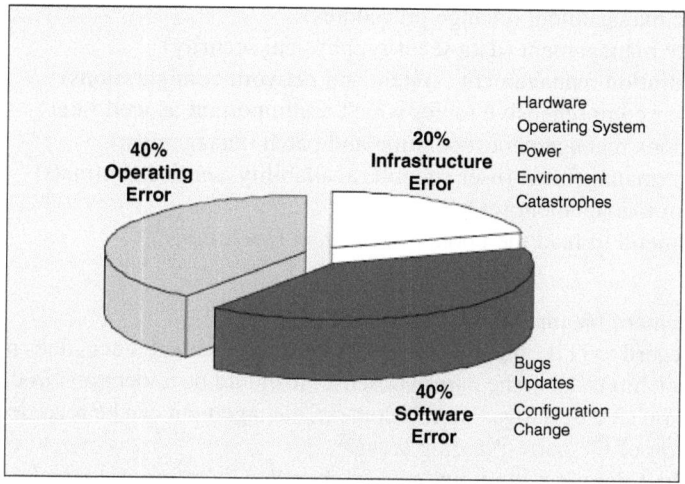

Fig. 3.1 Causes of trouble with IT Systems (Source: Gartner Group)

Particularly the last example demonstrates that the stability of cloud services is affected not only by technical deficiencies that can be solved technically but also by a lack of knowledge and carefulness regarding the monitoring and maintenance of the systems.

In real life, it is often a misconfiguration that causes the DNS service to fail, and an extension not done in time is the reason why a volume is used up to 100 %. To which extent the human factor influences the quality of IT services is shown in Fig. 3.1, which illustrates the distribution of causes for unplanned downtimes in the IT operation.

3.1 IT Service Management Reference Model

▶ *Best practices for cloud operation*

The principles of the *Information Technology Infrastructure Library*[2] (ITIL) have proven their worth also for structuring the operation of SAP systems on clouds. In the following sections, we will limit our focus to the most important areas necessary for operating SAP systems on Cloud infrastructures:
- Service level management (definition and monitoring)
- Performance management (capacity and resource planning)
- Availability management (backup and recovery, monitoring)

The topics of system operations will be discussed in the next chapters:

---

[2] Developed by the British government, now under support of the IT Service Management Forum (http://www.itsmf.com).

- Change management (change procedures)
- Security management (data security, physical security)
- Configuration management (system and network configurations)

For other comprehensive topics which are important as well like:
- Operations management (operation and patch management)
- Incident management (user support, availability, service contracts)
- Problem management (escalations)

we recommend to read the book: *SAP System Operations*[3]

> **Management Means 'Taking Care of It'**
> With regard to ITIL, the inflated use of the term "management" does not refer to leadership tasks in the narrower sense. It should be understood in the sense of "taking care of things." In this context, management can be regarded as the provision of the corresponding service.
>
> In the following, the term "management" is therefore used exclusively in the context of operating SAP systems on cloud infrastructures and not in the context of corporate governance. Accordingly, processes describe organizational procedures in the IT department instead of software processes on a computer.

3.2 Service Level Management

▶ *IT is always a service*

SAP solutions on public or private clouds are not an end in itself but a service used by the line of business (LOB) departments for fulfilling their respective tasks. These are the "end consumers" of the business processes which will be charged by the IT department for the supplied services. In principle, it does not matter greatly whether these services are provided by a private cloud or public one.

The quantity and quality of the provided services must be defined in *Service Level Agreements* (SLA) using measurable criteria so that their adherence can be verified. It is then the task of the *Service Level Management* to track and document the compliance with the SLA.

An SLA is often misunderstood as wish-lists of the various business departments. However, in reality, the SLA is the basis for the orchestration of the necessary processes and infrastructures by the cloud provider and therefore for the costs charged back.

---

[3] Missbach, Stelzel, *SAP System Operations,* SAP PRESS 2004.

A service that has to be 100 % available all year round has to be orchestrated differently than a service that is required only during normal business hours. Similarly, a system landscape that must guarantee short response times under extreme loads, and tolerate breakdowns of individual components has to be orchestrated differently than from a training system. This also applies to the required degree of safeguarding specified in maintenance contracts with suppliers and technology partners.

▶ *Service levels define quantity, quality and costs of a service*

If the LOB departments make high demands in the SLA they must be willing to bear the higher costs for the necessary efforts. It is the job of service-level management to reconcile as much as possible the expectations of the user as the internal customer, and the reality of what is possible under the given conditions.

3.3 Performance Management

Performance of an SAP system depends on the ratio of the available resources to the current load. Therefore, it is the task of *performance management* to ensure that sufficient resources are allocated at any time to be able to fulfill the performance requirements defined in the SLA.

3.3.1 Response Time

As discussed in the previous chapter, a user's productivity is essentially determined by the response time of the system. From the user's point of view, the response time is the period during which he must wait after having pressed the Enter key until a system response is displayed on screen.

▶ *Response time influences productivity*

During this period, the user usually cannot perform any other tasks. Therefore, short response times are the ultimate objective of every cloud implementation of a SAP system. Average response times below one second are generally perceived as good, while anything longer is generally regarded as disruptive for the workflow.

From the business departments' point of view, it is usually only the performance of SAP production systems that matters because these systems directly influence the productivity of the enterprise. However, the performance of the development and test systems matters as well because they indirectly influence the project costs via the productivity of the developers.

▶ **Response time from the system's viewpoint**

From the cloud provider viewpoint, response time is the average length of time required to process a transaction. This refers to the time from the arrival of the processing request at the application server until the moment when the response from the application server is transferred to the network.[4]

▶ **Response time from the user's viewpoint**

From the point of view of the user, response time include also the round trip time on the network infrastructure and the processing on the end-device.

Every transaction has a minimum response time. This ideal value can only be achieved after a certain time after the system starts up, and the buffers are filled; that is, when the system has 'warmed up'.

▶ **Relationship of response time to CPU load**

Even with a relatively low average system load, the randomly distributed user activities now and then temporarily cause a CPU usage of 100 % and thus wait times. This is shown in Fig. 3.2 as an example of a medium CPU load of 50 %. These wait times are so short, however, that the user will hardly notice them.

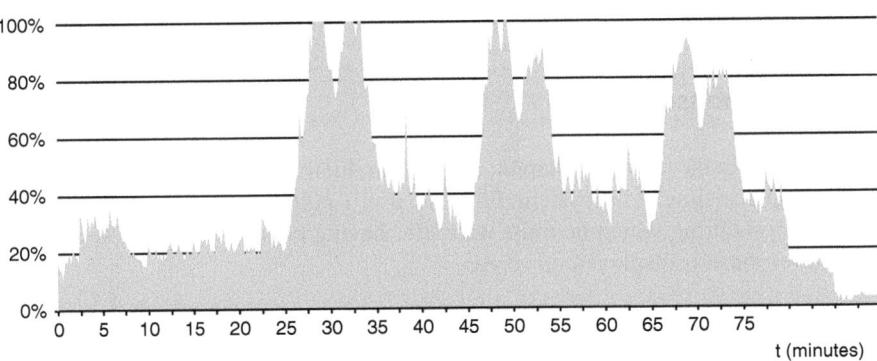

Fig. 3.2 Example of CPU load distribution with average of ca. 50 % utilization

As the number of users increases, the probability that wait times will increase and thus the average response time increases as well. The response time is thus in direct proportion to the CPU load, or, to put it more precisely, to the CPU wait time.

---

[4] The time displayed in the DIALOG field of the CCMS also includes the runtimes on the network up to the SAP GUI. The CCMS transaction DINOGUI display the execution time of the dialog step on the servers.

3.3 Performance Management

Figure 3.3 shows the situation with an average CPU load of approximately 70 %. Here, the 100 % peaks are actually small plateaus, with the result that some users must sometimes wait a little longer for the system response.

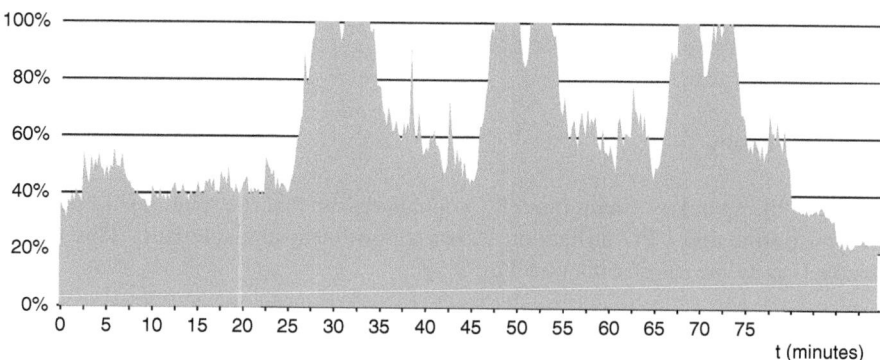

Fig. 3.3 CPU load distribution with average of ca. 70 % utilization

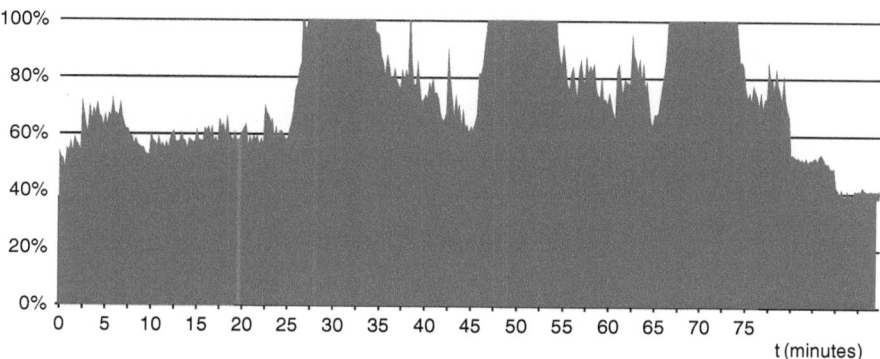

Fig. 3.4 CPU load distribution with average of ca. 80 % utilization

In Fig. 3.4, the 100 % plateaus have become so wide that, despite an average CPU load of only 80 %, long periods of unsatisfactory response times – and dissatisfied users – can hardly be avoided.

Experience shows that the users in business departments are less interested in the average response times per hour than in how long, based on their subjective perception, they have to wait. Therefore, based on the required response times, the cloud infrastructure has to be designed in such a way that a specific medium-level CPU load is not exceeded, in order to ensure that load peaks do not turn into prolonged 100 % plateaus.

> In theory system utilization of 100 % could be achieved easily if all users sent their requests in regular intervals, like the load generators in a benchmark. In reality, with an average CPU load of almost 100 % the response times will be unacceptable.

▶ **Queue theory**

From the "Markov Chain model"[5] you can derive that the relationship between response time and CPU utilization shows a non-linear characteristic. This is also backed up by measurements (see Fig. 3.5).

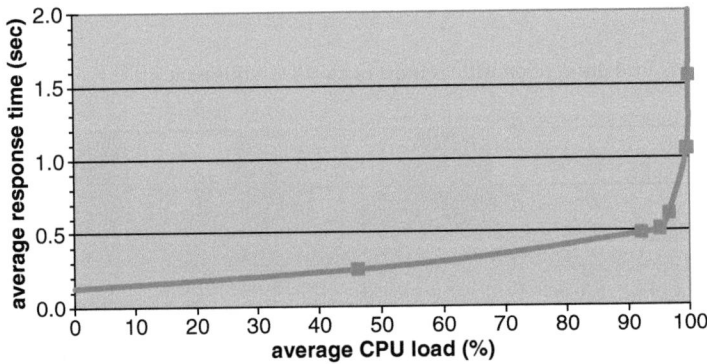

Fig. 3.5 Response Time Depending on CPU utilization

At first, the response time increases in an almost linear way together with the average CPU load. At a specific threshold value, there is a characteristic bend from which the response time very quickly increases to unacceptable values.

Depending on the response times stipulated in the SLAs, the system therefore must be designed in a way that the average CPU use does not exceed this threshold. You need to consider that the average values apply to hours while the peak loads causing the CPU congestion partially only last for split seconds. During these congestion situations, use does indeed reach 100 %, as shown in Figs. 3.2, 3.3, and 3.4.

---

[5] See Queuing Networks and Markov Chains. Modeling and Performance Evaluation with Computer Science Applications (Wiley 1998).

3.4 Units of Measure for SAP Applications

While the size of main memory and disk space can be specified in simple giga-, and terabytes, with system throughput, we first need to define a unit of measurement that can be used to specify the performance requirements of the business processes, independently of CPU type, computer technology, and manufacturer.

▶ *SAPS: the horsepower of an SAP system*

System throughput refers to the transaction volume that is processed in a given period of time. SAP has developed the *SAP Application Performance Standard (SAPS)* unit of measure for system throughput, based on the SD benchmark. One hundred SAPS correspond to the standard processing of 2,000 order items per hour, which requires 6,000 user interaction steps (screen changes) or 2,400 Sales & Distribution (SD) transactions.

SAPS can therefore be regarded as the horse-power of an SAP system. Having said that, SAPS has as much in common with the practical usage of the SAP Sales & Distribution module as horsepower does with the strength of an actual horse.

▶ *Release dependency of SAPS*

Application load in SAPS is release-independent; in other words, 100 SAPS are always equal to 2,000 order items per hour, regardless of the release of the SAP system. Due to the fact that the resource consumption of the SD-module rises with nearly every SAP release, a given server can process fewer order items per hour with newer releases. The number of SAPS the server can be accounted for is lowering accordingly.

This results in the paradox situation, that in spite of more and better functionality provided with every new release, in principle the "consumed" number of SAPS of a 1,000 user SAP System does not change from R/3 3.1 to ECC 6.6 as long as nothing changes but the release (i.e. no changes in customizing, usage of functions and so on). However the hardware that was able to support these 1,000 users with release 3.1 might only support 500 users with release ERP 6.0, because more and better functionalities consume significant more CPU power.

▶ *The donkey and the bag*

The situation can be literally compared with a farmer's donkey that has to carry a bag of 50 gal. As long as the farmer filled the bag with hay the donkey was running fast. After a while however the farmer made a "release change" to grain. The bag has still the same 50 gal, but the donkey slows down significantly. After the farmer found gold on his property and changed the content of the bag to ore the poor old donkey was only creeping. The good point in the case of IT is however, that thanks to advanced technology today's donkeys are stronger than elephants compared to their ancestors.

The moral of the story is however, that customers who use the opportunity of a SAP release change to move their SAP system from a legacy platform to a cloud just have to tell the provider the number of SAPS his old system consumed on the old release to enable him to select the right cloud infrastructure.

3.4.1 Predicting the System Load

The process of predicting the number of SAPS for a new implementation is called *sizing* and consists of two parts: the estimation of the maximum system load to be expected and the determination of the minimum required hardware configuration.

▶ **Greenfield sizing**

Cases where the customer is totally new to SAP or is implementing a SAP solution for the very first time are called Greenfield Projects. Typically not much of the information's necessary for a sizing are available in such projects. Therefore most of the parameters have to be estimated based on experience and best practices.

At least the number of users and which functionality they will use should be known. Assuming that the numbers of transactions to be processed scale with the number of users this can be used for a coarse estimate of the necessary resources.

▶ **What is a user?**

However we have to distinct between several types of users:
- The number of licensed or *named users* is irrelevant for sizing, because it is unlikely that all named users are active in the system at the same time.
- The number of simultaneous *logged-on users* is essential for sizing of main memory because the SAP system allocates memory for the context of each user.
- The number of simultaneous active users (*concurrent users*) *is the most relevant*, because they execute business processes that in turn require CPU ressources, generate IO operations, and write data to disk

The various SAP transactions generate very different loads because of their complexity, the interaction with other modules and particularly in the number of database tables that must be accessed. These differences are factored in considered by load *factors* specific for every solution. For sizing users need to be assigned to the solutions they use most.

> **Rule of Thumb**
> 30–50 % of the named users are logged-on simultaneously; 30–50 % of them are concurrently active

3.4 Units of Measure for SAP Applications

▶ *How active is a user?*

Not all users strain the system to the same extent. By their degrees of activity, the concurrent users can be classified into three categories:
- *Low activity users* execute at least one interaction step every 5–6 min. This could be a manager whose main activity is to analyze information.
- *Medium activity user* executes an interaction step every 30 s. This is the most common active user profile in the SAP ERP system.
- *High activity users* execute an interaction step every 10 s. Such a high degree of activity is at the limit of human capability, and only occurs in the case of users who are entering mass data.

> **Rule of Thumb**
> 40 % of users are low, 50 % are medium and only 10 % high activity – in retail 10 % low, 60 % medium, 30 % high

▶ *Transaction based sizing*

While for a classic ERP system the number of employees in an enterprise represents a natural upper limit for the number of users (for example in *Employee Self-Services*), this does not necessarily apply to a web shop. During a successful marketing campaign, dramatic peak loads can occur that must be processed by the CRM and ERP system before customers change to another site due to excessively long wait times.

Besides user-initiated online transactions, the sizing also has to consider the batch jobs. The general assumption is that batch jobs require fewer system resources than online transactions because they are not critical in regards of the response time. However, this assumption may not apply in all cases.

In certain scenarios, the nightly batch load can actually be much bigger than the maximum load caused by online users during the office hours and their total run time is critical for the business. A typical example is the SAP solution for the retail industry (IS-Retail), in which the nightly replenishment planning run absolutely must finish in time so that the trucks can be loaded and depart early in the morning. Other examples are the invoice runs in the SAP solutions for utility companies (IS-Utility), banks (IS-Banking), or insurance companies (IS-Insurance). In all these cases, the transaction load of the night-time batch jobs is several times bigger than that of the online users. Heavy batches happening in all industries are payment runs, dunning and financial closings.

Additionally, the system design must consider the uneven distribution of the system load over time. A realistic activity pattern contains typical daily and yearly maximums. In most enterprises there is a load peak at the beginning of lunch time which quickly decreases in the course of the early afternoon. This peak is caused by managers who start a large report shortly before they leave for lunch, hoping that they will find the result upon their return.

▶ **Seasonal peak loads**

Depending on the industry in question, there also might be seasonal peak loads. Examples are ice-cream manufacturers, whose peak season is summer, and gift item manufacturers, whose busiest time of the year is at Christmas. Considerably more important to the system-design process than the indication of how many million orders are entered per year is the maximum number of orders that must be processed by the system during a specified time window.

> **Averages Are Useless: Be Aware of Peaks!**
> As a matter of fact the average speed of your car is below the one of a snail if you average over 24 h – considering the time the car is running at zero miles per hour waiting for your return at the parking lot. In spite of this the car manufacturer has to dimension motor, gear and brakes for top speed (especially in Germany).
> The same is true for SAP systems. Therefore the system orchestration must consider the uneven distribution of the system load over time. In contrast to the synthetically generated load in a benchmark, real users do not perform their transactions steadily during the day or year.

Be aware that there are several SAP solutions that can't be sized by user numbers in principle – either because they do not have users like the process infrastructure PI, or because a single user can generate a unpredictable high resource consumption especially in analytical solutions like SAP BW, APO, MI, BWA and HANA.

After all the business relevant information's been collected, they have to be transformed into hardware architecture. The *SAP Quicksizer* on-line tool (http://service.sap.com/quicksizing[6]) is available to every SAP customer and partner to calculate the minimal necessary SAPS, memory, disk space and IO throughput numbers based on the input given.

▶ **SAP Quicksizer**

- Every SAP Application has own requirements and therefore its own section in a Quicksizer project
- Quicksizer does both user based and transaction based sizing (the greater of the two has to be used to determine the hardware requirements).

---

[6] To use the Quicksizer you need a SAP S-user account and credentials.

3.4 Units of Measure for SAP Applications

- Quicksizer assumes a moderate customized system (less than 20 % customer code)
- Quicksizer results include a 40 % security margin for "uncertainties".
- The output considers productive systems only, no development, quality assurance, test, training or Sandbox systems.
- Quicksizer does not consider resource demand of operating systems and Hypervisors!
- As any tool Quicksizer follows the garbage in – garbage out concept, there is no check against nonsense entries.
  For more details have a look at the SAP Quicksizer Guide.

Like the SAP solution portfolio, the SAP Quicksizer is continuously extended and adapted to the practical experience from customer situations. To ensure that old versions are not used unintentionally, there is no offline version of Quicksizer.

> **Questionnaires Are a Waste of Time (Mostly)**
> Usually the information mentioned above is collected off-line with questionnaires and later fed into the Quicksizer tool by a sizing expert. If something is forgotten or obviously wrong, the expert has to call back. A customer requesting offerings from multiple cloud providers has to fill in literally the same data into practically identical questionnaires which end up that the same data is keyed into the Quicksizer several times, just multiplying the work for anybody for a result which must be identical if no typing errors happen.
> Because all SAP partners have also access to the Quicksizer, it is sufficient if a customer enters his data and clicks the "send also to" boxes at the result section of the Quicksizer to get offerings from several vendors. This way an "apple to apple" comparison is ensured.

3.4.2 Can the Performance Be Guaranteed?

Every customer naturally expects that the cloud service provider guarantees the level of performance defined in the SLAs at all times. As shown above however, the response time is a dependent variable that results from the ratio between transaction load and available resources. Therefore, it is generally impossible to guarantee a constant response time if the system load is not constant either.

The situation of the cloud service provider is comparable to a shipping company that can guarantee the horsepower of their trucks but not how fast they will get from A to B if neither the payload, nor slopes, weather, road conditions, or traffic situation are known. In the same way, the cloud service can guarantee the number of SAPS available in his data centre but cannot grant the response time of the system if transaction load and user behavior is unknown. Guaranteed response time over the Internet are completely unrealistic, as we cannot even know the route the data packets will take.

▶ **Response time varies with the transactions**

Furthermore, the unpredictability of the capacity requirements of business processes has a much greater effect than the above-mentioned technical conditions. The sizing process is based on measurements of the performance requirements for used transactions which cover only a tiny part of the whole functionality in an SAP system.

Adding extra, generalized estimates to the main calculated estimate is the only way of allowing for the influence of customizing, reports, batch jobs, and hot spots. These generalized estimates are average values for systems with average reports. Experience shows that systems with an above-average level of customizing to specific requirements can differ greatly from these values.

▶ **Response time increases along with the database size**

Further, the response time for almost all transactions inevitably increases together with the size of the database. Examples are operations such as online availability checks and price determination. To return to our truck metaphor, this is the same as an increase of the load during a journey. The condition and incline of the road are equivalent to the number of users and transactions in the system. Customer written code then corresponds to potholes, and user exits to detours.

3.4.3 Measurement Based Sizing

Fortunately greenfield implementations with all their uncertainties become quite rare today. Most enterprises and public services wanting to move SAP systems to the cloud already use the complete SAP suite for many years in-house or at a classic outsourcer. In this case the individual resource demand can be derived from measurement rather than fiddling around with estimations. For obvious reasons a measurement based sizing is by far more accurate than a greenfield sizing using Quicksizer because it considers all individual parameters of a company.

▶ **How big is my current system?**

In an ideal world the system administrator know exactly the resource consumption under peak load of their existing SAP systems as well as the SAPS ratings of all his servers. In reality customers expected that the cloud provider find this numbers by looking into a magic ball, especially if the current system admin is afraid to loose his job when the system is moved into the cloud.

Therefore the necessary information has to be derived by analyzing "SAP Early Watch Reports" of the system to be "clouded" or tools like the SAPS-meter have to be deployed to determine the resource consumption as well as the load pattern of an existing SAP installation.

As part of the maintenance contract, SAP customers receive two Early Watch Reports per year or alternatively an Early Watch Alert on demand after a major

3.4 Units of Measure for SAP Applications

system chance. These reports show a number of system parameters automatically captured and checked against default settings. The status of the individual parameters is represented by a traffic light so that you can see at a glance whether everything is in green or whether a traffic light is yellow or even red. For every area, the services recommended for optimization are indicated.

▶ **Analyzing Early Watch Reports**

The reports focuses on the health status of the system, but shows also information about the platform and utilization figures that can be used to determine the actual resource consumption of the SAP solution.

From the title page the type of SAP solution, the database and the SAP release can be derived. From section "Performance Indicators" (mostly on page 3) you can derive:
- Number of active users
- Maximum number of Dialog Steps per hour
- The actual DB size
- Last month DB growth

Unfortunately the number of "users measured in the system" has nothing to do with the "concurrent logged on" or "concurrent active" users necessary for sizing.[7]

Of much better use for determining the resource consumption is the section "Hardware Capacity Check". From "Hardware configuration" you can derive the hardware manufacturer and model of the database and application servers, the number of cores and the amount of memory installed. The most essential section however is "Hardware Capacity" displaying the maximum CPU load and memory used of each server.

Together with the "nominal" SAPS number published as SAP benchmarks or other sources[8] it is easy to calculate the maximum SAPS consumption at each server and by adding them up the total number of SAPS the system "draw" under peak load – actually exactly the number we tried to estimate with cumbersome best practices in a Greenfield sizing.

---

[7] Actually the numbers are calculated from the numbers of dialog steps measured and are therefore a kind of hypothetical equivalent to a standard user. Depending on the number of dialog steps per week the users (identified by their user name) are sorted into categories according to:
   low < 400 dialog steps per week
   medium < between 400 and 4,800 dialog steps per week
   high > 4,800 dialog steps per week
The number of "Active Users" in table "Performance Indicators" is only the sum of the high and medium users. "Low Users" are neglected. If the number of Low Users is very high compared to Medium and High Users, 10 Low Users will be counted as 1 Medium User.

[8] It is always astonishing that customers do not remember the SAPS ratings of the servers they bought a few years ago taking into account all the battles between the different vendors about this topic. Maybe it's a good idea to write the SAPS rating to the housing of a server directly after installation. At least you should file it in the inventory.

Without any doubt orchestrating a cloud infrastructure based on early watch analysis is by far more precise than estimates and best practices as with the Quicksizer. However the early watch reports where never intended for this purpose. The primary focus is to report the health status of a system and sell additional SAP services to the customer.

This is why most of the pages are dedicated to patches, security, operation and ABAP code sanity and link you to SAP services available to improve the system status. You must plough through plenty of pages to get the handful of facts usable for determining the resource consumption of a single SAP solution

The biggest caveats are

- The averages for response times, users, transaction/time profiles are derived from a full week (from Monday to Sunday).
- The maximum CPU load is the highest average over a full hour, relative small load peaks which usually cause the most trouble are ironed out.
- The numbers can be totally misleading in virtualized environments if an older version of the SAPOSCOL agent is used which is not capable to distinguish between multiple SAP systems running on the same server
- The report covers only 3 weeks. If a high load generating activity like a year's end closing is not within these weeks, you miss the real peak.
- CPU resource consumption is only measured as a percentage and not an absolute number independent of server and CPU type.
- Addition, removing of a SAP instance or move of an instance to another server is not reflected in the report
- Parameters like the IO throughput which have become essential are not measured at all.
- For each SAP system you have to analyze another Early Watch report

Performance analysis tools from different vendors like IBM and HP have the same shortcomings, because they derive their information from the same source as Early Watch Reports.

3.4.4 SAPS-Meter

To resolve all these shortcomings, one of the authors developed the SAPS-Meter Web Service in conjunction with several bachelor studies at the University of Cooperative Education Stuttgart[9] to measure and analyze the resource consumption of complete SAP system landscapes in legacy and cloud environments. The SAPS-meter web service features:

- Averages are calculated over 5 min instead of hours
- Allow access to all measurements over any timeframe selected
- Calculate the absolute SAPS numbers rather than relative percentages

---

[9] Christian Bornholdt (2006) automated report generating tool for hardware resources in SAP server landscapes. Andreas Nisch (2007) Web Service zur Abrechnung der Ressourcenverbräuche von SAP-Systemen. Markus Bukaowski (2008) Tool zur automatischen Messung des Ressourcenverbrauchs von SAP.

3.4 Units of Measure for SAP Applications

- Measure correctly the individual resource consumption of multiple SAP systems sharing the same server in a virtualized environment
- Sum up correctly the resource consumption of database and SAP application instances distributed over multiple servers
- Detect automatically the addition, shut down and move of an instance to another server with other CPU numbers and calculate the correct numbers
- Auto detect any SAP system in a datacenter and list them all in one report
- Monitor the IO throughput per second for each individual system

This made the SAPS-meter an excellent tool to determine load patterns, peaks and trends. In addition it also offers one unique feature of great significance for cloud architectures:

- Like a utility tells the consumption of electricity in Kilo-Watt-hours (kWh) the SAPS-meter service reports the monthly consumption of CPU power in Kilo-SAPS-hours (kSAPSh)

This unique feature enables cloud provider to charge the real consumption of CPU resources rather the number of virtual cores allocated for the peak load.

> **A Comprehensive Unit of Measurement for SAP on Cloud**
>
> While the size of the memory allocated by an SAP system and the disk space occupied by its database needs no further definition, it is not that simple when it comes to the consumption of CPU resources.
>
> Generally SAPS are accepted as the "horsepower" of the SAP system or server. However, the numbers of SAPS a SAP solution is consuming at a given point of time is like the Watt consumed by an electrical motor just a unit of momentary "work". For billing purposes the time has to be taken into account this work is delivered. Therefore the performance is equal to the work per unit of time ($P = W/t$)
>
> In analogy to the usual unit for utility services kilowatt hour (kWh) the SAPS-Meter Web service provides kilo-SAPS hours (kSAPSh) and Kilo-IOPS-hours (kIOPSh) as comprehensible units for the resource consumption of SAP systems. One kSAPSh corresponds to a system load of 1,000 SAPS during an hour, a kIOPSh to a throughput of 3,600,000 IO operations completed during an hour (IO per second times number of seconds per hour times 1,000).

The SAPS-Meter Web Service is technically designed as a Web service. SAPS-Meter agents installed on each server of a legacy SAP landscape or SAP cloud data center are collecting the raw data. The agents are able to distinguish between multiple SAP solutions installed on the same operating system instance. The agent can detect if the number of active CPU's are changed dynamically. Agents are available for literally every OS used in SAP (Windows, RedHat, Suse, AIX, HP-UX, Solaris) and virtualization technology.

▶ **SAPS-meter architecture**

The data collected by the agents is transmitted once a day to the SAPS-Meter analytical engine. The numbers of consumed SAPS are calculated from the relative CPU load, the number of CPUs detected and the SAPS rating of each individual server for each SAP instance detected.

Using knowledge based strategies; the analytical engine is able to detect the move of a SAP solution between servers with different ratings as well as the distribution of a SAP solution over multiple servers. This process also considers SAP components which are added or completely removed during the reporting period. The analytical engine transforms the raw data into absolute numbers relevant for sizing and accounting, determine correlations and trends and generating the reports.

Finally the monthly resource consumption reports for each individual SAP solution are generated and either actively sent to a customer's E-mail address (push mode) or made available on the SAPS-Meter Web page for download (pull mode).

In addition, the analytical machine generates correlation diagrams for each individual SAP solution, showing not only the up and downs of the various parameters, but also their correlation and dependencies among each other. These diagrams are made available to the customers for further evaluation as required.

▶ **Why a web service?**

Traditional tools have to be acquired for a substantial budget and need weeks to be installed and customized. Utilizing the web service and cloud paradigm the SAPS Meter can be subscribed for a low service fee per day and is ready to use within a few hours. A complete data center is usually "SAPS Meter ready" in about half a day. Customers only need to download and install the agents and configure the network connection. The agent automatically identifies the SAP and database instances installed.

This data transferred once a day is encrypted, however the raw data collected by the agents can be checked at any time on the servers' file system by internal security staff.

Basis service provides the measurement and analysis of the individual SAP systems' consumption with regard to CPU, main memory, and IO resources at operating system level. Besides the average and peak load curves correlations between SAPS and IOPS can also be displayed. Additionally, a "SAPS-meter Plus" service monitors the number of users, transaction steps, and response times at SAP application level, and provides advanced analysis or trend correlations.

The simulation mode enables you to optimize the distribution of the SAP systems on the existing servers in order to optimize their utilization, or to simulate the behavior of the existing SAP systems on a new infrastructure which is not yet procured.

3.4 Units of Measure for SAP Applications

▶ *Subscription based payment*

There is no purchase price as such for this genuine "Software as a Service." Instead, you pay per day and for the SAP system for which the service is used. Like SAP solutions, SAPS-meter can be utilized for 90 days free of charge.

The demand for a tool like the SAPS-Meter is demonstrated by the fact that several customers volunteered to act as pilots during the development phase. Currently more than 1,500 SAP systems on approximately 800 servers are monitored worldwide using the SAPS-meter.

> **How Do Cloud Providers and Consumers Benefit from SAPS-Meter Service?**
> The SAPS-Meter Web Service is modeled according to the monthly utility bill. In such a bill, the costs aren't simply calculated according the maximum available output of the power plants, transformers and utility lines. They also do not split the costs for the individual houses in a village simply by the numbers of tenants living there.
>
> In IT however, it is still customary to split the costs simply by the number of users, regardless of how much and to what extent each of them utilize the systems. This is comparable to a situation where the bill for electrical power is calculated according the number of installed lights in an apartment and the costs for heating according to the number of radiators, no matter how long they are switched on.
>
> Practical experience in such a situation shows that nobody really cares about the efficient use of resources because the bill will not change even if all the lights are switched on in bright daylight, or if you leave open the windows while the heater is on. We find a matching behavior in IT with the widespread habit of business departments not willing to invest too much in efficient programming of their applications, because they have to pay the same fixed price for their operations anyway.
>
> Thanks to cloud and virtualization technologies, IT resources can be orchestrated on varying hourly demand and dynamically re-dispatched between different applications according to their specific need. As a consequence, the billing procedures for IT services have to be adjusted accordingly.
>
> The SAPS-Meter Web service has been designed to fulfill that function. It enables companies to meter the resource consumption for each SAP solutions in a virtualized cloud landscape and bill the business departments according to their resource consumption. This creates an incentive for departments to utilize these resources in a more efficient way.

▶ *Further scientific analysis*

Due to the web service architecture and wide proliferation the SAPS-meter also provides a massive repository for scientific studies. In cooperation with the Hasso

Plattner Institute of the University of Potsdam several master studies have been done on the IO behavior of SAP systems[10] and typical load patterns examine the key factors influencing SAPS and IOPS load.

3.5 Load Profiles

One of the most praised benefits of cloud architectures is the ability to respond dynamically to changing resource demand. However even the most elaborated orchestration software need some time till additional resources are made available. The better changes in demand can be predicted, the better the cloud architecture can be adjusted avoiding extensive "safety margins". This will also reduce energy consumption because any unused server can be switched off completely if it's known in advance when it's time to switch in on again.

For this purpose, a master study was initiated by one of the authors with the Hasso Plattner Institute of the University of Potsdam,[11] analyzing approximately three million datasets measured on a multitude of productive SAP systems over several months with approval from the customers to find possible recurring load patterns of SAP solutions.

In the utility industry such load profiles are commonly used to optimize the utilization of power plants and grids as well as a basis for billing. It would be a straight forward strategy for cloud providers to use load profiles in a similar way to define SLA's.

For obvious reasons the outside temperature is known as one of the most influencing factors for utilities. Also for obvious reasons we expect the day of the week as one most influencing factors for cloud infrastructures as well as the different types of SAP solutions.

3.5.1 Load Profiles of Transactional Solutions

The load of on-line transaction processing (OLTP) systems depends mainly on the activity of its users. Typical examples are SAP enterprise core component (ECC), SAP customer relationship management (CRM) and SAP supplier relationship management (SRM). Figure 3.6 show the load profiles of the ECC systems of three different customers monitored by SAPS-meter for workdays (left) and weekend (right) (Fig. 3.7).

---

[10] Analyse des Ressourcenverbrauchs in virtualisierten Systemen am Beispiel der E/A-Last betriebswirtschaftlicher Standardanwendungen. Robert Wierschke, Masterarbeit Hasso am Plattner Institut Potsdam, 2009.

[11] Analyse des aktuellen Ressourcenverbrauchs in konsolidierten Umgebungen am Beispiel betriebswirtschaftlicher Standardsoftwaresysteme. Daniel Richter, Masterarbeit am Hasso Plattner Institut Potsdam, 2009.

3.5 Load Profiles

The diagram visualizes the scatter of SAPS consumption measured over several weeks
- Light gray area represents data between the 5 % quartile and 95 % percentile (90 % of all measurements are within this band)
- Gray area displays all measurements between 25 % quartile and 75 % percentile (50 % of all readings)
- The dark line in the middle represents the median (i.e. the 50 % percentile).

The narrower the bands, the less spread the values are at a given time. So the less gray, the more constant daily load profiles and the better the system behavior can be predicted

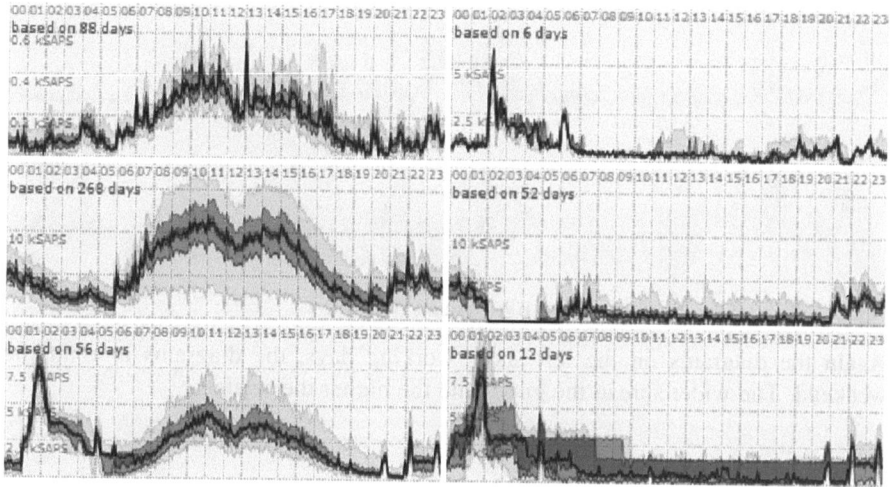

Fig. 3.6 Typical load profiles of SAP ECC Systems (OLTP)

All ECC-Systems show consistently a steady raise of resource consumption during workdays beginning 6:00 a.m. reaching its maximum at 10:00 a.m. There is a significant drop between 12:00 a.m. and 1:00 p.m. followed by a rise to an afternoon maximum and a steady decline by 7:00 p.m. Load patterns during night is quite different between the different customers depending on the individual batch runs and back-up strategies which also influence the load pattern on weekends. In one case this load is significantly higher than the load generated by the users.

Now you may argue that it is quite obvious that users come to the office in the morning, went to lunch at noon and went home in the evening, so the load generated by their transactions will correlate accordingly. The main result of this analysis however is how exactly predictable this behavior is for the individual customers. Sometimes the same peak load happens at exactly the same time with the same load every workday. Such systems, running like "on rails", are ideal candidates for actively managed cloud architectures where additional resources can be added just in time before the peak and removed shortly afterwards.

3.5.2 Load Profiles of Analytical Systems

Typical for on-line analytical processing systems (OLAP) like SAP business warehouse (BW) or supply chain management (SCM) is the relative low numbers of users which however cause significant resource consumption.

The load profiles of two BW systems of different customers in Fig. 3.7 show no significant rising or decline. The high load phases at night are caused by the transfer and loading of data from the source systems and pre-processing of the reports.

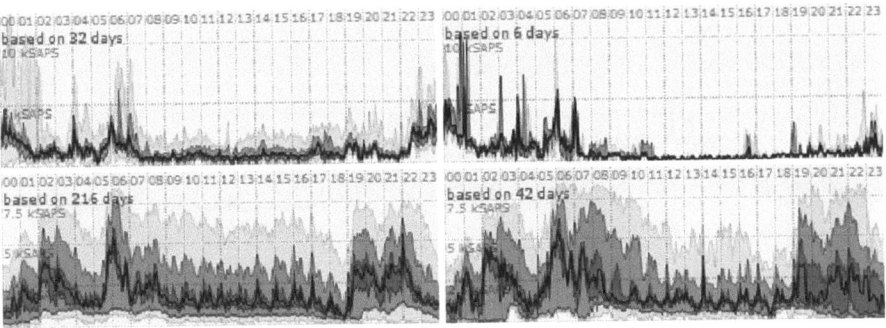

Fig. 3.7 Typical load profiles of SAP BW Systems (OLAP)

Again the diagrams on the left show working days, the diagrams at right the weekend. The wider spread the gray band the higher the scatter.

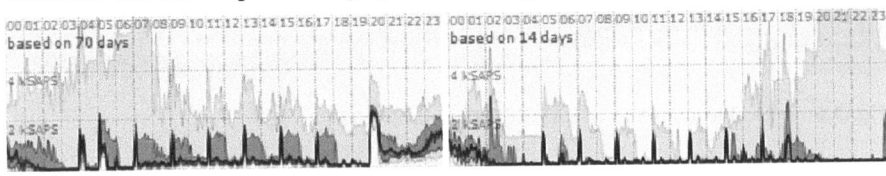

Fig. 3.8 Typical load profile of a SAP SCM System (OLAP)

The load profile of a SAP SCM-System in Fig. 3.8 reflects the planning runs scheduled every 2 h.

In comparison to OLTP systems the analysis demonstrates a significant higher scatter. It must be concluded that OLAP systems are much less predictable and therefore always need more "safety headroom" than OLTP systems.

3.5.3 Load Profiles of Other SAP-Solutions

NetWeaver systems like Enterprise Portal (EP) and Process Integration (PI) can't be characterized as OLTP- or OLAP-Systems. User driven systems like EP have load profiles with the same characteristic as OLTP systems as picture 9 demonstrates for workdays left-hand and weekend on the right.

3.6 Availability Management

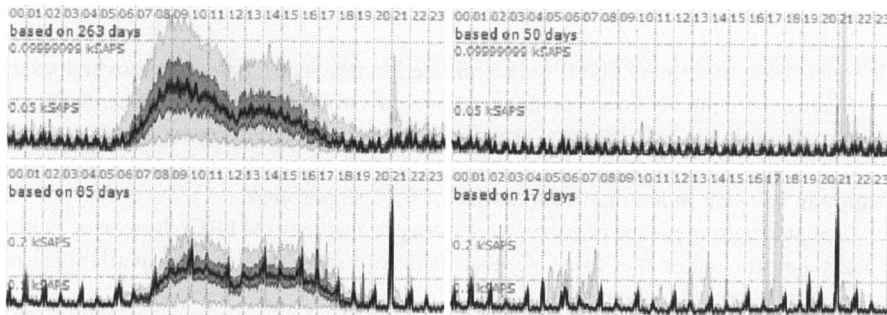

Fig. 3.9 Typical load profile of a SAP NetWeaver EP Systems

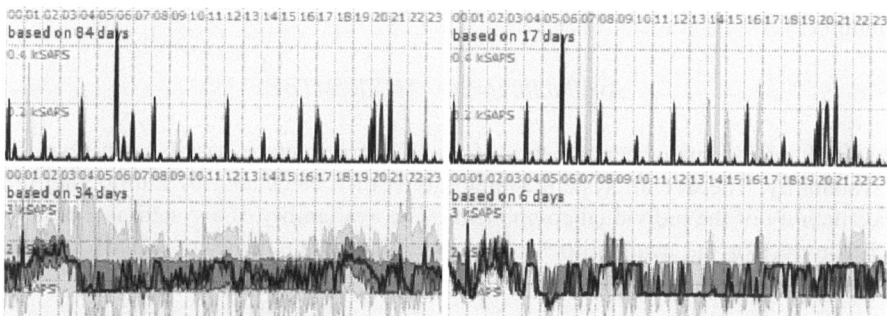

Fig. 3.10 Load profiles of SAP XI-Systems

For the PI Systems analyzed however no common pattern could be indentified even if the SAPS consumption of the two SAP systems was quite similar.

The analysis demonstrates that the load profiles of user driven SAP solutions like ECC and EP are relatively predictable. This made them ideal candidates for cloud environments where resources are actively managed to reduce costs and energy consumption. The individual load profiles however have to be determined case by case with tools like the SAPS-meter.

3.6 Availability Management

Last but not least SLAs for business-critical applications must define the necessary availability. However, high availability comes at a cost even in cloud infrastructures. This is like taking measures against fire and accidents: You accept a considerable amount of expenditure as insurance against an event that you hope will never happen. When evaluating the different solutions available in cloud architectures you shouldn't think in terms of how much availability the company can afford, but rather how much downtime it can survive.

3.6.1 How to Define Availability?

In most cases, system availability is expressed in terms of a percentage over 1 year.

Such a percentage however does not reveal anything about the frequency of system downtimes, only the total downtime aggregated over the year. A system that loses network connectivity twice a month for 10 min will not make users very happy in spite of an average availability of 99.9 % per year.

The alternate measure of *mean time between failures* (MTBF), however, is not totally helpful either if it takes several days to restore operational availability in case an incident does happen.

A meaningful measurement for system availability is therefore the relationship between MTBF and the time required to repair the system. Availability is thus defined by the *mean time to repair* (MTTR) divided by the mean time between failures:

$$Availability = 1 - MTTR/MTBF$$

Each of the many components of an IT infrastructure has its own level of availability. The overall system availability is then calculated by multiplying the availability of the individual components. The availability of a system is therefore the product of the availabilities of its individual components in a mathematical sense as well as in a practical one.

▶ *Serial components reduce availability*

The result is that the total system availability is always lower than that of the individual components. For example, two serial components with an availability of 99 % percent each have an availability of only about 98 % (99 % × 99 %), which is more than a week of downtime per year.

▶ *Parallel components increase availability*

On the other hand, by redundantly merging two components with an individual availability of 99 % each, you obtain a total availability of 99.99 %. This is the reason why in a Cisco UCS system all network components are implemented redundant by default. With three redundant components you could even achieve an availability of 99.9999 %, which corresponds to approx. 30 s of downtime a year.

The availability is then calculated as the combined probability of all three components failing at the same time; that is, the product of the three probabilities of failure:

$$A_{total} = (1 - A_1) \times (1 - A_2) \times (1 - A_3)$$

- Ai = availability of the individual component

For this we assume, however, that the individual component is still able to operate the system when all other components have failed. Therefore, three redundant power supplies do not ensure an increased availability if the power of all three power supplies is necessary to cover the power requirements when the server is fully utilized.

In the book "SAP Hardware Solutions"[12] various methods are introduced that can be used for implementing completely redundant infrastructures down to the cabling level.

▶ *Planned downtimes*

Still, it is inevitable to ensure sufficient time windows for maintenance when defining SLAs. In particular, you need to take care that the time intervals between maintenance windows do not become too long. For example, if you have only one maintenance window per quarter in a 24×7 operation, this means that errors identified by the manufacturer cannot be eliminated for 3 months via patches, bug fixes, or corrections. It is just such an error that can cause an unplanned downtime. Too few and too short maintenance windows are therefore counterproductive for total availability. The times for maintenance, like times when availability does not need to be ensured, are counted as achieved availability.

3.6.2 How Many Resources Are Needed in Case of a Disaster?

Even if cloud infrastructures for mission critical applications should always feature internal redundancies, a single data enter is like having none if a disaster strikes. In case the power has to be switched off because the data centers' raised floor has been flooded, having an emergency power supply is of not much help.

▶ *Cutting resources in half means half the number of users*

Most disaster recovery (DR) concepts stipulate that reduced resources are acceptable for a limited period in case of an emergency, as long as the system is available at all.

However, you must understand the consequences of such a reduction of resources. Having half of the CPU and main memory resources does not mean a doubling of the response time but rather that only half the number of users can still work with the system in case of an emergency.

One reason is the non-linear relation between CPU usage and response time as described above. Also a system that only has 50 % of main memory left but that is

---

[12] Michael Mißbach, Uwe Hoffmann, Prentice Hall 2001, ISBN 0-13-028084-4.

used for logging in 100 % of users is forced to perform massive paging, which renders the response time totally unacceptable.

3.6.3 How Much Stability Is Required?

Availability and stability are terms often mixed, but they are two different things. While availability defines that sufficient capacity is available, stability defines whether the business processes also run as required. The stability is something an application service provider has to cater for in addition.

In service oriented architectures the interfaces between the interconnected systems have become critical key points for the stability of cross-system business processes. Another problem with distributed but tightly coupled business systems arises if one of the involved systems must be reset after a fatal error of its database to the state before the system failure occurred, causing inconsistencies within the business process chain.

With the vision of one single In-memory database as the single data repository for all SAP solutions the consistency problem is solved at the root cause at least for SAP-only implementations.

3.7 Summary

SAP systems are mission-critical applications for companies. Service level agreements between the consumer of SAP services and the providers of the various cloud models are necessary to define quantity and quality of the services to be consumed in mutual agreed units of measure. The following basic principles apply:
- The performance of an SAP system depends on the ratio between the available resources and the current load. An under-dimensioned system will, at best, cause unsatisfactory response times; at worst, it can jeopardize the whole enterprise.
- For new SAP implementations (greenfield) estimating the maximum expected system load is part of the mutual agreed SLA. It is the task of the service consumer to deliver the necessary information.
- For existing SAP systems moving to cloud infrastructures the necessary information can be derived from measurements. At least the most recent SAP Early Watch reports should be made available for analysis.
- Tools like SAPS-meter can be used to provide the necessary data before the migration to a cloud infrastructure, but also for the ongoing monitoring of the SLA and even the automatic generation of utility like billing.
- For the resource consumption of SAP system the kilo-SAPS-hour has to be defined as a new unit of measure for a utility like billing.
- Defining the system availability in terms of a percentage over 1 year is not reflecting the real demands of business critical systems. In addition the maximum acceptable downtime has to be defined.
- Even in cloud infrastructures sufficient maintenance windows have to be granted.

Security Aspects for SAP on Cloud

Since the early days of the internet, security has become a major topic in enterprise computing. Confidentiality, integrity, and availability of applications and data are of utmost importance for any public cloud provider to maintain customer trust and confidence. For obvious reasons the same apply for private cloud operations.

Protecting confidentiality, integrity and availability (CIA) is probably the most controversially discussed subject around cloud computing. Similar to conventional deployment models of SAP, we need to be able to protect the software, hardware and communication end to end.

In contrast to most traditional hosting options, cloud environments are highly shared, multi-tenancy computing environments which potentially increase the risk of getting exposed to external and internal threats.

No matter which deployment model a SAP customer chose, it is absolutely vital to understand the responsibilities around security of each supplier who is part of delivering the service. Apart from protecting enterprise applications such as SAP from internal and external threats, many organizations have to meet legal standards for compliance and regulation.

The introduction of internet based services into enterprise critical software required new approaches for IT security departments.

Over the last decades, new holistic concepts and technologies have been developed to respond to those threats and became best practices in any professional managed enterprise IT. Compared to a traditional hosted IT environment, an IaaS cloud offering does not create entirely new risks. In fact, we will learn in this chapter that the technologies to approach security risks in a cloud environment do not fundamentally change.

Moving, hosting and running mission critical applications like SAP to the cloud creates a shared responsibility model between the customer and cloud provider. Therefore cloud solutions add an additional layer into a security framework. It is

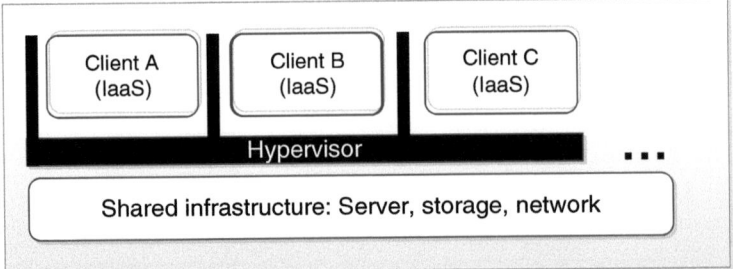

Fig. 4.1 Hyper visor as a potential security risk

therefore of utmost importance to understand the security responsibilities for a specific cloud delivery model.

▶ *The cloud add a new layer to the security framework*

Cloud computing is based on virtualization and associated technology which means the underlying infrastructure (server, storage and network) is shared among a potentially large number of customers. Ultimately, this introduces an additional risk for security breaches: the hypervisor. Although the risk of penetrating the hypervisor through an internal or external attack is rather small, it exists (Fig. 4.1).

SaaS applications like Ariba, SuccessFactor and newer SAP PaaS developments described in Chap. 7 will release customer IT departments to a large extent from actively managing security.

However, for the "classical" SAP business and NetWeaver solutions demanding an IaaS model, the customer IT department still assumes responsibility from the guest operating system up to the SAP applications and database systems. The shared model relieves SAP customers to some degree from operational burden of the infrastructure and the data center, but configuration and patch management as well as access control is still within the client responsibility. This is true also for SAP appliances like BWA and HANA.

SAP customers must therefore still carefully consider what cloud services they choose since the responsibilities might vary depending on the specific part of their SAP systems they want to move to the cloud. The fulfillment of applicable regulations and laws is always in the consumer's responsibility.

To highlight the importance, we will first discuss the different types of threats and security risks in detail. Readers familiar with this topic and the legal aspects of security might skip this section and move on directly to Sect. 4.3.

4.1 The Threat Landscape

Most large companies take information and access security of their IT systems serious. The protection of business-critical information is not only important because of the loss of credibility but also from a legal point for view.

Companies increasingly invest in information security because a deluge of new laws and regulations make boards of directors and management personally responsible for failures in this area. This increasing legal pressure made IT security, identity management, and data privacy acknowledged as a vital requirement.

In the struggle for budgets, resources and the competing priorities within IT departments, it can become a challenge to get funding for IT security since there is no immediate return on investment and the actual risk is difficult to quantify. The chief security officer (CSO) find themselves in the difficult situation of justifying investment into security.

Other than in the early times when hacking was a computer nerds "sport", cybercrime has become a profitable business with a growth rate any stock market analyst would give a "triple A" rating.

▶ *Cybercrime – a profitable business*

Knowledge about vulnerabilities and resources to use them are traded on the black market. Even governments are suspect to play a role in this hidden war which means there are literally unlimited resources available to the attackers.

Eventually, it comes back to manage the risk of a security breach. Any security risk needs to be identified, assessed and prioritized followed by coordinated application of countermeasures in order to minimize and control the probability and/or impact of a security breach.

▶ *Become familiar with security threads*

Unfortunately IT Managers but also Security Administrators are often unaware of the relative risk profiles from external threats versus internal sources.[1] In principle there are three main security threats to most companies.[2,3]

4.1.1 External Threats

Typical examples for threats originating outside an organization are social engineering attacks, Worms, Botnets, rootkits[4] and other Malware. The intent behind the vast majority of external threats is to cause malicious disruption. Sometimes the motivation is to steal data, very occasionally external threats are politically motivated and directed at specific organizations.

---

[1] http://newsroom.cisco.com/dlls/2008/ts_102808.html.

[2] http://www.networkworld.com/news/2008/111208-cisco-study-internal-security.html.

[3] http://www.cisco.com/en/US/solutions/collateral/ns170/ns896/ns895/white_paper_c11-506224.html.

[4] http://technet.microsoft.com/en-us/sysinternals/bb897445.aspx.

Based on the experience of the author, external threats usually come as "mass" attacks (DoS). Attacking a well-defended organization is a relatively poor risk vs. reward ratio for the hacker. Even if an organization was not only able to detect an attempt and alert law enforcement[5] but also collect enough evidence to trace and prosecute an individual the legal consequences usually far outweigh the possible gain.

Phishing, identity theft and fraud from external sources are topics that are usually not seen relevant to business applications such as SAP. However, an attacker who successfully "phish" the account/password of a SAP user assumes all the rights of this user and could cause severe damages.

4.1.2 Internal Threats

An internal threat originates from employees or contractors within an organization. The motivation generally falls into three categories: Disgruntled employees (malicious damage), Industrial Espionage (theft of Intellectual Property) and Criminal Theft (defrauding money or other liquid assets).

Employees have the most important elements in unauthorized data access available to them: Time and internal knowledge of systems and procedures. There is little more than separation of responsibilities (or duties, SoD) and access rights to tackle this problems.

In many cases however employee's unintentionally breaching compliance and security "Accidentally".[6,7,8]

Even if SAP data is stored on the servers transmitted encrypted, users have a tendency to export them to Excel and save it locally.

▶ *The e-mail gap*

The classic example is using the *Reply to All* option when sending an email with confidential information derived from a SAP system, without noticing that external addressees are also included on the distribution list.

Laptops and especially memory sticks that disappear from hotel rooms or are left in a taxi are also a potential risk.

---

[5] http://www.theregister.co.uk/2012/02/06/marriott_hacker_jailed/.
[6] http://www.cisco.com/en/US/prod/collateral/vpndevc/ps5707/ps5057/lippis_report.pdf.
[7] http://www.cisco.com/en/US/solutions/collateral/ns170/ns896/ns895/white_paper_c11-499060.html.
[8] http://www.cisco.com/en/US/solutions/collateral/ns170/ns896/ns895/white_paper_c11-503131.html.

4.1.3 Technical Attacks: Viruses, Worms, Trojan Horses, etc.

Malware is a generic term for malicious software. These threats usually originate externally, but employees often unintentionally help to introduce them from outside the company, for example by connecting infected laptops to the company network.

Even virtual desktop infrastructures (VDI) are not immune because most Trojans, Viruses, etc. are introduced by visited Web-Sites and email attachments. If the User in a VDI environment is affected, he is closer to the Datacenter than he would be with a classical local installation. For both cases, there are threat mitigation technologies that help to address these security issues driven by users' behaviors, but they are not yet mainstream on the enterprise and yet incipient on the cloud providers as part of their services

▶ *Zero-day exploits*

Immediately after security vulnerabilities become public, hackers start scan for companies which did not yet implement the counter measures. In general, these attacks are called zero-day exploits and are based on the assumption that it will take some time before the corresponding patches are implemented.

A famous example was the SQL Slammer worm which significantly impacted the Internet by overloading networks in 2003. The worm used a gap which had been published by a corresponding patch by Microsoft 6 months earlier. This is just one of many cases in the recent history which demonstrates the necessity of patch management.

▶ *Trojan horses and rootkits*

A Trojan horse is perhaps the most sophisticated type of malware. It is basically a program which ostensibly executes an useful application, while carrying out a hostile function in the background without the user's knowledge.

This function usually involves the installation of a rootkit, the most dangerous type of malware which often "sniff out" passwords, log keystrokes or implement a permanent Backdoor into an affected system.

As a worst case PCs infected by rootkits can be misused as "Zombie PCs" or bots in a criminal way by selling their resources to a third party; for example for sending masses of spam mails.

▶ *Man-in-the-middle attacks*

You could think that the proliferation of wireless communication has made eavesdropping much easier than in the past, when you need physical access to the network cables for a man in the middle attack.

Actually it is much more difficult to get into a WLAN as long it's properly protected.

The threat is that someone may just plug a wireless device into a network Jack to install some man-in-the-middle tools which use WLAN or 3/4 G to send the Data to the attacker.

SAP client server communication is not encrypted by installation default and vulnerable to such an attack.

4.1.4 Non-Technical Threats

Besides technical type of attacks, it is the non-technical ones that usually threaten IT systems. These attacks target the user as the weakest link in the security chain and are generally known as "social engineering." Any experienced hacker will try to find an unintentional ally in the company.

▶ *Social engineering*

The classical social engineering attack is the faced telephone call from the internal helpdesk requesting the user name and passwords in order to resolve a fictitious IT application problem or to prevent a user account from being locked.

Another example is a USB stick infected with a virus, which is openly placed in the employee parking lot in the genuine hope that someone will pick it up and insert it into his or her company PC to find out whether they can delete the data on the stick or use it privately. Without knowing, the employee has thereby unleashed the virus, which "opens a backdoor" into the company internal network.

▶ *Phishing*

The state of the art type of social engineering is "phishing" (password fishing) where attackers send bogus emails that look like internal ones to make employees reveal their access codes.

The only method that helps against social engineering and phishing attacks is to make the users in a company aware of those risks and to use good email security software (e.g. Scansafe, Ironport to name only a few).

4.2 Legal Aspects

Today legal regulations (*compliance*) add the additional element of corporate accountability to IT security. Executives may be fined or in worst-case even imprisoned if financial control and risk management cannot be guaranteed.

▶ *Compliance and corporate governance*

Corporate governance focuses on defining rules of behavior that apply to all employees of a company. Examples include the Sarbanes-Oxley Act (US), Basel II and KonTraG (Control and Transparency in Business Act in Germany).

Also included are general privacy policies at national and international levels like the European Privacy Directive, the Federal Data Protection Acts in Germany and Austria, the Health Insurance Portability and Accountability Act (HIPAA) and Gramm-Leach-Bliley Act (finance industry) in the US, and the Online Privacy Protection Act (OPPA) for California.

In addition, the Payment Card Industry (PCI) Security Standards provide a real financial incentive (via fines or loss of payment capability) for e-commerce businesses to be compliant with the suggested security practices for handling sensitive information, such as account holder data.

However the legal regulations only define the target, not the way to achieve them. Practical hints can be found in IT control frameworks:

▶ *IT control frameworks*

ISO 17799 (http://www.iso.ch) covers areas like: Security policies, HR security, physical security, communications and operations management, information security management, incident and crisis management, and compliance.

ISO 27001 defines the implementation and documentation requirements of an *Information Security Management System* (ISMS) as a basis for an information security certification.

Control Objectives for Information and Related Technology (COBIT) have become popular in the US and provide a broader scope for IT initiatives. It is intended for General IT management, in which security is only one topic among many.

COBIT and ISO 17799 are designed as best practices of a control frameworks that a company can follow to create IT and security-relevant processes. Business-critical processes or tasks that require greater proof of security measures can be certified individually according to ISO 27001.

4.3 Classical IT Security and the Cloud

Like availability, security is a process that is implemented with the aim to minimize the possibility of damage occurring. And, like availability, security involves identifying and eliminating the weakest elements, given that a company's entire security is only as strong as its weakest link in the organization.

One of the most important objectives is to do a risk analysis that leads to the implementation of a security policy. However, it is not enough to document this policy on paper; it must also be put into practice using appropriate personnel and management techniques. This also includes emergency training for reacting to security incidents.

▶ *Security is a never ending process*

In an ideal world this "search and eliminate" has to be done only once. In reality organizational requirements, software releases and regulatory and compliance frameworks are continuously evolving. Therefore the process of security is never "finished". Cloud deployment models are an opportunity for organizations to improve security by leveraging the manageable homogenous platform and advanced provisioning that cloud infrastructures offer.

The classic procedure in the area of IT security is to harden the network perimeters by establishing firewalls. However such an approach leave the internal infrastructure vulnerable if an attacker breaks through the outer defense layer.

▶ **SAP infrastructure need hardening**

SAP infrastructures are built on multiple layers on top of the servers, storage and networks hardware: hypervisors, operating systems, databases and finally the SAP solutions itself – none of these are delivered "secure by default".

▶ **Defense in depth**

Because the entire SAP system is only as secure as its weakest point emphasis must be put on end-to-end security processes and procedures. This leads to a defense-in-depth strategy containing multiple layers of defense from the physical access to the datacenter through the whole stack up to the database and SAP application itself.

▶ **Key questions for SAP on cloud security**

The next step directly after the installation must therefore always be to set up the security-relevant parameters specific to the infrastructure layer and in response to the following questions:
- How to implement a SAP system securely on a Cloud platform?
- How to protect data within the Cloud and on the way to the client?
- How to ensure secure user authentication to SAP applications?
- How to deploy identity management and single-sign on?

In simple words, the application is secure if nobody can illegally connect into the network and spy the data communication between front- and backend, log in to the hypervisor, operating system database or SAP application server and install malicious software or compromise my data.

These classical questions of IT security have to be also answered on cloud deployments; therefore clouds require security hardening to achieve acceptable security standards and "defense in-depth" like conventional SAP landscapes, however with a boost of multi-tenancy.

▶ **Who control what in the cloud?**

However Private and Public Cloud deployments differ in the degree of control that an IT organization may have over various layers. Table 4.1 show the extent an organization can control infrastructure and application components on a Public IaaS (such as Amazon EC2) in comparison to classical in- or outsourcing models.

Table 4.1 Degree of customer control for applications running on a IaaS

Infrastructure layer	Private cloud on premise	Private cloud hosted	Public cloud IaaS
Datacenter	Full control	Limited control	No control
Network	Full control	No control	Little to no control
Storage	Full control	Limited control	Little to no control
Hyper-visor	Full control	Limited control	No control
Operating system	Full control	Full control	Limited
Database	Full control	Full control	Full control[a]
Application	Full control	Full control	Full control
Backup/Restore	Full control	Limited control	Limited

[a]Some cloud providers put restrictions around this

4.4 Security on Public Clouds: Who Is Responsible?

For public cloud providers, it is of fundamental importance to provide confidentiality, integrity and availability of customer data on their platforms. Therefore, public cloud providers have to implement security concepts that go far beyond a standard on-premise deployment.

However it must be always transparent for all parties "who is managing what" and has subsequently the responsibility for the security of this layer of the infrastructure. "We assumed that the cloud provider take care for this" is not an acceptable excuse.

In any case, public cloud providers take responsibility for the physical security of the datacenters. The same applies for the hypervisor layer since this component is the core component of the service.

Transmitting sensitive data over a Public Network (the Internet) to a remote shared environment which is outside the control of the owner is not exactly a new concept in hosted environments.

Looking at an IaaS setup which necessary for classical SAP solutions the responsibility for hardening the guest operating system is still a responsibility of the customer.

4.4.1 Security Concept of Amazon AWS

As with clouds in the sky, every public cloud offering is different. As the only public cloud supported for the classical business suite by SAP at the time of writing we will discuss the security concept of Amazon AWS as an example.

The security concept of Amazon AWS is based on the 'shared responsibility model'. In a few words: Amazon takes responsibility from the virtualization layer down to the physical security of the cloud datacenter facilities.

The customer keeps responsibility for the guest operating system, the application software installed including updates and security patches as well as the configuration of the security group firewall provided by AWS.

Customers can further enhance security by implementing host based firewalls, host based intrusion detection/prevention, encryption and key management.

The concept ensures that not even the system administrators of Amazon have access to anything above the hypervisor level. Only the owner of the private key has access to guest operating system, the database and the encrypted data and network connections.

Physical access to AWS datacenters is strictly controlled and granted only to employees and contractors who have a legitimate business need for such privileges. The datacenters feature state of the art fire detection and suppression systems, fully redundant electrical power systems backed-up by Uninterruptible Power Supply (UPS) units and diesel generators.

The data centers are built in clusters in five Regions: Northern Virginia (US East), Northern California (US West), Singapore (Asia Pacific), Tokyo (Asia Pacific) and Ireland (EU). This allows customers to meet location-dependent privacy and compliance requirements, such as the EU Data Privacy Directive.

However Amazon didn't tell anybody where the cloud datacenters are actually situated. Even most Amazon employees don't know the places, only the ones who 'need to know required'.

Because of this customers can't check in person the actual measures to protect the premises, however there are ongoing audits to ensure that even most stringent certifications like ISO-27001 are fulfilled.[9] The Security and Compliance Center provide customers with security and compliance details about AWS.

According to **Amazon Web Services Overview of Security Processes** "Security within Amazon EC2 is provided on multiple levels: the operating system (OS) of the host system, the virtual instance operating system or guest OS, a firewall, and signed API calls."

Virtual instances are completely controlled by the customer. Customers have full root access or administrative control over accounts, services, and applications. AWS does not have any access rights to customer instances and cannot log into the guest OS.

AWS recommends a base set of security best practices to include disabling password-only access to their hosts, and utilizing some form of multi-factor authentication to gain access to their instances (or at a minimum certificate-based SSH Version 2 access). Additionally, customers should employ a privilege escalation mechanism with logging on a per-user basis. For example, if the guest OS is Linux, after hardening their instance, they should utilize certificate-based SSHv2 to access the virtual instance, disable remote root login, use command-line logging, and use 'sudo' for privilege escalation. Customers should generate their own key pairs in order to guarantee that they are unique, and not shared with other customers or with AWS.

---

[9] http://aws.amazon.com/security.

Amazon EC2 provides also a mandatory inbound firewall which is configured in a default deny-all mode which customers must explicitly open the ports needed to allow inbound traffic. The firewall can't be controlled through the Guest OS; but requires the customer's X.509 certificate and key to authorize changes, thus adding an extra layer of security.

4.5 Public Cloud Security Automation and Management

Utilizing the services of a public cloud provider relieves a client from the task of running and securing a datacenter, the actual servers, storage and the physical networks including the virtualization layer.

However as Table 4.1 demonstrates, it is still within the client's scope to harden the operating system and most obviously the actual application. This chapter provides an overview on various means to improve security within a hosted environment and does not necessarily apply only to cloud deployments of SAP.

Given the complexity of the subject it is obvious that the author can only touch on some aspects of security in a public cloud. As a guiding principle, automation is the key to a successful cloud deployment – this aspect particularly applies to security. Automation and central security management reduces the factor of 'human error' and provides a consistent configuration across a large number of systems.

Most operating system vendors provide more or less sophisticated tools for centrally managing and automating security. Depending on the built-in tools of an operating system and the specific requirements of a customer, a separate third party tool might be required.

Every operating system vendor has different approaches to optimize and improve security in a cloud deployment. The chapter will focus on mainstream operating systems for the cloud; Red Hat Linux and Microsoft Windows.

4.5.1 Hardening Red Hat Linux as Guest Operating System

Red Hat provides various offerings for Cloud computing. For public cloud computing, Red Hat follows a completely new approach in where the cloud provider essentially becomes the *"next generation OEM"*. Red Hat has established a cloud certification program to certify that public cloud providers have tested the cloud and have support processes in place to quickly resolve problems should they occur.

Each cloud provider needs to undergo a rigorous testing and certification to be able to ensure the delivery of a secure, scalable, supported, and consistent environment for enterprise cloud deployments.

Once a cloud provider has been certified by Red Hat, customers, independent software vendors (ISVs) and partners can use Red Hat technologies in this public cloud. Integral part of the Red Hat's "Certified Cloud Provider" program is a tool called "Red Hat Update Infrastructure" which provides consistent updates to Red Hat Linux Systems in a public cloud.[10]

For managed Linux systems in a private cloud, Red Hat offers an on-premise tool called "Red Hat Network Satellite" or a hosted system called "Red Hat Network". These tools manage and update a Red Hat Enterprise Linux system environment through a web based interface.

Updates to the operating system can be scheduled/pushed through the "Red Hat Network Satellite server" or pulled from the "Red Hat Enterprise Linux" server using the command line (yum) or a GUI tool. Updates and patches can be scheduled on a regularly basis using CRON or other system schedulers.

If a "Red Hat Satellite server" is used, Linux systems can be grouped and updates can be scheduled when appropriate. Using groups, updates and patches can easily be cycled through your software release lifecycle: development, test and production systems.[11]

Red Hat Enterprise Linux six comes with IPA (Identity Policy Audit) for identity and access management. IPA manages Linux users, groups and authorizations across a wide system landscape (including *sudo* access). Authentication is handled via Kerberos protocol. User information can be fed to a central IPA server even from Microsoft Windows Active Directory in order to enable cross-platform security management.

4.5.2 Hardening Windows as Guest OS

Similar to other vendors, Microsoft provides hardening guidance in the form of whitepapers in order to reduce the attack surface area of Windows.[12]

Windows includes features such as Windows Update Server and Windows Security Configuration Wizard. These tools ship as standard features with the Windows operating system and allow an administrator to uniformly deploy and enforce security settings and patch levels.

▶ *Active Directory design for SAP*

Using Microsoft's Active Directory as an identity management layer it is considerably easier to secure Windows servers because Active Directory can be used to centrally control and enforce security policies and configuration for both SAP and all access management requirements throughout a company's IT assets.

---

[10] https://access.redhat.com/knowledge/docs/Red_Hat_Update_Infrastructure/.
[11] http://au.redhat.com/products/enterprise-linux/rhn-satellite/.
[12] http://blogs.msdn.com/b/saponsqlserver/archive/2012/05/28/sap-on-sql-server-security-whitepaper-released.aspx.

4.5 Public Cloud Security Automation and Management

The Active Directory Domain Service (AD) is a prerequisite for an SAP system landscape on Windows Server operating systems. Active Directory supports user management and Single-Sign-On (SSO) integration for SAP systems using a central LDAPv3 directory and Kerberos domain functions.

There are a number of factors to consider in deciding which design is suitable for SAP systems: separate organizational unit (OU), domain, or forest. SAP suggests two basic variants for integrating SAP solutions with Active Directory. The advantages and disadvantages in terms of security are outlined briefly below:

Scenario 1: Users and SAP System Are in the Same Active Directory Domain
Microsoft recommendation: Single forest, single domain, if possible
- Advantages: Less to manage; straightforward; you can implement SSO Kerberos integration and IPSec more easily; you can implement group policies and settings from SAP systems in a dedicated Active Directory Organizational Unit; follows Microsoft's single forest/single domain recommendation (whenever possible)
- Disadvantages: All Active Directory users and computers would have access to the SAP systems by default unless additional isolation measures are taken; more care is needed to implement a delegated administration model.

Scenario 2: Users and SAP Systems Are in Separate Active Directory Domains Within a Forest
- Advantages: Separate user administration in separate domains; you can continue to implement SSO Kerberos integration and IPSec
- Disadvantages: Somewhat more configuration and operating effort required; no protection against "malicious" domain administrators because the real security perimeter is the Active Directory forest; multiple identities for each user (one for each domain) can be generated, which may lead to a greater identity management problem; no real technical advantage in delegated administration to previous scenario.

Scenario 3: SAP Systems Are Hosted in Separate "Resource Forests;" for Example, in Outsourcing Scenarios
- Advantages: You can specifically implement dedicated group policies and settings for the SAP systems in a highly-secure environment; protection against "malicious" domain administrators, as a separate forest offers better isolation

(continued)

- Disadvantages: Significantly more configuration and operating effort is required; SSO Kerberos integration would require cross forest trust; separate synchronization of users with LDAP is likely necessary; IPSec domain isolation and encryption may not work or be permitted.

Placing the SAP systems into a dedicated Active Directory container enables the administrator responsible for security to implement specific security settings on the SAP servers in a controlled manner.

▶ *Using AD to harden windows*

For example the Active Directory administrator can delegate limited control of the SAP Organizational Unit (OU). This also allows the SAP administrator to create the <sid>adm and SAPService <SID> accounts prior to running the SAP installation program. This avoids the need to install SAP using a domain administrator account or to install SAP using local service accounts (not recommended).[13]

If the SAP administrator is familiar with Active Directory the Active Directory team may delegate authority to reset password or create new accounts to the SAP administrator. In any case the SAP administrator will only have permissions to change accounts inside the SAP Organizational Unit.

To prevent other polices from "undoing" the SAP specific policies it is recommended to activate the policy block setting on the SAP container.

Use one Single Policy for all SAP Containers.
Use one single policy for Sandbox, Test and Production containers. This ensures consistent behavior on all SAP systems. When changing policy settings it is recommended to copy the Policy to a new name, block Inheritance on the Sandbox container and apply the policy to Sandbox to perform testing. This process can be repeated on the Test container.

Extra care must be taken on extending security policies on cloud environments as they must still be unique regardless of how wide the SAP container on cloud may scale out (even further for hybrid cloud environments).

Cloning of virtual machines and then adding them to the initial pool is a common practice on the cloud. With that, some properties of the new cloned VMs might need to be changed to reflect uniqueness' on the SAP landscape which would also require that all the previous security polices follow and cover the new VM and its users.

This is usually done via the cloud orchestration tool, so attention must be taken on how the security calls via API would be done versus how the SAP landscape growth on cloud is planned to happen for a particular end-customer environment.

---

[13] http://technet.microsoft.com/en-us/library/cc732524.aspx.

4.5 Public Cloud Security Automation and Management

Windows includes a utility called the "Security Configuration Wizard". This wizard based tool can create a XML policy file that contains security hardening settings. The policy can then be uniformly applied on the entire SAP Cloud infrastructure

The SCW XML file can be converted to an Active Directory Policy. This allows the configuration to be applied to individual servers or groups of servers.

▶ *Upload policy to AD using the SCW transform command*

After uploading the standard Cloud XML security configuration policy to Active Directory the Group Policy Editor can be used to further harden the Windows operating system.

Using Group Policy Editor Tool check the system audit policy and adjust as required

> **Uninstall Internet Explorer.**
> Many security vulnerabilities require a web browser to be installed in order to run malicious code hosted on a web server. Critical security patches are issued for example for Microsoft Internet Explorer (IE) and this software is sometimes the delivery mechanism for security vulnerabilities. As a matter of fact there is no valid reason to have any web browser on a production SAP server.
>
> Internet Explorer can be removed completely from Windows 2008 R2 and Windows Server 2012. However it is not sufficient to just delete the IE directory because the code is tightly integrated with Windows, therefore you must follow the steps in the relevant Microsoft knowledge base article.[14]
>
> With Internet Explorer removed from the Windows guest OS you can safely ignore security patches addressing the IE issues in Microsoft's monthly security bulletin.[15]

Data Execution Prevention (DEP) is a function as of Windows that is intended to help prevent (malicious) software from being executed in protected areas of main memory. DEP can be used to ward off some buffer overflow attacks caused by code injection (for example, MSBlaster). This setting is activated by default.

▶ *Protecting the windows kernel and main memory*

However, an Active Directory service must be implemented and hardened correctly to allow for these functions with the necessary security.

---

[14] http://support.microsoft.com/kb/957700#stepsforwin2008r2.

[15] http://www.microsoft.com/technet/security/current.aspx.

All commercially available operating systems require patching without exception. This was recently validated when the SSL "Beast" vulnerability was discovered. Constant improvements to software systems or eliminating known security weak spots require the controlled implementation of patches in the production systems.

▶ *Never touch a running system?*

Microsoft release security patches on the second Tuesday of each month. All patches need to be individually assessed to determine if they are relevant. It is not recommended to blinding apply all patches released.

A general policy enforcing all security patches to all servers immediately is not a sophisticated security policy for many reasons, chiefly that many security patches are issued reactively after vulnerabilities have been discovered by third parties.

▶ *Sometimes it's better to delay a patch*

In some cases security administrators may rely too heavily on patching as a means to secure a system, potentially under-investing in technologies such as firewalls, dedicated VLANs and Active Directory policies. A security administrator may mistakenly believe that if all Windows servers are patched then the entire Windows infrastructure is "secure". Clearly this is not the case.

Microsoft Security patches are only one part of a security solution[16] and there are many more aspects to building a well secured system. Therefore it is the recommendation of the author to secure SAP servers by isolating them from the general network, reduce their attack surface area and review each patch issued each month.

If a patch is relevant for an SAP system it should be implemented in production after adequate testing – this document has shown that in most cases these patches are generally not relevant if the SAP systems have been adequately secured.

If patches are clearly not relevant for an SAP system they can be delayed until the next planned downtime. Alternatively the patch can be delayed until Microsoft releases the next Windows Service Pack which will include a "rollup" of all previous security patches.

The fact that these unused components are disabled or blocked eliminates the *immediate* requirement to patch these components. The system administrator may decide to patch during the next planned outage some months after the security bulletin is released. Often the system administrator patches unused or disabled functionality for consistency reasons rather than security reasons. Some customers have requirements that all Windows servers should be patched to a consistent level, even if the functionality is completely disabled. In such cases the security solution may alleviate the need for immediate emergency outages even on adequately secured SAP servers.

---

[16] "Formulate A Database Security Strategy To Ensure Investments Will Actually Prevent Data Breaches And Satisfy Regulatory Requirements" – Forrester January 2012 http://www.oracle.com/us/corporate/analystreports/infrastructure/forrester-thlp-db-security-1445564.pdf.

4.5.3 Hardening the Hypervisors

Last but not least the hypervisors should not been forgotten. For public cloud environments like Amazon AWS the hypervisor security is granted by the provider. On private cloud implementations the administrator would need to also take care of hypervisor hardening aspects.

There are some "hypervisor hardening" guides from the major hypervisor vendors[17,18] which are worth to review before any major private cloud implementation and also for a better understanding of what is expected on the hypervisor security area from a public cloud virtualized offering.

4.6 SAP on Private Cloud: A Practical Example

After we discussed how public clouds can relieve SAP customers from tasks related to security and what they still have to do by themselves we will introduce an example of a SAP on private cloud infrastructure at the IT service organization of a large chemical Company in German, operating one of the world's largest SAP environments, with about 60,000 SAP users.

The organization faced the challenge to extend existing SAP hosting offering to the cloud. The solution was to deploy a service-oriented infrastructure across two sites based on FlexPod.

FlexPod is a private cloud architecture consisting of Cisco Unified Computing System; NetApp unified storage and VMware Virtualization. The FlexPod architecture is optimized for a variety of pre-validated workloads including SAP.[19,20]

The achieved benefits after a implementation time of only 6 months are
- SAP on-demand services with dynamic operations and utilization-based billing
- Use cases, including SAP system provisioning usingOS templates, system refresh, project and sandbox, repair, and systems in a DMZ-I
- Accelerate system refresh from days to a few hours
- Back up 3 TB SAP data in minutes, not 3–4 h
- Rapidly adapt to change and customer requests

The security concept of SAP Applications built on FlexPod starts on the infrastructure level by introducing a secure multi-tenancy architecture on the shared storage environment using NetApp MultiStore to isolate data of different tenants. The MultiStore software creates multiple virtual storage systems within a single physical storage system without compromising privacy and security.[21]

---

[17] http://www.vmware.com/support/support-resources/hardening-guides.html.
[18] http://technet.microsoft.com/en-us/library/dd569113.aspx.
[19] http://www.netapp.com/us/technology/flexpod/.
[20] http://www.cisco.com/en/US/prod/collateral/ps10265/cisco_ucs_flexpod_netapp.pdf.
[21] http://www.netapp.com/us/products/storage-security-systems/multistore.html.

On network level the shared FlexPod network infrastructure is separated into dedicated tenant VLANs (virtual LANs), on server level by VMware. For more details see Chaps. 8 and 9.

Tenant user access is granted by routing tenant networks (VLANs) into customer networks using VPN (virtual private networks) tunnels. Administrative access on the other hand is granted via internal jumpboxes, i.e. dedicated servers acting as gateways into the infrastructure. Administrators are required to use strong authentication methods to access the jumpboxes and can then proceed to hop into the tenant networks. Access is monitored and audited at the jumpboxes. This is one example of infrastructure level security in shared cloud environments.

4.7 Summary

- Defense in Depth approach applies equally to Cloud solutions as it does to traditional deployment models
- Hypervisor security is critical to overall system security. Patching cycles on a Hypervisor can disrupt system availability. The vSphere hardening guides should be considered for VMware, Windows Core should be the default deployment form for Hyper-V hosts. For open-source hypervisors information related to security on Linux is available mainly from Citrix (referring to Xen) and RedHat (referring to KVM);
- Cloud hosted operating systems must be hardened – there is no Operating System that has demonstrated "Secure by Default"
- Windows Active Directory provides a enterprise wide management framework to centrally control firewall, security and software configuration using standard built in tools
- Linux Systems can achieve similar outcomes with the purchase, setup and configuration of additional utilities and scripting
- Hardening greatly reduces the need to apply security patches. Well hardened Windows operating systems can run for more than a year before a security patch needs to be applied.
- Windows Update Service is a tool bundled with Windows that can centrally manage an Enterprise Cloud solution. Similar tools exist for Linux though scripting might be needed on some cases to provide central management and reporting.

Change and Configuration Management   5

> *In the cloud, the change and configuration management processes necessary for SAP include not only multiple logical systems working in concert, but also new cloud constructs and specific technology and organizational factors. Combined, these elements work together to create and enable the SAP-on-cloud system lifecycle.*

The old advice "never touch a running system" can't be followed anymore in cloud environments built with the intention to enable fast change. Practical experience shows that insufficiently prepared changes are the main cause of malfunction. Therefore, change management has particular significance as a central quality assurance instrument in the context of cloud management.

▶ *Never touch a running system ... without CCMS*

This way the change and configuration management system (CCMS)[1] represents the hub or nexus of a cloud infrastructure, enabling to create, regulate, tune, and manage SAP on the cloud in a trustful manner. The new cloud-specific constructs like resource pools, failure domains, scale units, health models, service profiles, etc., must be planned for, configured, and maintained.

In a public cloud like Amazon or Microsoft as well as in private or hosted clouds, the cloud owner controls all of these logical systems and constructs. In the end, though, it is this CCMS function that brings together everything necessary to create the cloud.

---

[1] Don't confuse the acronym CCMS in this context with the SAP Compute Center Management System

5.1 Introduction to Change and Configuration Management

Like any other computing platform, a cloud infrastructure is nothing more than a vehicle for running business software solutions. To do so, the cloud depends on several logical systems—systems that do the behind-the-scenes work of supporting the cloud.

These logical systems make it possible for SAP and other business applications to do the real work of the organization (such as creating sales orders, moving materials, paying the bills, and so on). Cloud infrastructures minimally require the following processes:
- Service catalog and contracts management
- Network fabric and service management and reporting
- Change and configuration management
- Monitoring and health management
- Financial management

▶ *Cloud elements tie into CCMS*

Combined, these logical systems enable the cloud to pool its resources, provide a foundation for elasticity, enable usage-based management, and allow cloud administrators access to a self-service management portal. But it is the change and configuration management system that is the heart of the cloud.

And therefore the robustness and resiliency of this system, combined with robust enterprise-ready infrastructure, are paramount to giving IT organizations the confidence they need to host their "last mile" applications, such as SAP, on the cloud.[2]

Unfortunately these logical systems generally have currently no hooks into SAP's applications and components. Instead, these hooks must be fashioned through SAP–aware tools or utilities.

5.1.1 Elements of the CCMS

The accuracy of data that resides in the CCMS is critical to the flawless processing of the other logical systems. The change and configuration management system's data store is essentially the system of record for operating a cloud; it contains detailed information about the cloud's specific services, fabric, profiles, and more.

Governance measures should focus on ensuring that this data store is safeguarded, maintained, backed up, and secured. The change and configuration management system comprises several elements related to the cloud's data and information flows:

---

[2] IDC. 2011.

- **Data types.** The structure of information's and their categorizing by purpose and addressing any differences introduced by usage in a private cloud.
- **Data stores.** The information stores and flows required by a private cloud infrastructure. The term store is a generic term that refers to long-term storage (such as databases, file systems, or blob-based storage) in addition to more transient forms of storage, such as queues.
- **Information management.** The processes to secure and govern information used in operations that occur in a private cloud.
- **Information flows.** The paths that information takes, and the transformations it undergoes as it flows through the change and configuration management system and interacts with data types, data stores, and information management processes.

5.1.2 Change and Configuration Data Types

Data types used as inputs to and outputs from the CCMS include[3]:
- Service class requests
- Service class configuration change request
- Service requests
- Service configuration change request
- Catalog update request
- Update configuration request
- Service/fabric update
- Service reporting update
- Service/fabric configuration requests

Each one of these data types ties into a relevant data store, discussed next.

5.1.3 Integrating Change and Configuration Management with SAP

Use automated scripts or workflows, and establish automated auditing and control checks to connect the CCMS to SAP and provide the following functionality:
- Change a service, service class, or service template
- Perform service, fabric, and catalog updates
- Perform service reporting updates
- Request and release resources and update configurations
- Update the change and configuration management data store

Unfortunately, many of the private cloud systems do not yet provide native SAP API-aware tools or scripts. One solution might be to develop a SAP API-aware

---

[3] Slater, Paul. *Reference Architecture: Technology View for SAP on a Private Cloud Infrastructure.* Microsoft. 2011

scripting "bolt-on" to your specific cloud provider's configuration and change management system using an SAP-approved scripting utility such as Connmove's SAP scripting utility, HP's utilities, or Microfocus's Borland/Segue products.

▶ *Script your own SAP-aware tools*

In this way, a private cloud could effectively scale up or scale down (drain and shrink) SAP resources on the fly (once those resources are no longer needed by SAP). This functionality would help compensate for the fact that the SAP login load balancing mechanism, for example, was never intended to work with resource pools and other cloud constructs necessary to provide real-time elasticity.

In lieu of the ability to natively peer into (and automatically respond to) SAP's performance metrics, a private cloud provider might create an SAP API-aware bolt-on that peers inside the system's SAP MONI table. Similarly, in cases where SAP MONI access is prohibited, the private cloud provider might access a copy of this table through a third-party (which automatically updates the copied table every few minutes). While not real-time, such an approach could conceivably provide reasonable scale up and scale down functionality.

Before we take a closer look at more of these technical challenges, a brief view into the business side of change and configuration management is necessary.

5.2 Managing SAP Business Changes

In the context of introducing necessary business changes, change management is based on an approval mechanism (determining what will be changed and why). The following change management adages set the stage for running SAP within an organization:
- The business doesn't care about technology
- However, the cloud might enable new capabilities
- On the other hand, the cloud might inhibit ways things are done today

For example, public cloud network latency might affect the business's ability to run real-time SAP reports as fast as managers like. Certainly SLAs and quality of service metrics could be established to tackle this just as in traditional data center environments – if the public cloud infrastructure can provide the necessary physical properties at all.

On the other hand, the business might instead be better served by pursuing workarounds and other changes that ultimately take its business capabilities to new levels. Several practices serve to minimize business disruption and maximize an organization's ability to thoughtfully navigate a new course in the midst of change, outlined next.

5.2.1 Change Management Drives the Business and IT Lifecycle

The change management process controls the life cycle of all changes. The primary objective of change management is to eliminate, or at least minimize, disruptions while changes are made to services.

Change management focuses on understanding and balancing the cost and risk of making a change against the benefit to either the business or the service. Minimizing human involvement and driving predictability are two core principles for achieving a mature change management process, and ensuring that changes can be made without compromising the perception of continuous availability.

5.2.2 IT and Business Accountability and Alignment

Arguably an organizational perspective as much as a technology or business aspect to change, managing the alignment between the business and SAP IT is critical. Achieving transparent and accountable alignment is probably the number one factor positively affecting change processes across the board.

> ▶ *Transparency facilitate the business/IT relationship*

As discussed in Chap. 5 such transparency goes a long way towards ensuring that the two vital ingredients of "business" and "IT" not only march together in lockstep, but do so in the right order: business before technology.

The necessary deep-seated alignment must absolutely start at the top. The relationship between the business (CEO) and technology (CIO and CTO) teams forms the baseline for communication and alignment.

IT must actively listen to the business and do its best to solve their business problems through the application of technology. The business must accept that what they would like to have comes always for a price, even minimizing the costs.

Both sides of the business/technology teams must be prepared to give and take, too, in the interest of gaining a mutual win in the marketplace. If that means contracting, outsourcing, or cloud-sourcing a piece of the business or a subset of the technology support staff, so be it.

5.3 Managing Technology Changes

In the context of the cloud, managing technology changes is paramount to managing new cloud constructs. For example, private and public cloud providers typically talk of the following constructs:

- **Resource pools** – infrastructure assets such as server CPU, memory, disk and other resources are pooled to run SAP.
- **Physical fault domains** – provide cloud platform resiliency which in turn enables SAP to remain up and available.

- **Upgrade domains** – enables the SAP IT organization to replace, repair, or otherwise up date the cloud platform's physical resources without negatively affecting eitherits availability or the availability of SAP.
- **Resource decay model** – describe an acceptable level of decay for each asset class or resource pool (at which time the pool would be refreshed or replaced altogether). Effective resource decay models reduce the cost of maintenance by avoiding expensive one-off maintenance on the cloud's failed infrastructure assets.
- **Reserve capacity model** – describes how much infrastructure capacity to hold in reserve to deal with hardware failures or the need to physically upgrade resources.
- **Scale units** – a standard unit of capacity (such as a virtual CPU or a block of disks capacity or a quantity of RAM) that is added to the cloud when workload or resource decay warrants such an addition.
- **Capacity plans** – indicate when and to what extent resources are added to the cloud to maintain its capability (to maintain a minimal level of capability)
- **Health models** – used to detect whether the cloud and its resources are operating as expected, operating less than optimally, or in a failed state. The health model drives automated configuration changes to preserve system performance and availability.
- **Service classes** – reflect whether an application is running in a stateful class, stateless class, or in an incompatible or unknown class.
- **Cloud costing and chargeback models** – encourages certain behaviors related to how infrastructure is allocated to the SAP cloud, ranging from 'use only what you need' to 'use only what you can afford.'

Maintaining SAP business process functionality requires not just managing the above, but "hardening" these constructs to maximize SAP system uptime.

5.3.1 Understand the Configuration Management Process

The configuration management process is responsible for maintaining information on the technology assets, components, and infrastructure needed to run the cloud. Critical configuration data for each component, and the data's relationship to other components, must be accurately captured, maintained, safeguarded, and secured.

This configuration data should include past, current, and future-state forecasts, and be easily available. In this way, access is preserved and predictability is achieved, again decreasing service delivery risk.

The CCMS uses a single change and configuration management data store. This store contains the entire configuration information about the service classes, services instances, and fabric infrastructure. Again, it is the system of record for all configuration information about the SAP system's cloud infrastructure and therefore needs to be treated and safeguarded as such.

A uniform technology stack based on standard configurations makes change and configuration management much easier. In this way, for example, patch management implementation and change control testing are easier, timely, and more reliable. How a uniform technology stack is subdivided and managed to provide the foundation for SAP services is covered next.

5.3.2 Manage Service Templates and Profiles

Service templates or profiles define configuration specifics, such as allocated CPU, memory, network bandwidth, storage, and so on. Cloud service providers (internal or hosted) should offer only a small number of service options to their consumers.

Simplicity allows the provider to provide greater predictability at a low cost. And the consumer surrenders only minimal flexibility but benefits from the cost savings that come with simplification and standardization.

▶ **SAP service templates for different designs**

Given that SAP is a multi-tiered application, however, comprised of database, SAP Central Services (SCS), application servers for ABAP and Java each, developing and managing service templates could prove to be cumbersome.

Ensure your cloud provider's service template capabilities are adaptable to different SAP design and architecture philosophies. Ensure the provider supports different scalability profiles (for example, to scale up, out, down, or in), capabilities, and sizes and types of scale units.

In lieu of this flexibility, consider adopting a simpler architecture or design, one that creates a standard application server comprised of a set number and type of work processes or functionality. Conversely, to create the most flexible or "modular" SAP environment, consider abstracting each work process into its own service template or profile.

Use these "modules" to assemble complex configurations in a standardized and repeatable way. Because the SAP application workloads and work processes are abstracted from physical hardware, consumers need not be concerned about hardware specifics; they need only choose the service template or profile with the right balance of availability, performance, security characteristics, cost basis, and so on.

▶ **Consider modular templates**

Important questions that need to be answered and reflected in the templates or profiles include the following:
- What classes of service will the templates support?
- What templates are needed to meet the different workloads or server roles that each service class will host?

- How will these templates vary based on SAP application component (ERP, SCM, PLM, etc.) or role (application server running only dialog work processes, dedicated batch servers, and so on)?
- What will each template for each service class cost?
- How will costing be calculated (by IOPS transmitted? SAPS consumed? Disk space used? RAM utilized? A specific combination for each different templates?)
- Are there any special eligibility requirements for each class of service?

5.3.3 Use a Technical Sandbox

Like SAP highly recommends a Quality Assurance system (also called a test or burn-in system) to make sure that no change to the SAP application destabilizes the productive SAP software environment, deploying a technical sandbox (also called a T-Box, Crash-and-Burn or Phoenix system) is recommended to make sure that no change to the hardware configuration destabilizes the SAP platform. Examples for such tests are fire drills for HA and DR setups after changes to the cluster scripts, updates or changes of the virtualization solution etc.

▶ *The SAP technical sandbox*

In an ideal world, the technical sandbox replicates the complete production environment. In the real world, though, an exact replica is prohibitive expensive. Here you can benefit from the stateless computing technology described in Chap. 9. This technology for example available through Cisco UCS allows applying any change possible (including even changes to the BIOS) temporarily through service profiles.

This way you don't have to have to spend the expenditures for the technical sandbox all day long but only the hours you really need them. For example the same resource could be shared between the Quality Assurance system and technical sandbox, toggling between test SAP software changes and changes to the infrastructure.

Doing so provides a multi-purpose test landscape for any changes to the productive SAP system and validating that the production system will indeed not "break" under any testable conditions. And it provides a training capability and re-tooling mechanism for new-hires or rusty support personnel.

5.3.4 Protect the Development System

If a technical sandbox is not available, consider changing where the Development environment sits in the promote-to-production change control processes pertaining to the SAP technology stack. In most cases, the Development environment is either the first or second system in this process. SAP configuration changes originate here, and in the absence of a technical sandbox, technical change management typically originates from here as well. A test or quality assurance system typically follows the development system.

Consider the value of swapping these two systems, though, and testing changes in a test or quality assurance system *before* Development. This is especially compelling in environments where the Development system is heavily used, such as in highly customized systems or in short-lived systems.

The idea is to mitigate the risk that a technology change like a firmware upgrade or component swap might knock out the heavily used and therefore critical Development system, by first testing the planned change somewhere else.

5.3.5 Review the SAP Technology Stack and Tools

Review new SAP technology stack options and tools annually if not more frequently, and plan not only for how new technologies may be incorporated into your current cloud platform but help you better manage the change and configuration processes. Keep your options open, your vendors on their toes, and the opportunity to take advantage of gains in technology or reductions in cost real.

And then be bold (in a conservative mission-critical SAP kind of style, of course). Be quick to evaluate, and even quicker to implement changes to your system if they look to equate to a significant increase in performance or a significant decrease in cost – in the former case, assuming you're on the road to requiring the additional bandwidth.

By all means, do not circumvent your lifecycle management and promote-to-production processes, but instead take advantage of opportunities to realize significant advantages typically afforded only to early adopters. And of course, do so with the understanding that the risk must of course be carefully evaluated and mitigated throughout the review process.

5.3.6 Leverage Regression Testing Tools and Capabilities

Conduct regular regression testing to validate a particular business process executes as fast or faster after a given change to a configuration – this lets you validate change management processes in a "backwards" fashion.

In the realm of testing, functional testing has little bite – it's not sexy, or particularly exciting. But it represents an excellent real-world application-layer method of validating performance tuning exercises, a role well beyond its intended purpose of ensuring that developed code continues to function after a change to that code.

5.3.7 Maintain Technical Change and Configuration Management Rigor

A certain amount of rigor is required to maintain an effective change and configuration management system.

One key is to baseline new systems and then re-baseline after every configuration change. Deploy each SAP service template or profile individually and then baseline each business and technology "layer" in the SAP Technology Stack. Only a defined performance "starting point" enables a validation of the effect of changes to the stack result in a decrease or increase of performance of SAP in a cloud environment.

▶ **Define the baseline**

The need to balance the speed with which changes may be deployed in an environment against conservative due diligence is a challenge, but one that can reap great rewards when optimized.

Another key to high rigor involves leveraging the resources germane to resource pools as a load testing component within the end-to-end promote-to-production process. Develop a load testing methodology, be it large or small in scope, as an integral part of your change management strategy.

▶ **Run load tests**

Create a process whereby each change promoted to production is at some point in time load tested prior to turning the system back over to its end user community.

Make it the final "check box" to be marked off in your change management checklist, as a planned change works its way from a Technical Sandbox through non-production systems prior to landing in Production.

5.4 Managing Organizational Change

As discussed in Chap. 2 the characteristics of most SAP applications demand IaaS as the only supported cloud flavor. Therefore all the operational tasks down to the management and patching of the operating system are still necessary to be done by the company consuming cloud services. Only the operation of the hardware itself and the virtualization layer has to be managed and patched by the cloud provider.

Therefore moving SAP systems to the cloud doesn't allow companies to run their mission critical systems with less skilled and experienced experts – with the exception of experts skilled only in installation, operation and patching of proprietary servers hardware and operating systems.

The greatest factor that decreases system stability lies in the realm of human resources, particularly in cases today where IT departments have few resources in the wake of cost-cutting, unaddressed employee attrition, and poorly executed shoring strategies.

▶ **Risk of ultra-lean SAP service operation**

Consider the potential situation where an IT organization chooses to staff its SAP team so lightly that their focus can only be on day-to-day operations, which

5.4 Managing Organizational Change

means there is little budget or time left to address the spectrum of operations and service delivery in their entirety.

Characteristics of such diluted or "ultra-lean" service operation organizations include the following:

- **Little time to stay up to date.** The strategic long-term needs of the business made possible through IT innovation and process diligence suffer.
- **Little time to improve or harden processes.** Lack of time or personnel bandwidth to pursue, much less achieve, operational excellence through incremental improvements and best-in-class efficiencies.
- **Little time to pursue automation.** Lack of bandwidth to pursue or deploy process automation, systems management, and so on.

When the burden of system uptime and availability is placed in the hands of very few key technologists, one human error, one extended leave of absence, or one unhappy IT pro operating in the midst of a hardware or software failure could further exacerbate an otherwise manageable issue.

Certainly, such a situation might represent a risk with which an organization's leadership team is comfortable. But does such a situation really preserve budget dollars in the midst of mission-critical service operations?

▶ *SAP service operations problem areas*

Remember that running SAP on public cloud is IaaS only and consider how the following "worst practices" related to system uptime, availability, and disaster recoverability affect service operations:

- **Manual processes.** When SAP process automation is overlooked, it creates an environment in which the organization depends too much on error-prone manual processes and people.
- **People-related Single Point of Failure.** When SAP operation knowledge is maintained in the heads and on the laptops of one or a few people, rather than in a robustly protected and highly accessible knowledge repository, business systems are put at risk. Such a practice negatively affects troubleshooting, the speed with which real-time on-the-job and informal training can be absorbed, cross-training, new-employee onboarding, and so on.
- **Poor documentation and testing.** When key IT processes, such as database restores, disaster fail-over and failback processes, and capacity planning, are bereft of documentation, and have not been proven through real-world testing, business systems are put at risk.
- **Incomplete processes.** When key IT processes are missing components or practices that are essential to availability, simple issues can quickly escalate to major business system outages. For example, a promote-to-production change management process devoid of a load testing component means that changes to the technology stack are not proved under load. Under such conditions the organization's user community acts as the stress testing component. Obviously such practices risk poor performance and downtime.
- **Poor workload balancing.** When key members of a service provider or internal IT department find themselves overworked with steady-state as well as new project

activities – while less-equipped or less capable colleagues (with presumably more time on their hands) are underutilized simply because they are unable to take on additional workload and responsibilities – more errors and greater unplanned downtime are inevitable.

Such situations point primarily to people and service delivery issues rather than flaws in technology and architecture, providing an interesting maxim: mission-critical systems are typically affected much more by the people and processes used in the delivery of the Service Operation domain than by issues related to technology and architecture. Automation is the essential method of remediating this situation.

5.4.1 Understand the Four Technology Perspectives

An enterprise IT management must decide on a *technology perspective* or how it views its investment in information technology resources. Some companies look at IT spending from a long-term perspective, and try to purchase assets with a useful life of perhaps many years. Other companies subscribe to the belief that regular hardware and software refreshes will provide a competitive advantage or a performance advantage over time.

Though other methods exist, organizations often pursue technology investments based on one of the following four perspectives:

- **Conservative.** As the least risky of all approaches, an IT management with a conservative technology perspective places SAP system availability above all else. They seek mature technology, mature practices, and tried-and-true solutions that work, day in and day out. What they potentially sacrifice, then (though in their eyes this is not a sacrifice at all), is anything new – for example new architectures described in Chaps. 8 and 9.
- **Mainstream.** Like their conservative brethren, these IT management prefer established platforms and products to newer ones. However, they are comfortable with changes when in good company. Said another way, they want to be able to point to a slew of other companies in the same boat, and feel confident that they are not alone, that most of the industry is doing things in a manner similar to their approach.
- **Close Follower.** Many SAP customers are close followers. They leverage their IT investments in proven technology, but with exceptions. Although maximizing uptime always remains central, close followers are willing to try new technologies to gain a competitive advantage and position themselves better for the future.
- **Leading Edge.** This is the most challenging approach, hence the more popular label "bleeding edge" assigned to this technology perspective. Competitive positioning is key, as it's all about getting a jump on the competition in terms of minimizing cost, minimizing response times of business transactions, maximizing system accessibility, and so on. Therefore, a leading-edge SAP IT team must be prepared to invest heavily in change and configuration management than their less risky counterparts.

5.4 Managing Organizational Change

▶ *In-sourcing – the new trend?*

Out sourcing SAP system operation and infrastructure to cut costs has become a mainstream during the last decade and public clouds are seen as the ultimate ratio in these regards. Ironically some large enterprises which are usually not leading edge in terms of IT currently in-sourcing their SAP system operation again while implementing private cloud technologies.

5.4.2 Minimize Human Involvement

Minimizing human involvement is a proven principle for achieving infrastructure resiliency; a well-designed private cloud infrastructure can dynamically perform operational tasks, automatically "detect and respond" to failure conditions in the environment, and elastically add or reduce capacity as required by the workload.

▶ *Automate to decrease errors*

However, all of these actions are changes, and all changes pose risk. The following questions must be answered and defined in the change approval process:
- What human intervention (proactive management outside of automated processes) is still needed to evaluate the risk of a particular change and then approve or reject the change?
- Who will make a decision on the intervention?
- What information does the Change Approval Board (CAB) need to be able to make the decision?
- What must be done to ensure the CAB has the necessary information as quickly as possible?
- After the decision has been made to proceed with the change, can the rest of the change process be automated?
- How can the system be "rolled back" if the change is not successful?
- What steps or checks require human intervention?
- After the change, what steps need to be taken to ensure that the change was successful?

It is important to maintain a record of all changes, including standard changes that have been automated, especially for mission-critical infrastructures. The automated process for standard changes should include the creation and population of the change record per standard policy to ensure auditability, which is an important support-specific quality attribute.

▶ *Automate to accelerate processes*

Finally, don't forget the basics! The simplest method of automating human involvement is "the checklist." Automated checklists help speed up processes, ensure accountability, encourage process diligence, and make for a simple audit process. Regardless of the format, checklists make sense in ensuring that daily, weekly, monthly, and other regularly scheduled tasks are completed at regular intervals. Use the data collected via SAP transactions SSAA or RZ20 as a starting point.

5.4.3 Optimize Organizational Change Processes

More so than the technologies deployed, or the SAP IT organization's people and organizational limitations, inefficiently executed processes impinge most on an SAP IT organization's agility, and therefore its timely ability to address business needs. Measure the organization's process efficiency against itself over time (for example, quarter to quarter), and against its peer groups. Arguably the most common inefficiencies include inabilities to:

▶ *Organizational change process optimization*

- Provision new systems or platforms quickly, in response to just-in-time business needs.
- Re-provision or reconfigure existing systems quickly, in response to changing business needs.
- Conduct basic capacity planning, much less capacity management.
- Conduct performance management.
- Conduct holistic and proactive systems management (from the private cloud's logical systems to the hardware and software infrastructure, to applications and business scenarios/processes).
- Conduct reactive systems administration.
- Deploy change management practices.

Some of these process inefficiencies may reflect technology limitations. Identify those limitations and standardize and rationalize them as possible. In other cases, though, limitations directly reflect a lack of process automation and controls. Replace manual checklists and other manual processes through tools like Cisco Intelligent Automation. In this way, the organization's process discipline may start to mature through stabilization. Once stable, the organization can pursue the next level of maturity geared towards greater process efficiency, and ultimately process agility.

5.4.4 Plan for SAP Staffing Backup Before Disaster Strikes

Ensure each individual team member within your SAP IT team has a backup. For instance, each Basis team member, by name, should have a backup identified for him or her. This helps avoid confusion when people come up missing in an emergency, call in sick, or simply wish to take a vacation now and again.

Groups or teams need to backup other teams, too, just as each individual within your organization should have a backup. For example, your SAP Operations team might backup your Basis team in terms of monitoring, and your Basis team might backup your DBAs. Your server team might backup your SAN team, and vice-versa.

Don't forget to maintain "both" types of Staffing Plans, too – plans that reflect the individual employees, contractors, and third party consultants already tasked with actively supporting your environment, and plans that include obtaining backfills and replacements from sources outside of the organization.

For example, one of our favorite customers maintains a large org chart box "underneath" their SAP Basis and DBA technical support boxes labeled "Vendor SAP Services." Another box labeled "Contract Operations Services" resides underneath their SAP Operations and Data Center support groups.

In this way, a three dimensional organization chart is created, one with the resiliency and structure capable of meeting daily needs while also positioned to respond to emergencies. And such a dual-staffing approach helps them understand where they might locate incremental bandwidth not only for disasters but for new projects and initiatives, too.

5.4.5 Leverage Help Desk and Operations Support Teams

As we have seen many times over the years, organizations like the SAP Help Desk often represent a company's best kept secret when it comes to maximizing customer satisfaction. The same goes for the behind-the-scenes SAP Operations team. As discussed before, operating SAP on a cloud infrastructure will not change the need for Help Desk and Operations teams maintained properly to function at their peak.

Train your Help Desk to be "fence straddlers" – individuals capable of understanding, working with and talking to both the business and the technical folks they support. The best Help Desk technicians are a combination of business analysts and junior SAP Basis administrators, and possess excellent knowledge management skill sets as well. In this way, they understand and can speak "business" as well as "SAP," including the acronyms, vernacular, and so on necessary to be well understood by their customers across the board.

▶ *Leverage your best kept secrets*

In the same manner, train your SAP Operations team as backfill for key SAP technical support roles (if not the entire technology stack!). The best SAP Operations teams are ready to step into junior DB administrator, SAP Basis, and Operation system management. In case of using the IaaS services of a public cloud provider you may not need deep technical infrastructure knowledge of virtualization layer storage and network support.

Regarding both the Help Desk and SAP Operations teams, be sure to equip them with the proper tools necessary for troubleshooting and working through issues. Effective knowledge management is the lifeblood of an organization, especially one tasked with supporting a breadth of activities like those that span multiple business processes and virtual IT support organizations within the umbrella of SAP support. That is, it's vital that these teams are given access to, and training relevant to, using a knowledge management tool that helps them manage their unique SAP business and technical environment.

5.4.6 Thoughtfully Outsource and Augment

Look deep into your SAP IT organization to determine strengths and weaknesses. Conduct a staffing assessment to identify gaps that can be filled through training and directed experience (or on the job training) versus those that require new people with new skills and experience. Consider your organization's self-efficacy or ability to learn, change, and adapt to new technologies and business paradigms. And then consider staff augmentation or outsourcing areas where gaps are identified that are too wide, non-core, or simply too non-strategic to pursue.

Talk with similar SAP support organizations to understand why other companies are driven to make similar staffing choices, particularly their key lessons learned. And remember:

▶ *Explore new staffing paradigms*

- Focus on investment in skill, not in IT infrastructure
- Outsourcing SAP specific skill may reduce costs, but leave companies with few options in negotiations with the outsourcer.
- Standard OS and infrastructure support functions however can be considered for augmentation or outsourcing.

Especially for SAP deployments on public clouds it is important to craft a well-defined mutually agreed set of expectations about what management services are provided by the cloud provider and what has to be still be managed by the cloud consumers along with an engagement model. And cultural nuances absolutely must be understood, especially relevant to communication, accountability, meeting deadlines, and sharing risks. This is just as true of technology and people as it is of how processes are employed, covered next.

5.4.7 Mitigate Risk by Open Exchange of Real Life Experience

New vendors will try to convince you to migrate to new platforms and tools, incumbents will require you to stay with proprietary ones (to stay "supported," for example). Finally, SAP AG itself will nudge you to move into newer releases of their products as well. For obvious reasons you can't always expect unbiased information from any of these parties.

A proven method to minimize the risk is to establish relationships with the SAP technical community in your area – other companies, also betting their business on SAP. This should include your local SAP user group, even if most of their focus lies outside of the platforms underpinning your SAP solutions.

▶ *Mitigate risks – share experience*

To the point, establish relationships with other SAP customers running SAP systems similar to yours in terms of technologies employed, version of the SAP component, and key technology components (SAN vendor, DR approach, etc.).

Don't forget to look outside the core SAP system, too – other SAP sites running the same bolt-on tax software, or inter-enterprise middleware, or SAP-aware enterprise systems management tools all prove useful in times of crisis, or simply when it's time to consider upgrades. All of this makes for an effective risk mitigation foundation.

It must be mentioned however that establishing such relationships comes for a price – like in a marriage they don't work if only one party try to get all the benefits. Other than in the relationship to hardware vendor competency centers which are mostly misused as "consulting for free" departments, relationships in SAP user groups work only if information flows in both directions.

Such "two-way" information exchange would also enable the hardware vendors SAP competence centers to support you better – only when you feedback changes of the release, number of users and database sizes of the SAP solutions deployed you can expect to be alarmed if issues with such configurations become known.

5.4.8 Increase IT's Process Discipline

As a final step in maximizing organizational effectiveness in the midst of changing business priorities and technology capabilities, focus on continuously improving your process discipline.

The cloud will necessitate more automation, after all, requiring greater attention to developing and managing processes over time. While many business and IT processes may be individually implemented and refined, the best SAP support organizations take advantage of the following in the name of incrementally increasing their "process discipline":

▶ *Incrementally evolve your process discipline*

- Repeatable processes, which implies well-documented and well-understood processes.
- Reusable templates, including project plans, various levels of deliverables (such as those geared towards executive audiences, those geared towards end user communities or particular business entities, and those geared towards technical audiences).
- Knowledge management tools, such that key learning's can be retained within the organization to avoid recreating the same wheel over and over again.
- A dedicated Project Management Office, or PMO, with a charter to maintain and hone the aforementioned tools and processes, along with the skills of its core PMO members (and dotted-line or virtual project managers typically aligned along either major business processes or IT centers of excellence).

In our experience, effective business change management and overall IT governance is only made possible with excellent process discipline – position your team to make a noticeable difference and work to improve your process diligence over time.

5.5 Summary

In this chapter, we reviewed the change and configuration processes that together enable stable and secure operation of mission critical SAP deployments.

New cloud constructs were examined alongside tried-and-true methods of managing change. We also reviewed a number of areas shown to be effective in minimizing the impact of change, including the use of templates and checklists, methods of testing the SAP technology stack, and more.

This chapter concluded with discussions of several practices shown useful in helping the SAP IT organization manage change, including minimizing human involvement, optimizing organizational change processes, planning for the worst, using the organization's hidden resources, and developing a people-centric risk mitigation process, all of which help the organization to increase its process discipline and more effectively navigate change.

How Private and Public Clouds Work   6

> *Cloud Computing – both, Private as well as Public Clouds – introduce new technical and operational concepts. This chapter explains how these solutions differ from traditional IT infrastructures and describe how these concepts improve service quality and lower the cost of IT.*

One of the major observations over time in the evolution of IT is the fact that major innovations have been driven by the idea of lowering Total Cost of Ownership (TCO). Along many technology changes, three pillars of innovation have always included Automation, Standardization, and Consolidation.

This story is still true when we look closer into how cloud computing really works internally. From a 10,000 ft perspective, the final goal of providing and consuming IT-Services as a utility has come very close to realization with cloud computing – and utility computing is the way things are going to happen in the future.

▶ **The driving forces**

Much like there is a power outlet in any room of a house right now, there will be access to data and services any time and at any location in the future. The only major question in the future will be whether data is exposed to a public, shared cloud or kept in a Private Cloud.

6.1 Cloud Services Principles

Before we take a closer look at what technologies are used for cloud services today, it makes sense to recap the characteristics – the essential features which make cloud computing distinctive against hosting and traditional IT – and attributes of this technology. The following characteristics are fundamental for cloud services:

▶ **Description of the service model**

- On-demand self-service
- Service consumption over the Internet
- Resource pooling and sharing
- Rapid elasticity in the used resources
- Metered services
- Pay only for what you use

In order to achieve these characteristics, a number of attributes apply typically to cloud based solutions. These attributes may be described as follows:

- Commodity HW and SW to deliver best price/performance ratio
- Massive scale in the hardware infrastructure to enable low costs
- Homogeneity and standardization of hardware and software
- Virtualization for easy deployment and optimal utilization
- Resiliency against failures built-in by architecture (based on redundancy and replication)
- Geographic distribution among datacenters for disaster recovery scenarios
- Service orientation in the consumption. Allocation of resources can be changed at any time.
- Self service oriented and highly automated
- Speed of service provisioning as well as recovery from a failure

Finally, there are also differentiations in the service model how cloud services are consumed. There are three basic types for cloud computing:

▶ **SaaS for provisioning of applications**

- Software as a Service (SaaS) provides the capability to use an application package over the internet without taking care about hardware, operating system, or operational considerations of the application installation.

▶ **PaaS for provisioning of platforms**

- Platform as a Service (PaaS) provides the capability to deploy an application into a (managed) platform

▶ **IaaS for the utilization of infrastructures**

- Infrastructure as a Service (IaaS) allows to request a Virtual Machine and to use this VM the same way as a server on premise.

The service models differ in the responsibilities of those who manage and maintain the respective cloud setup. In general, control but also responsibility to manage the installation is least in SaaS and highest in IaaS solutions.

This means in practical terms, in the case of SaaS, that a potential end-user can work directly with the application and no IT is enforced for maintaining the work environment. In IaaS however, patching and OS configurations usually requires IT to provide additional services for using the cloud based infrastructure.

6.2 Technologies for Public Clouds

Public clouds are shared infrastructures, which are exclusively consumed over the Internet. In general a large amount of pooled resources shared among many customers results in an attractive price/performance ratio.

Highly automated infrastructures and sophisticated solutions for resiliency against failures provide further support for this attractive solution. The major difference for Private Clouds is certainly the fact that Public Clouds are not dedicated to a certain group of users but open to anybody.

In order to provide more insight into how Public Clouds technically work and how they achieve their proposed features, we are going to make an assessment of the technology and concepts behind Windows Azure and Amazon Web Services (AWS). There are of course more than these two Public Cloud providers available but the description the technology of the two examples should be sufficient to get the concept.

6.3 Windows Azure Cloud Fabric

In our first assessment, we will have a closer look on the technology behind Windows Azure. Windows Azure was originally defined as a Platform as a Service solution which has now been extended to support the Infrastructure as a Service model as well.

We will see how this is realized in technology and operational considerations. In a second assessment, we will have a closer look at Amazon Web Services which provides an example of an Infrastructure as a Service solution.

The base philosophy behind the hardware structures in a cloud data center is to create homogeneous infrastructures to reduce the maintenance and administration effort. Like most of the commonly known public cloud services Microsoft Azure uses the x86 platform based on Intel or AMD CPUs.

Microsoft divides their Windows Azure Data Centers into clusters for the sake of manageability. A cluster is typically built up from approximately 1,000 individual computers which are called nodes. All computers are mounted in racks, and typically roughly 20 racks comprise one cluster.

▶ *Highly automated infrastructures*

Every cluster in the data center is controlled by its own Fabric Controller (FC)[1] – actually one of the compute nodes with a special role, which is responsible for

---

[1] Not to confuse with the acronym FC for Fibre Channel

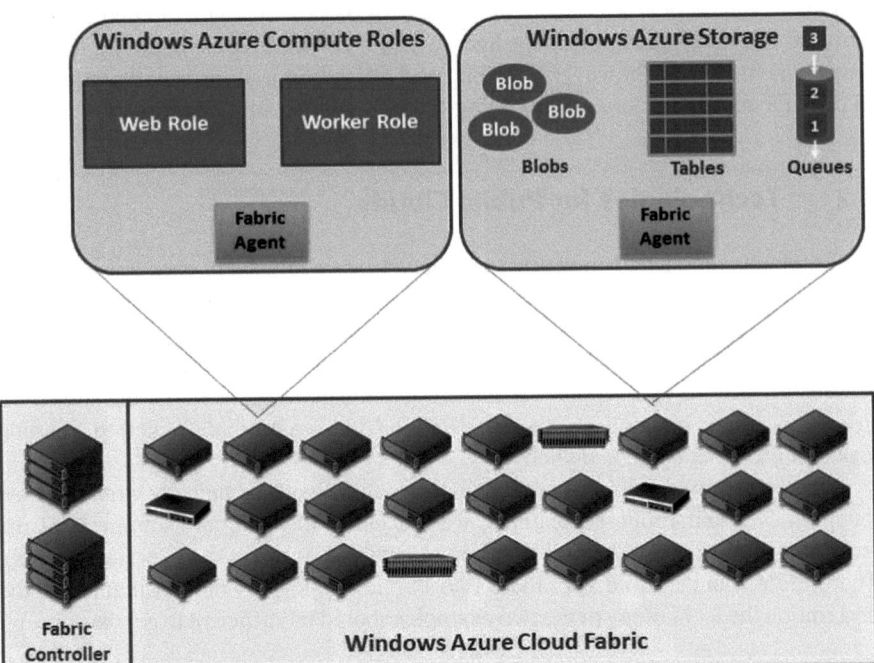

Fig. 6.1 Windows Azure cloud fabric

deploying a single node, provide the ability to manage and monitor all nodes in the cluster and control the deployment of services as well as their lifecycle on the cluster's nodes.

Fabric controllers take their configuration out of a huge XML-file which tells them what nodes are associated with their cluster, what IP-Addresses are assigned, what network routers are associated with the cloud, and so on. A cluster controller is bootstrapped by a single Utility Fabric Controller (UFC) which distributes the XML file to all existing FCs.

If we look a bit more into the layout of a cluster, we will see that each rack is equipped with its own router (called a Top-of-Rack router, or TOR) and one or more nodes which run a copy of the FC function. One of these nodes is always the Primary FC, while all the others are synchronized with the primary and act as standby. This level of redundancy provides effective protection against hardware failure and even allows for rolling software upgrades without service interruption. The fabric controller itself is a multi-instance service within the Windows Azure data center. 'Multi' here typically equates to between 5 and 7 instances.

The nodes inside the Windows Azure cloud fabric can either be utilized for compute services called the Windows Azure Compute Roles or for Window Azure Storage Role (WAS).[2] Picture Fig. 6.1 shows an overview about the Windows Azure cloud fabric.

---

[2] Not to be confused with the acronym WAS for the SAP Web Application Server

6.3 Windows Azure Cloud Fabric

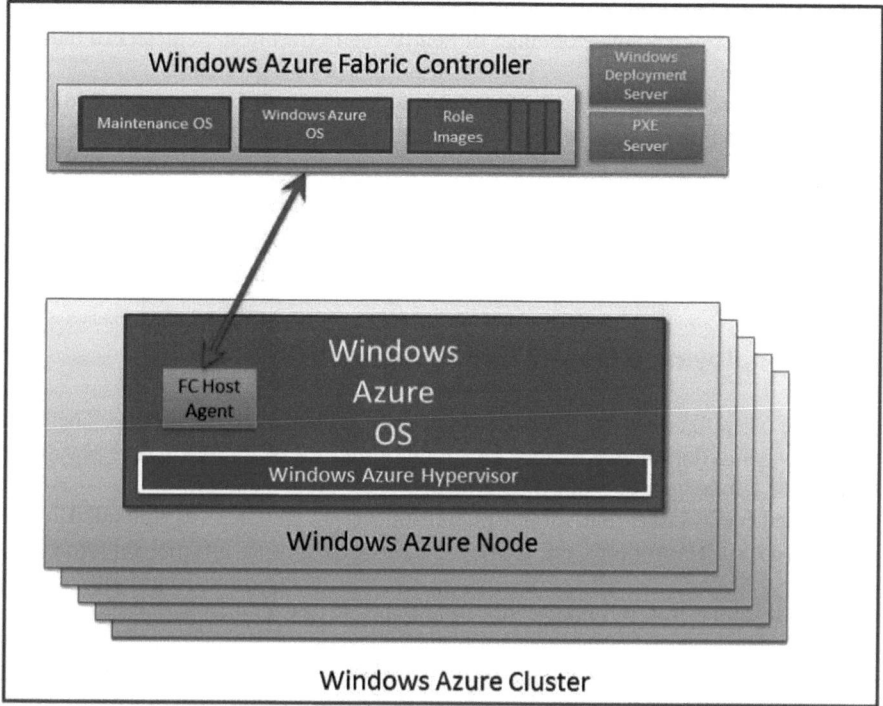

Fig. 6.2 Deployment of a compute node in Windows Azure

6.3.1 Provisioning a New Node in Azure

The fabric controller is in charge of managing all physical resources of a pool of compute or storage nodes and also controls the deployment of services into the managed cluster. One task in this regard is adding new nodes to the resource pool when needed. Whenever a new node is added to a FC, the Power Distribution Unit in the respective rack (which is also manageable via TCP/IP) switches the node on and the node will boot a PXE image from the fabric controller.

▶ *Deployment of Azure OS*

The first image which is then booted on the new node is a maintenance OS. It prepares the new node for its final configuration and then installs the Windows Azure OS image by using a Windows Deployment Server on the fabric controller. The Windows Azure OS is actually a preconfigured and customized version of Windows. After this step, the new node is installed with a Windows Azure OS which in turn runs on top of a hypervisor – a special version of Hyper-V – and is equipped with the FC Host Agent to allow the fabric controller to control and monitor the new node (Fig. 6.2).

The Fabric Controller polls the availability of a service running in the cluster by a technology similar to the exchange of heartbeats in traditional clusters to indicate the health status.

In case of failures, the fabric controller is able to re-distribute a running role to a spare node and thus automatically assure the service continues to work. This automatic service recovery is however only guaranteed for the role types Web role and Worker role. Any other application type needs to address the service recovery by itself.

6.3.2 Deploying a Service into Windows Azure

Any kind of application that runs in a Windows Azure cloud is a service. There are several ways to deploy a service it the cloud: either the Windows Azure portal can be used or a management tool like System Center AppManager.

The service – either the service definition or a VM role – is uploaded to the respective tool. From there, the package is forwarded to an internal service called Red Dog Frontend (RDFE) – the name has obviously some Microsoft internal meaning – which in turn chooses the right Fabric Controller to deploy the service.

▶ *Azure Red Dog Frontend*

RDFE is the front end of all services in Windows Azure and is responsible for deployment, billing, user access, and service management. The decision where a service is deployed is based on the datacenter region where a cluster belongs, and also to an optional affinity group which determines whether a new service should be located somewhere in a cluster where other customer services run.

Affinity groups help make sure there is network proximity between different services in the Windows Azure cloud. A good example where this is desirable includes the configuration of an SAP database and its application servers.

▶ *Azure affinity groups*

Once the service definition has been forwarded to a fabric controller, the FC determines the resource requirements for the service from the service definition and creates a role image – actually a virtual machine image – and deploys this image to nodes in the cluster.

The same time the role is deployed, virtual IP addresses and packet filters are configured on the VMs and network connections to the internal load balancers are configured for this role.

As soon as the service has its resources assigned, Windows Azure automatically takes care about network load balancing and maintains the availability of the service.

6.3.3 Roles and Instances in Azure

Any Windows Azure compute instance is actually a virtual machine which is deployed as Virtual Hard Disk (VHD) file from the Fabric Controller. VHD files are the file format used in Microsoft's Hyper-V virtualization for VM storage.

Microsoft provides pre-configured VHD images for using a Windows Azure compute instance VM as a front-end or web server (called a Web role) or as a back-end .NET application server (called a Worker role).

▶ *Predefined role templates for web and .Net server*

If neither of these is appropriate, the VM can be used as a generic VM role. In this role, Microsoft does not provide a SLA on the VM's OS because you upload your own VM virtual hard drive image (and Microsoft does not perform any updating on the OS). The obvious consequence here is that applications such as SAP default to an IaaS model in Windows Azure once they are supported – which result in the fact that customers still have to take care for the correct OS patch level by them self.

Web and Worker roles are fully handled by the Fabric Controller, and they ease the task of creating a web server of a .NET application server by providing these capabilities in preconfigured way. A user only needs to upload website code or the .NET application to this setup.

Web and Worker roles fully support the redundancy concepts which maintain in combination with Network Load Balancing the availability level of 99.95 %. In contrast, when a (generic) VM role has been deployed, this level is not guaranteed but instead must be specifically architected in the applications and in terms of their initial setup.

6.3.4 Fault Domains and Upgrade Domains

As described in Chap. 3, an important consideration for utilization of a public cloud is to maintain guaranteed availability levels in the Service Level Agreement with customers.

In order to achieve maximum availability, lots of redundancies and replication are involved in the infrastructure and services. The base unit for fault isolation inside the cloud datacenter is the cluster. It is an encapsulated unit consisting of replicated nodes for the fabric controller and a potentially huge number of compute nodes which are all identical in size and function – these are redundant.

Racks inside a cluster are the units of fault isolation and are called Fault Domains. A single rack is equipped with compute nodes, network gear and possibly a copy of the Fabric Controller. If an application needs to survive hardware or software failures, it needs to have instances of the application service running on different fault domains. Fault domains therefore address the aspect of unplanned outage due to unexpected failures.

Another possible reason for unavailability of an application service is patching or updating of the OS or software components used. In order to avoid this, Windows Azure provides the concept of an Upgrade Domain. Very similar to a Fault Domain, several copies of a role instance are distributed over a different group of compute nodes.

▶ *Avoiding planned downtime*

Since all maintenance work in Windows Azure is performed by the Fabric Controller, the task of the FC is now to ensure that only one instance of a compute node at a time is upgraded or patched while the others remain available for the user. After finishing this task on one instance, access is switched internally to another copy of the instance, and the upgrade continues in a round robin fashion on the remaining nodes within the Upgrade Domain.

If a service in Windows Azure is deployed in different Fault Domains and Upgrade Domains, Microsoft states in the Windows Azure SLA an availability of at least 99.95 %. Distribution of a service over at least two Fault and several Upgrade Domains is actually done by the Fabric Controller at the time when the service is established.

6.3.5 Azure Storage

As described before any nodes inside the Windows Azure cloud fabric can be utilized in a Storage Role. Windows Azure provides public cloud storage capacity in Microsoft's six data centers which are geographically distributed over three regions: America, Asia, and Europe. The total capacity in Windows Azure exceeded 200 PB at the start of 2012.

The available cloud storage is used both from the cloud computing nodes for persistent storage and externally as a location independent and cost efficient storage service. The provisioning of storage as a cloud service is widespread across essentially all public cloud providers. Compute clouds are an extension of these services and depend on them (though not all cloud providers offer a compute cloud solution).

▶ *Azure storage for PaaS and IaaS*

In Windows Azure, the storage is accessed via RESTful web service calls (http/https). Access to storage is possible not only from a computing instance in the cloud but also from on-premise by using web services-based calls. There are four options for storage services:
- Blobs are large chunks of binary data such as videos, backup files, and so on. From the perspective of an application on Windows Azure, blobs look like a drive formatted with the ubiquitous Windows NTFS file system. Blobs are also used for file storage whenever Windows Azure storage is accessed from outside the cloud. A single blog can be up to 200 GB in size.

- Tables are a set of entities (rows) – not to confuse with tables in a relational database – which in turn contains sets of properties (columns). Tables are best used for massive scale-out, entity-based storage. Tables are often also named in the context of NoSQL (Not only SQL). Tables can be very large, ranging up to several terabytes in size, storing billions of objects or entities.
- Queues are a reliable method for the delivery of messages. Windows Azure provides APIs to store messages in a queue in order to enable communication and synchronization between independent services running on separate compute nodes. While one service may request an action by writing a message in a queue, participating services can read messages and delete them after a task has been executed. A single message can be up to 64 k of data in size.
- A Windows Azure Drive enables the use of a blob as a single NTFS volume in the Virtual Hard Disk (VHD) format. This VHD file can be relocated between a private cloud on-premises and the Windows Azure public cloud.

In order to use storage in Windows Azure, a user needs to create a Windows Azure storage account which is based on a worldwide unique name. One of the attributes in the account settings identifies the storage location – one of the currently six data centers – where all the data will be physically stored and all the read and write access is going to.

Here, the user typically decides to have the closest physical proximity and thus least access time. Once a storage account exists, a user can create blob containers in it. Blobs are chunks of disk space which used for raw storage capacity. When blobs are created they are subsequently put into those blob containers and used from there.

Additionally, tables for entity storage and queues for message bases storage can be created as needed for the cloud application. Access from the outside to blobs, tables, and queues is possible by using HTTP or HTTPS calls such as:
- https://<nameofaccount>.blob.core.windows.net/<nameofcontainer>
- https://<nameofaccount>.table.core.windows.net/<nameoftable>
- https://<nameofaccount>.queue.core.windows.net/<nameofqueue>

Windows Azure storage used for blobs, tables, or queues is replicated three times inside the same data center that has been specified upon creation of the storage account. By using different fault domains in a data center for these three copies of data, Windows Azure provides an SLA of 99.9 % availability per month for storage services.

In addition to the internal replication, there is the option to use geographic replication in one region for the data at no additional cost. Geographic replication is always asynchronous. Since Windows Azure is hosted across two different data centers in each European, Asian, and American geography, this replication enforces several 100 km between each copy of the data. In this way, Windows Azure enables disaster recovery by protecting against common environmental risks including earthquakes, fires, floods, hurricanes, and more.

6.4 Amazon Web Services

Amazon offers Amazon Web Services (AWS) since 2006, a suite of web services which provide public cloud services. Similar to Microsoft's Windows Azure, AWS is a scalable and reliable platform for compute and storage services and has altogether many similarities with Windows Azure.

One of the major differences however is the fact that AWS focus entirely on a pure Infrastructure as a Service (IaaS) solution for compute and storage cloud services. This makes it very easy for a broad range of applications including SAP to be installed and supported in the Amazon public cloud.

The base services for compute cloud solutions in AWS are called Amazon Elastic Compute Cloud (EC2). EC2 is similar to Windows Azure based on virtual machines which can be requested by a user as UNIX (Solaris x86), Linux or Windows server (however only Windows and Linux are supported for SAP instances).

The virtual machine contains an image of the operating system that needs to be administrated and configured by the IT department using the services of EC2. The AWS cloud infrastructure hosts and monitors these virtual machines and also provides storage and network services for their usage.

Each time a new instance of a virtual machine is requested by a user on the Amazon Management Console, a server template for the VM is used in order to create the final VM. The process of copying the template into a new VM and booting this VM takes just a couple of minutes.

▶ *Amazon machine images*

The templates are called Amazon Machine Images (AMI) and contain preconfigured images of an OS which can be used as baseline for the installation of an application – for example a SAP All-In-One or BusinessObjects solution.

There is a large selection of preconfigured AMI's available at Amazon and the EC2 community which serve the various purposes of a VM. Upon ordering a new instance, a user can size the VM in a kind of Starbuck's coffee sizing according to the categories Small, Medium, Large and Extra Large which in turn defines the amount of CPU cores and main memory available in the VM. The following table shows the available resources and their possible usage for SAP applications:

Instance type	Cores	Memory	Prod	SAPS
Standard large	2	7.5 GB	No	N/A
Standard extra large	4	15 GB	No	N/A
High-Mem extra large	2	17.1 GB	No	N/A
High-Mem double extra large	4	34.2 GB	Yes	3,700
High-Mem Quad extra large	8	68 GB	Yes	7,400

While the first three lines represent configurations which are not recommended for productive use with SAP solutions, the last two are supported. The SAPS numbers reflect the measured performance in SD benchmarks with the SAP version ECC 6 EHP4.

▶ **Keys for secure access**

Once the new instance has been created, Amazon provides a key pair for a secure access to the VM. With Solaris x86 or Linux, the VM is accessed via Secure Shell ssh (which uses the created keys for encryption), while with Windows, Microsoft's Remote Desktop is used. In the case of a Windows VM, the default administrator password is also encrypted by using these keys.

6.4.1 Amazon EC2 Availability

Similar to Windows Azure, AWS is organized in several data centers which are distributed across different geographical regions. Any of the data centers follows the principle to be completely isolated from any other data center and thus form an Availability zone for the VMs which are running in it.

▶ **Replication between datacenters**

Replication of a VM instance is by default configured within one Availability zone. Replication over geographical regions is possible but must be configured manually and at additional cost. The Amazon SLA specification of 99.95 % reflects the availability of an entire Availability zone and does not refer to an individual instance (Fig. 6.3).

6.4.2 Storage in AWS

Amazon Web Service provides three different types of storage service with different characteristics and use cases. The following description shows their main features:

> Amazon Simple Storage Server (S3) is a highly durable storage typically used as object store. The main characteristics of S3 are as follows:
> - Object or file based storage
> - Highly durable, Amazon claim 99.99 % availability and 99.999999999 % durability – theoretically 1 out of 10 billion data files could get lost per year
> - Cannot be mounted directly by EC2 instances

For SAP solutions S3 storage can be utilized typically for backups and SAP archiving.

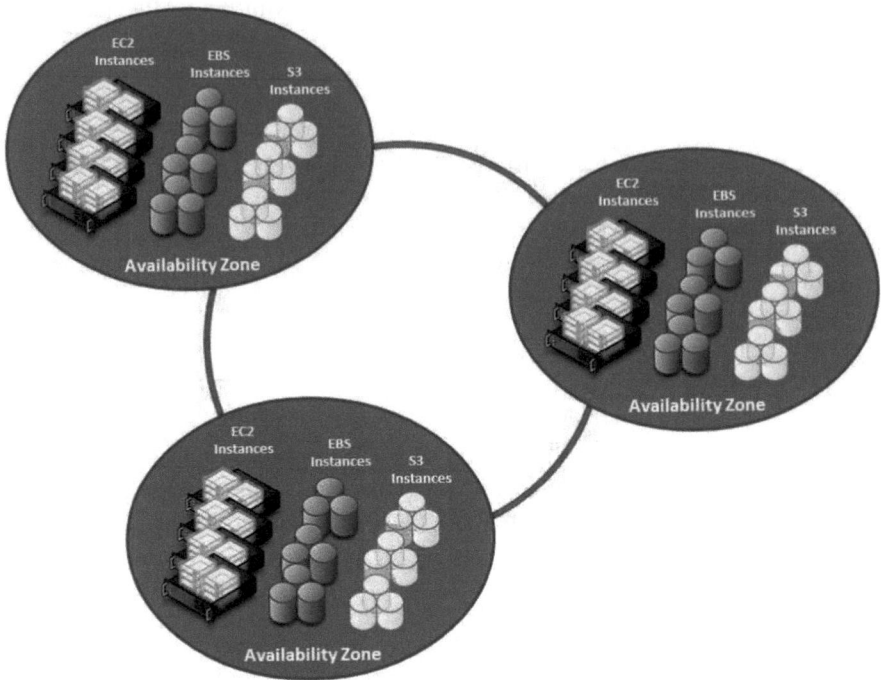

Fig. 6.3 Distribution over Amazon availability zones

Amazon Elastic Block Store (EBS) is the storage volume used for all data storage inside an EC2 instance. It provides a block structure for the persistent storage and maintains a reliable and highly available storage subsystem for the EC2 instance. The main characteristics of EBS are:

- Persistent block level storage volumes for use with EC2 instances.
- Contains a file system and appears as storage volume
- Can also be used as intermediate backup target

For SAP solutions, EBS volumes are typically used for installation of SAP as well as for the database software, log and data files.

The throughput of provisioned IOPS EBS volumes goes up to 1,000 IOPS (for 16 K block size) per volume. Striping 10 of these volumes result in 10,000 IOPS. Most important is that this IOPS can be guaranteed.[3]

Ephemeral Storage provides each instance of Amazon EC2 a certain amount of instance-related storage (volatile DAS). This storage is called ephemeral because it only exists for the lifetime of the EC2 instance and does not persist after its shutdown.

---

[3] http://aws.typepad.com/aws/2012/08/fast-forward-provisioned-iops-ebs.html

The typical use of this storage is for temporary purposes associated with the OS or the SAP application. SAP installations typically use ephemeral storage for swap or pagefile, or for temporary areas of the database

6.5 Technologies for Private Clouds

While Private Clouds share many of the characteristics of Public Clouds, such as service orientation, pooling of resources, elasticity and self-service orientation, and fast provisioning of services, there are a few fundamental differences.

Contrary to public clouds, the resources of a Private Cloud are always dedicated to an organization or a group of users (regardless of whether the Private Cloud's physical implementation is on premise or hosted remote). Furthermore, Private Clouds commonly follow the Infrastructure as a Service model.

Private Clouds may be seen as an abstraction layer which allow for the granular and flexible utilization of compute resources without requiring knowledge of the true infrastructure behind the scenes.

Real implementations of Private Clouds are based on servers, storage, and network fabrics across potentially many different vendors, and they may be installed in different locations. There may be a mix of AMD and Intel CPUs, for example, as well as different storage protocols such as FC or iSCSI. Virtualization can be based on hypervisors like VMware ESX, Citrix XEN Server, or Hyper-V. Deploying these resources in a service oriented way requires an abstraction of the infrastructure and an efficient handling by a controller instance – the Private Cloud controller.

The major advantage of Private Clouds versus traditional IT processes surrounds the flexibility and speed of operation at optimal utilization of existing infrastructures. Consider the process of requesting a new installation of an SAP Application server.

In the past, hardware provisioning or deployment of a new VM first had to be requested. Once available, the new server needed to be integrated into the existing infrastructure including OS installation, network configurations, patching etc. After that, the SAP installation could be done and the SAP Application server was able to handle user logons or batch operations.

With the concept of Private Clouds, a user is able to request a new VM on a self-service portal. The user can specify resource requirements as well as pre-configured features of the new VM. Deployment is based on templates which may already include the latest patch or special configurations for dedicated purposes (like the installation of a SAP instance). Furthermore, the automated deployment of a new SAP Application server can be part of the deployment process and will be orchestrated by the cloud controller. The result is a SAP service which is available in 1–2 h instead of several days if not weeks.

One development of Private Clouds that is already being realized today is the combination of Private and Public Clouds in a hybrid model. In this concept, users can choose through the Cloud UI whether they want a dedicated private infrastructure (at possibly higher cost) or a shared public infrastructure. The final request is then processed in the cloud controller and handled accordingly.

Another option is the possibility to upload (or migrate) a VM from a Private Cloud environment into a Public Cloud. This is also already possible today and becoming more prevalent. Due to limited network bandwidth, the process however is often not fully automated yet.

A very interesting question in this situation certainly will also be, if the uploading of a VM into a Public Cloud works seamlessly, can the process be executed the other way around?

Our assessment of the technology of Private Clouds starts with a closer look into Microsoft's Private Cloud solution followed by VMware's vCloud solution.

6.6 Microsoft Private Cloud

Microsoft's Private Cloud solution is centered on the Windows Server as OS, Hyper-V as the virtualization platform, and System Center for automation and control. Other hypervisors like VMware ESX and XEN Server are supported as well and can be included in the management concept introduced by the various System Center solutions.

The following figure illustrates the building blocks of a Microsoft Private Cloud (Fig. 6.4):

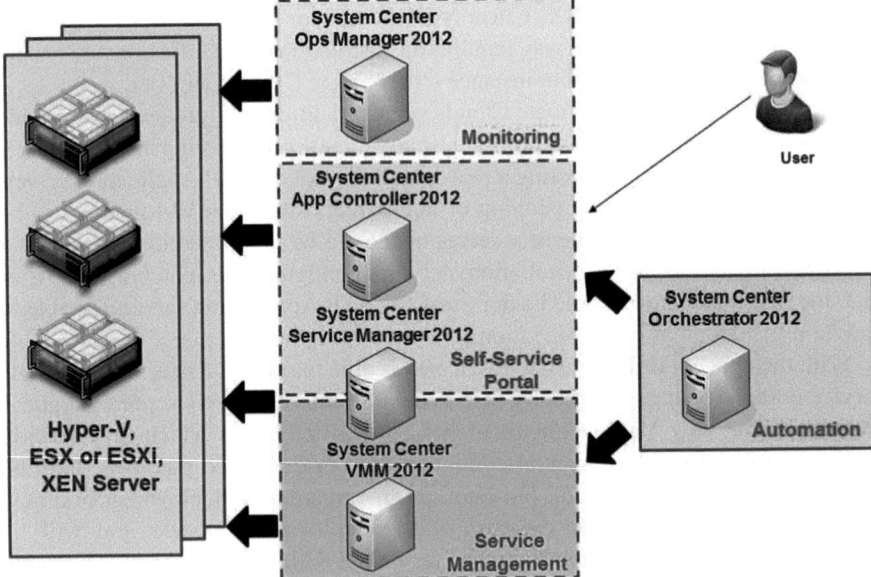

Fig. 6.4 Components of Microsoft private cloud architecture

▶ **Microsoft System Center as cloud controler**

Microsoft System Center Virtual Machine Manager 2012 (VMM) provides the fundamental services for creating and managing private clouds. VMM manages virtual and physical machines as well as storage infrastructures, network configurations, and clusters for high availability solutions. Templates for the deployment of new VMs and applications are maintained here in a library. VMM encapsulates all the tasks for managing the infrastructure of VMs.

Microsoft System Center Service Manager 2012 provides automated IT service management and an associated self-service portal. Service Manager enables also the definition of approvals processes with human interaction.

Microsoft System Center App Controller 2012 is a self-service portal for requests made directly to a private cloud created with VMM 2012.

Microsoft System Center Operations Manager 2012 is utilized to monitor health and performance of the complete stack consisting of virtual machines, physical servers, OS and applications. Operations Manager can also initiate actions to fix detected problems.

Microsoft System Center Orchestrator 2012 provides a way to automate interactions among other management tools such as VMM 2012 and Service Manager

6.7 VMware vCloud

VMware vCloud is another popular example of a Private Cloud solution. It supports a wide variety of different hardware vendors and is based on VMware virtualization technology combined with additional management solutions.

Figure 6.5 provides an overview of vCloud building blocks and architecture:

The vCloud solution consists of a Resource Group dedicated to the management of the Private Cloud infrastructure and one or more Resource Groups which provide the resources for the Private Clouds. All Resource Groups utilize VMware HA to provide resiliency against hardware failures. The management Resource Group provides the following functionality:

VMware vCloud Director provides the services for the management of the Private Cloud and is composed of several individual services. The main task of vCloud Director is to abstract virtual resources and to expose managed components to the users. This layer includes the vCloud Director itself, an MSSQL Database, and the vCloud API which in turn enables the management of vCloud components programmatically.

VMware vShield Manager is the management center for all security related tasks in a vCloud framework. It controls the various vShield solutions for perimeter security, role based access, and delegation of tasks. It is fully integrated into the vCenter management console.

VMware vCenter Chargeback provides dynamic resource metering, cost modelling, and report generation for pay per use of a Private Cloud. Data regarding resource

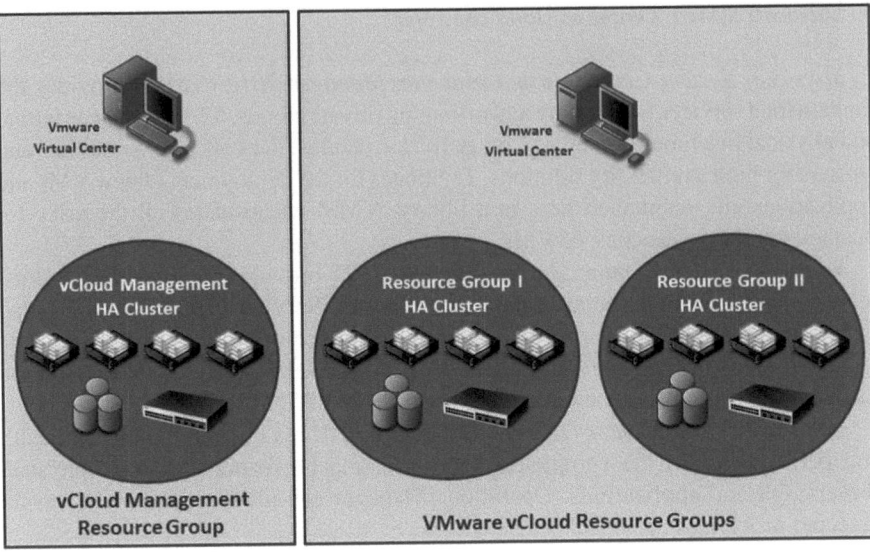

Fig. 6.5 VMware vCloud overview

utilization is collected inside the vCloud in the vCenter management console, and is forwarded to vCenter Chargeback in order to enable the automatic accounting feature.

VMware vSphere Management Assistant is a pre-configured Linux VM which allows administrators and developers to run scripts and agents to manage ESXi hosts and vCenter physical servers. It includes the vSphere command-line Interface CLI as well as SDKs for Perl. VMA represents the orchestration layer in the context of a Private Cloud.

6.8 Summary

- A high degree of automation and standardization as well as the scaling effect of large, shared pools of resources makes public clouds very cost effective.
- Windows Azure is a public cloud solution which followed the Platform as a Service principle only originally. In mid 2012, this solution was extended to also support the IaaS model. High automation and availability makes it a good choice for web server or .NET applications. SAP applications are currently not yet supported on Windows Azure but will very likely become available soon as VM roles.
- Amazon Web Services represents the longest publicly available public cloud service. An IaaS solution, SAP supports AWS for various applications including SAP All-In-One, SAP BusinessObjects, SAP Afaria, and SAP HANA.
- Private Clouds share many of the features of Public Clouds. Their service model in the context of SAP, however, is strictly Infrastructure as a Service. The main aspect of Private Cloud is the dedication of resources to a specific organization or group of users.

SAP Solutions on Public Clouds 7

> *In public clouds, enterprise-class computing capabilities are instantly available, easily accessible and come at a compelling price. However, the concept also triggers controversial discussions around governance, control and security of public accessible, highly shared, multi-tenancy computing environments.*

There is no doubt that particularly public clouds will become an integral part of our lives in the next decade. We don't have to look far for whether we use applications such as office-like-apps or services which are closer to the infrastructure such as storage on demand for our personal data.

▶ **SAP's way to the cloud**

While companies like SalesForce.com and SuccessFactor built their business models on cloud computing for many years, SAP cloud offerings such as PaaS or SaaS are relatively new.

For more than a decade, SAP had a rather difficult "relationship" to cloud computing given the roots of the company, the cultural difference between cloud applications and on-premise software which made SAP so successful.

It has been a long road from SAP's early efforts with SOA (project Vienna) in 2004 which took more than 2 years to develop. SAP "Business by Design" was released in 2006 and it took another 3 years to transform it into a commercially scalable and multi-tenancy service offering.

With the acquisition of SuccessFactor in 2011 and the announcement to acquire Ariba in 2012, SAP sent a signal to the market which leaves no doubt about the direction into on-demand software and cloud computing.

Given the current amount of change and transformation within SAP's cloud strategy, this chapter can only provide a snapshot of current initiatives on which SAP focuses.

In the previous chapters we've discussed the technologies that fuel public and private clouds and the advantages and limitations which apply for SAP application running on an IaaS.

The following chapter will focus on SAP applications in public clouds from a generic point of view and we will discuss open cloud-standards, cloud APIs and new areas within SAP such as NetWeaver cloud.

We will have a brief technical look at the current service offering of Amazon's cloud for SAP which is currently the only certified IaaS offering available. Finally, we will have a short outlook on some of the new areas in public cloud infrastructure and offerings by SAP.

7.1 Public Clouds: A Short Overview

Today, most large service and infrastructure providers offer cloud computing in different variants, scope and scale.

It is a challenge to provide a short and comprehensive overview on the current public cloud market. One approach to classify cloud offerings is to distinguish by service layer. Several cloud providers focus on the infrastructure layer (IaaS) whereas others provide more comprehensive offers such as databases or applications (PaaS and SaaS) (Fig. 7.1).

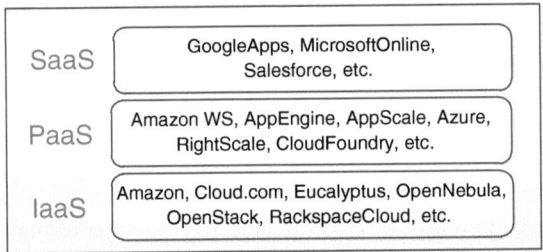

Fig. 7.1 Service layers of cloud computing

When we consider SAP applications on a public cloud as a sourcing alternative to a traditional IT environment, we will focus on IaaS offerings since most SAP solutions depends on its own runtime (all NetWeaver application server based solutions).

At the time of writing, there are various cloud platforms with a focus on IaaS on the market. Large service providers like T-Systems, Singapore Telecom or infrastructure providers such as HP or IBM offer cloud services in different forms and shapes.

▶ *Public cloud offering will be commoditized*

Besides, a number of consulting companies and specialized boutique providers like Freudenberg IT, Novis and others offer IaaS for SAP solutions. Some of the services are still in beta testing and others are fully released to the public. It is expected that most of the big players will support SAP applications in their cloud service offering in the near future.

It is important to understand that the public cloud market is still a reasonably new market and it is not very uniform. There is not one cloud standard, API, platform or software suite which everyone follows.

Consequently, deciding for a cloud offering should not only depend on the price of a particular offering, but rather on a number of aspects briefly discussed in Sect. 7.2. Cloud standards are still in development and platforms and frameworks might change in the near future.

7.1.1 Cloud Standards

Whenever the IT industry heralds a new paradigm that changes the very foundation of the market, one process always goes a long with it: the big players create a myriad of standards and technologies all proclaimed as the only future way to go.

It is no surprise that cloud computing is the same in that respect and in most cases it takes several years to shake out the markets. There are numerous organizations focusing on the development of cloud standards.

Some of these organizations center on aspects such as security or accessibility. Other groups focus more on generic subjects such as the management of cloud infrastructure or applications.

In previous chapters, we have already mentioned the "National Institute of Standards and Technology (NIST)" and the "European Telecommunications Standards Institute (ETSI)" to name just a few.

▶ *Compatibility is key*

When we look at SAP applications in a public cloud, an important characteristic of an IaaS offering is the degree of compatibility to standards. Similar to changing your electricity provider, you might want to be able to change your cloud provider in the future without a major interruption of the service and consequently the business processes. In a traditional IT environment, a change of the hosting provider comes usually with two options:
- SAP system copies: Copy a SAP system (as a file) to the new hosting provider via tape, disk or network is a straight forward procedure. Usually, this approach comes with shorter service interruptions but goes along with substantial changes and reconfiguration of the SAP technical layer.
- Physical move of infrastructure: Moving the physical SAP servers to the new hosting provider's data center comes with less configuration changes on SAP level but obviously come with a higher risk and longer outages.

A benefit of virtualization is obviously that it enables us to gain the benefits of both approaches: Virtualization enables us to copy a server on logical level (as a flat file) including all SAP applications and configuration items within the virtual machine.

Although virtualization is one of the main pillars for cloud computing, we learned in the previous chapters that cloud providers can use different types of virtualization technologies (e.g. different types of hypervisor technology or virtual machine containers) for their IaaS service.

Depending on the compatibility of each provider's technology, it leaves us with three different scenarios to move virtual machines from one cloud provider to another:

Online-transition of VMs: If the incumbent and new service provider's cloud platform are based on the same standard (e.g. OpenStack[1]), it is technically possible to move the virtual machines which host the SAP applications online or with a 'near-online' procedure.

Obviously, a secure, high-bandwidth and low-latency network between the old and the new service provider are a pre-requisite. If such a network is not available, the VM images can still be easily copied as flat-files started at the new provider with a minimum of change to the configuration.

Export/Import of VMs: In case one or both service providers use a proprietary cloud platform the procedure requires more effort. At the incumbent cloud service provider, the virtual machines in which SAP applications run need to be halted, exported and converted to a general accepted format.

Today, widely accepted formats are VMware ESX VMDK images, Citrix Xen VHD images or Microsoft Hyper-V VHD. The images will need to get transported to the new cloud providers' data center either via a private network or via a physical storage device. Subsequently the VM image needs to be imported and if required, converted to the new service providers cloud platform technology.

Lift and shift application data and configuration: Obviously, this is the worst case scenario for public cloud providers who do not offer an export/import functionality of virtual machines.

Moving from one cloud service provider to another is pretty much the same effort and costs as moving today from one traditional hosted infrastructure solution to a new. In the best case, only flat files such as SAP database or NetWeaver configuration files need to be copied. In case different OS or DB's are used, SAP data will need to get migrated[2] to the target operating system or database before the new systems can be setup at the new service provider.

The ability to be compatible to a widely accepted cloud standard should be taken into consideration when deciding for a cloud service offering. A proprietary cloud standard can be compared with proprietary UNIX platforms: moving your SAP applications to a different platform might come with high costs, effort and even risk – the reason why many organizations avoid 'vendor-lock-in' where possible.

---

[1] OpenStack is an IaaS cloud computing project launched 2010 by Rackspace and NASA. Today, more than 150 companies joint OpenStack, among others, Cisco, IBM, and HP.

[2] SAP heterogeneous system copy using R3load.

7.1.2 Cloud APIs

Cloud application programming interfaces provide a standardized way to access and consume services or content in a cloud. Software which is built and optimized for cloud computing use these pre-defined access points in order to communicate either with consumers or with software which can reside in another public or private clouds.

▶ *Mashup applications*

Applications which consume (web-) services of two or more sources are called 'mashup' applications. Mashup applications reuse and re-purpose public accessible services and content through defined and standardized APIs in order to create new value for its users.

Some of the best-known examples for cloud apps or mashup apps are:
- *Google maps API* – the most used web API being used by thousands of mashup applications all over the globe.
- *Salesforce.com* has opened its core services via SOAP to the external community.
- *EBay's* API – widely used by the EBay development community in order to access the marketplace directly via XML.
- Various network providers such as *AT&T* opened their networks via APIs in order to extend their service offerings to the public.

Cloud APIs can expose services and content to different areas within a company (e.g. sales department or procurement) and it can be made private or public accessible.

Developers can create or customize applications which use content from internal backend systems such as SAP as well as public available services in order to create value to a company. Development time as well as software quality benefits from re-using services and content.

Cloud API's expose their features usually via the Simple Object Access Protocol (SOAP)[3] or Representational State Transfer (REST).[4]

We should keep in mind that SAP applications are not per definition cloud application as such. Today, most SAP software components leverage the SAP NetWeaver application server (ABAP and JAVA) as their primary technology platform.

SAP applications rely largely on the integration capabilities of NetWeaver. Hence, cloud APIs play at least for most current SAP applications a rather minor role.

---

[3] A protocol for exchanging structured information based on XML messages for Web Services in networks.

[4] A software architecture and Web service design model for distributed systems such as the Internet.

However, some cloud augurs claim that APIs are the new middleware of the future since APIs will handle the integration layer of an application hosted in a cloud. The summary of this chapter will briefly discuss SAP's capabilities in that area (NetWeaver Cloud).

▶ *Amazon as de-facto standard cloud API*

Although most cloud service providers have designed their own APIs which are optimized for a particular cloud offering, many APIs are more or less compatible to the Amazon's EC2 cloud API. Since AWS was the first major IaaS cloud provider in the market, Amazon set the de-facto standard. If we look at IaaS offerings for SAP, we find management APIs which offer a certain control over the infrastructure resources which are provided to the cloud service consumer.

In the future, there might be infrastructure management applications that manage on-premise infrastructure as well as infrastructure within a public cloud offering in a transparent and unified way. In that context, we will discuss SAP's project Titanium in Sect. 7.4.2.

7.2 Can Public Clouds Meet SAP Application Requirements?

There will be no surprise that the answer is: *it depends*. Due to the economies of scale, public cloud offerings can be particularly attractive from a price point of view.

In Chap. 2, we discussed technical characteristics of SAP applications which might limit the functionality in a public or private cloud. However, there are obviously more decision points than price and technology particular when we look at hosting SAP applications in a public cloud offering.

▶ *Don't let the price cloud your judgement*

In order to set the context for this section we need to understand the driver for a particular hosting option for SAP applications. In the previous chapters, we have focused on technical or commercial drivers. However, equally important are organizational drivers which need to be considered.

Companies which intend to change their current way of hosting SAP applications will go through a decision process that needs to reflect a balanced view on all available options – public clouds should be just one of them.

In previous chapters we have learned that cloud computing comes in different service layers (IaaS, PaaS and SaaS) and in different deployment models (private or public).

As mentioned earlier, we will primarily focus on IaaS offerings for SAP – however, the line between public or private cloud is not as clear as some might think (Fig. 7.2).

It is important to recognize that technologies that fuel private clouds are not fundamentally different from public clouds. Whether a traditional hosting solution

7.2 Can Public Clouds Meet SAP Application Requirements?

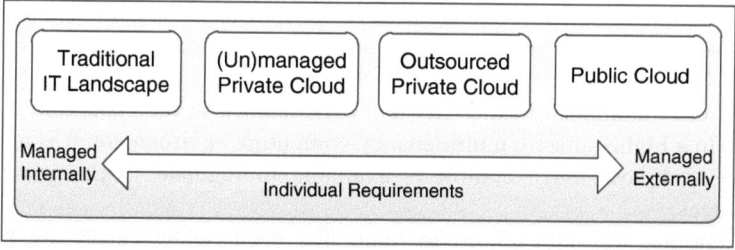

Fig. 7.2 Sourcing options for SAP

or cloud solution suits best depends exclusively on the individual requirements of the organization that uses SAP applications.

Most established infrastructure and/or SAP service providers added a utility and/or cloud offering for SAP to their existing service portfolio. Others teamed up with partners in order to provide jointly a sourcing option for their clients.

▶ *Among others, public clouds is one hosting option*

IT-heavyweights such as HP, Microsoft and IBM offer traditional hosting options next to private or public cloud services. While private cloud environments for SAP are widely available today, public cloud offerings are relatively new to the market.

There is little doubt that it will be a commoditized service offering in the future. However at the time of writing, few companies moved their production SAP systems from a traditional hosting arrangement into a public cloud offering.

Looking at the SAP hosting market in near-term future, it is rather unlikely that we will observe an imminent large scale shift. Whether private, public or hybrid clouds will dominate the future of enterprise critical applications has yet to be decided. The drivers for selecting a deployment model for SAP applications are evidently as individual as a company's requirements.

Hosting SAP applications in a public cloud might appear to a medium-size manufacturing company in a different light than to an organization which is in the financial or defense industry.

The following generic points are a list of criteria which might support and guide the decision process for a deployment model:

Business Criticality: We have discussed service levels in Chap. 3 and we have highlighted that SAP applications support the very core of the business processes of a company. The typical SAP customer will carefully weight costs against risk and in most cases, follow a conservative and risk adverse approach.

When it comes to service levels, most public cloud offerings provide a comprehensive availability for IaaS (e.g. 99.95 %). Beside availability it might be also very important to understand how quick the service will be back once it failed (Recovery Time Objective: RTO[5]) and how much data was lost (Recovery Point Objective: RPO[6]).

We already examined availability and *performance* in the context of SLAs in Chap. 3. In a highly-shared, multi-tenancy computing environment, it is important to understand how much control is available to regulate CPU, memory and IO resources.

Furthermore, we should keep in mind that even public clouds are built on 'traditional' infrastructure consisting of server, storage and network components. If a single SAP software component which does not scale-out[7] (e.g. the SAP database) exceeds the capacity of the maximum size of the cloud service providers virtual server capacity (i.e. virtual memory and/or CPUs), the particular component will negatively impact the business process.

In Chap. 4 we have learned that *security* is a process and not a product. Among other aspects, security relies on software and software will always have errors. At the end, it comes back to risk versus costs. Each company needs to decide which type of data can reside in a public cloud and which data needs to reside internally for security reasons.

In many cases, it might not be easy to separate confidential company data from data which is less critical from a security point of view. The overlaying application (SAP) might not support different data stores depending on the criticality of data for one and the same application.

Integration and interfacing requirements can be a limiting factor for a successful public cloud deployment of SAP software. In most cases, SAP systems are heavily integrated into other non-SAP systems.

Integration can become a major headache in cases where the interface scenario is very complex or relies on very large data volumes and real-time replication. In various industries such as the financial or the manufacturing industry it is absolutely vital that data from interfaced systems (e.g. from ATMs) is transferred within a given period in order to prevent timeouts or even worse, loss of transactions.

Organizational and operational requirements need to be considered well before moving SAP applications into a public cloud offering. A public cloud in its essence is just another souring option to host SAP applications by an external service provider. However, delivering a SAP service to a client can be obviously more than providing the infrastructure.

It is a common industry practice to keep the number of service providers who are entrusted with the delivery of a single service to a minimum. In most cases, this approach increases the transparency and accountability within a service. Service

---

[5] The duration of time a service must be operational after a disaster occurs in order to prevent a major impact to the overlaying business process.

[6] The maximum acceptable amount of data lost in a disaster.

[7] Due to the nature of a particular software component, it cannot be distributed over multiple servers (scale-out) in order to achieve load balancing.

level agreements can be easily articulated and the usual "finger-pointing-syndrome" can be avoided.

▶ **One throat to choke!**

Large global service providers offer end-to-end services from the infrastructure layer to SAP NetWeaver and from SAP Application management services to business process consulting. An important decision criteria for choosing a public cloud service provider for SAP is the vertical scale of services provided.

How Standardized is the current SAP environment? The highest level of adaptability is usually achieved if an organization operates its own IT landscape and delivers the service to its internal organizations.

In contrast to traditional IT landscapes and private cloud offerings, public cloud offerings are highly standardized services that leave very little to no room for exceptions or customization that exceed the service provider's specification.

The service provider offers pre-defined service packages to pick and choose from. The packages usually come in infrastructure building blocks (e.g. storage, memory or CPUs) and with service levels such as availability and scalability. A twenty year old application which is based on COBOL code running on DEC UNIX might be quite challenging to move into a current public cloud offering.

Apart from technical or commercial drivers, there are a number of other decision points that need to be considered when choosing the right sourcing option for SAP applications. Whether public clouds can satisfy the requirements of a SAP customer depends on the individual needs.

7.3 Amazon Web Service for SAP

In the previous chapters, we examined the technical layers and infrastructure details of Amazon's Public Cloud Service for SAP applications. This paragraph discusses how these building blocks compare to traditional infrastructure. Amazon Web Service(AWS) is constantly improved and extended. In that context, we can only provide a snapshot of the service at the time of writing.

▶ **AWS started in 2006**

Today, AWS supports large parts of SAP's application portfolio whether for production or non-production purposes. Amazon uses a proprietary technology for its cloud offering and does not follow an open standard.

Currently, AWS for SAP is a pure infrastructure cloud service (IaaS) only and should not be confused with other cloud offerings of SAP (e.g. NetWeaver Cloud).

Amazon Elastic Compute Cloud (Amazon EC2) comes in infrastructure building blocks of servers (referred as instances), storage and network. The building blocks come with different attributes and can be selected based on application availability and/or performance requirements.

Amazon offers a wide range of configuration options and provides a web-based interface in order to configure infrastructure resources in an easy and intuitive way via the AWS management console.

At the time of writing SAP certified the following solutions on AWS:
- SAP Business Suite
- SAP Business Objects BI solutions
- SAP Rapid Deployment Solutions (RDS)
- SAP Business All-in-One with a maximum size of 60.5 GB of memory for roughly 32GB of compressed data
- SAP HANA database servers for developers only
- Sybase provides various AMIs (AMIs will be discussed in the following chapters) for developers such as Sybase ASE and Sybase IQ

Like with most other IaaS offerings, costs to the end-user depend on the actual configuration and usage of building blocks (utility pricing).

SAP and Amazon supply various guides and other sources of information around implementation and operations of SAP applications in AWS.

The notes and guides are constantly updated and like with any other SAP implementation, it is important to get familiar with the latest information.

Most documents around SAP on EC2 focus on standard SAP applications based on the SAP NetWeaver application server architecture (ABAP and JAVA). Other, non-NetWeaver based SAP applications might require different configuration or fall short certain options or features.

7.3.1 Instance Types for SAP (Server Building Blocks)

AWS provides a wide range of instance types which come with different configuration of vCPUs and memory. Computing power is measured in ECU (Elastic Compute Unit) which has been introduced by Amazon in EC2.

AWS is built largely on commodity x86 hardware. Obviously this means that AWS is using more than one server model and more than one type of processor. ECU provides an abstraction layer for consumers of EC2 and it supposed to provide a consistent amount of CPU capacity across AWS.

SAP Note 1656250 provides a comparison between ECU and SAPS based on certain EC2 instance types. Although not specifically mentioned, ECU can be translated into SAPS with a rating of 1 ECU ~285 SAPS. In order to mitigate the risks of a highly shared, multitenancy environment, Amazon offers dedicated instances which run on infrastructure which is dedicated for a particular client at additional costs.

Although not specifically mentioned, ECU can be translated into SAPS with a rating of 1 ECU ~ 285 SAPS.

7.3 Amazon Web Service for SAP

Table 7.1 AWS instance types for SAP

Instance type	Cores	Memory	Prod	SAPS
Standard L	2	7.5 GB	No	N/A
Standard XL	4	15 GB	No	N/A
High-Mem. XL	2	17.1 GB	No	N/A
High-Mem. Double XL	4	34.2 GB	Yes	3,700
High-Mem. Quad XL	8	68 GB	Yes	7,400

Other AWS instance types such as "Standard Large", "Standard Extra Large" and "High-memory Extra Large" can be used for non-production SAP installations. SAP recommends the following AWS instance types for the deployment of SAP applications (Table 7.1):

Amazon provides operating systems in the form of pre-configured images called AMI (Amazon Machine Image). Of course, only SAP supported Windows and Linux versions are supported for AWS. At this stage, SAP supports Windows 2008 (R1 and R2), Red Hat Linux and SUSE Enterprise Linux (at the time of writing, Windows is not offered for production systems).

Sybase ASE, MS SQL server, MaxDB and DB2 are supported as databases for SAP systems – restrictions for Oracle database apply.[8]

Note that not all SAP kernels have been released for AWS – only newer versions come with support for AWS.

7.3.2 AWS Storage for SAP

The default storage that comes with a new instance is called *local* or *instance storage* which is assigned to a specific server instance upon creation. Local storage is ephemeral which means, it is bound to the life of an instance and is used for SWAP files or data which is of temporary nature.

EBS storage stands for persistent Elastic Block Storage and as the name suggests, it is persistent. It appears to the instance in a similar way as NAS (Network Attached Storage) to physical server. Volumes can range from 1 GB to 1 TB and multiple volumes can be assigned to an instance.

Volumes appear to the operating system as a block device and the data volumes are independent from the instance to which they are assigned to.

EBS comes with built-in resilience within the same availability zone (more about availability zones in the following paragraphs) in order to prevent data loss of a single hardware component. EBS volumes can be detached and attached to different instances within the same availability zone.

Similar to traditional storage, SAP recommends using multiple EBS volumes in a software RAID configuration in order to distribute the IO load that SAP

---

[8] Note 1618590 – Support: Oracle database on Amazon Web Services.

applications create. EBS storage is used for SAP database files such as data and log files.

Amazon S3 stands for Simple Storage Service and in the SAP context it is primarily used as a backup storage. S3 is an object based storage system and it can store objects between 1byte and 5 TB. It cannot be presented to an instance as a device like EBS.

S3 storage is by default "off-site" from the availability zones where instance might run and it is automatically replicated within the same region.

Amazon *EBS snapshots* are a method to backup point-in-time snapshots of data stored on EBS volumes to S3 storage. EBS snapshots are block-level incremental which means, only changed blocks of data between the new and the last backup are being stored.

In contrast to traditional incremental backups, Amazon S3 storage offers the ability to delete no longer required incremental backups without losing the ability to perform a full restore with the remaining active incremental backups.

Basically, this means that the customer benefit from the reduced space consumption of an incremental backup while at the same time, have the ability to perform a point-in-time backup with any of the remaining snapshots. There are many heaps of options to (re)use EBS snapshots for example to create or copy new instances (including SAP), resize, replicate volumes or simply share data. We will look at EBS snapshots again in Sect. 7.3.4 when we look into high availability and backup restore of SAP systems within AWS.

7.3.3 Network: Amazon Virtual Private Cloud

Apart from EC2 classic network which comes by default, Amazon offers the setup of a virtual private cloud (VPC) which can be considered as an extension of a company's local area network.

Customers have the option to set their own IP ranges, subnets, routing configuration and gateways within this network. The virtual private cloud inside Amazon data centers can be assigned a public IP address (Amazon Elastic IP) which makes the network accessible from the Internet (if required) or alternatively, a VPN connection (virtual private network) using an encrypted tunnel can be established between a client's local IT networks.

For customers with high bandwidth requirements, Amazon offers "Direct Connect" which provides a dedicated line between an AWS data center and a customer data center. Direct Connect offers bandwidths between 1 and 10 GBps and supports multiple connections.

In the SAP context, clients can for example run their non-production environments such as development or sandbox systems in AWS, whereas the production systems run on premise (hybrid cloud). SAP requires only production systems running in a VPC but given the nature of SAP systems, it can be considered as best practice that VPC are a good way to go for all type of SAP systems.

7.3.4 Backup/Restore of SAP Applications on EC2 Instances

A quite important aspect when discussing SAP infrastructure is its resilience against failures and how to recover from a major disaster. It is a fundamental requirement to be able to restore any production SAP instance to a given point in time.

Incidents that require a restore are referred as logical failures such as the accidental deletion of a SAP table which would require a point in time recovery of one or more SAP systems.[9]

AWS offers two different options for storing backups of a SAP system: backups can be copied directly to S3 or in a two-phase backup, first to an EBS volume and then to S3.

AWS offers the option to create an AMI image of an instance including all attached EBS volumes. In order to get a consistent snapshot of the image, the image needs to be halted for a short amount of time for the image process to be started in background (lazy load).

Image creation can be scripted and scheduled just as normal backups from within the image. Restoring an image is being done via AWS web interface and simply triggers a new instance based on the image taken. Obviously creating an image is similar to an offline backup since it lacks the ability to roll back or forward in time.

For SAP systems which are business critical or outages are impacting the business, online backups are mandatory. S3 storage is object storage and the data is organized in what Amazon calls "buckets". Buckets can help to organize and separate backups such as file system, database log and data.

For small SAP installations, the operating system and database built-in backup tools can be used. The backup and restore procedure is a two phase-backup again whereas the data is stored on an EBS volume in the first place and copied to S3 in the subsequent step.

For larger and more complex environment, it might be required to rely on 3rd party professional enterprise backup-software. If supported within AWS, the backup software can be setup in an AWS instance and be operated pretty much in a similar way as within a traditional IT infrastructure.

Some providers of backup software started to support S3 and provide a native S3 interface which appears to the backup software similar as a traditional tape library. If the backup software does not support S3, an EBS volume has to be used as an interim store before copied to S3. Obviously, the later procedure requires some manual effort (e.g. scripting).

Apart from logical disasters, we need to cater for physical failures such as the failure of a single component (e.g. a server or a disk), the failure of an entire site or data center and regional failures where a major disaster might impact an entire region.

---

[9] Applications which exchange significant amount of data might need to be recovered together even if only one of it fails in order to cater for cross application consistency.

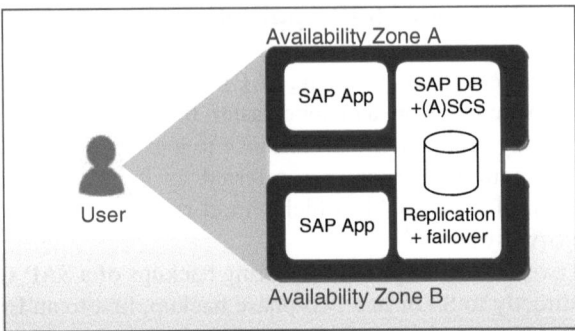

Fig. 7.3 Example of distributing SAP SPOF over two AWS Availability Zones

7.3.5 SAP High-Availability in AWS

As mentioned earlier, Amazon EC2 offers the concept of Availability Zones (AZs) which are similar to sites in the traditional sense. Availability zones are isolated zones which are supposed to protect from major outages if an application is distributed over two AZs.

Availability zones within the same region are interconnected with high-bandwidth, low latency networks (Fig. 7.3).

AWS offers built-in resilience for a lot of its components which cover failures of components within the same availability zone (e.g. automatic restart of an EC2 instance when underlying hardware fails, automatic EBS volume replication within the same availability zone).

However, AWS does not support traditional cluster software which is why single points of failures (database and SAP central services) will need to be protected in a different way.

In order to remove the SPOF from an EC2 image running SAP, Amazon suggests different options such as software mirrors (e.g. MS SQL server mirroring) between two EC2 instances and a standby EC2 instance for the SAP SCS/CI using a manual failover procedure. SAP Enqeue service replication can be setup between the two EC2 instances in order to protect the SAP lock information.

In case one or more EBS volume fail, AMI images or a standard restore from S3 storage can be used to perform a manual restore of the service. In order to increase availability, Amazon recommends staging the failover instances in a different Availability Zone.

Distributing SAP components over multiple AWS regions might be technically possible but come with certain limitations (e.g. no replication between regions, no high-bandwidth or low latency network connections between regions, etc.).

It is obvious that AWS does not offer an out-of-the-box bullet-proof HA solution for SAP. Every failover mechanism comes with manual steps and will therefore impact RTO and potentially RPO.

It is important to understand that when designing the technical infrastructure for SAP applications in AWS, similar rules apply as in traditional IT hosting environments. AWS offers infrastructure building blocks which need to get applied in the correct way to achieve a desired outcome (e.g. a particular SLA).

7.3.6 Monitoring with Amazon CloudWatch

Today, SAP Solution Manager provides monitoring functionality which exceeds the capabilities of traditional SAP CCMS (Computer Center Management System).[10]

Particular in a virtualized environment, it is important to gain insight into performance metrics which are collected at the hypervisor level. Amazon offers monitoring (called CloudWatch) for infrastructure in two different characteristics: basic and detail CloudWatch. Basic CloudWatch comes free of charge and monitors a set of infrastructure attributes in a 5 min interval. Detailed CloudWatch comes with a 1 min interval, offers higher granularity but comes at additional costs.

It would exceed the scope of this book to provide an insight into the attributes and options available. SAP provides only support to AWS instances which have permanently detailed CloudWatch enabled.[11]

7.3.7 Other Aspects of SAP on AWS

The following additional aspects should be considered when moving SAP applications to AWS:

Moving an existing *SAP landscapes to AWS* is a project of itself and it is far beyond the scope of this book. However, we want to provide a brief overview on the currently available options. Data less than 500 GB can be copied directly to AWS using additional tools to speed up the process.[12]

If the SAP data exceeds 500 GB, Amazon offers the data export/import functionality which provides the option to ship a physical storage device to an AWS data center from where it is copied to an S3 bucket or an EBS volume.

Amazon supports also the *import* of *virtual machines* from the following formats: VMware ESX VMDK images, Citrix Xen VHD images and Microsoft Hyper-V VHD images for Microsoft Windows Server 2003 R2 and Windows Server 2008 R1 and R2.

In case instances (virtual servers) supposed get moved back from AWS into an on-premise private cloud, AWS instances can be exported to VMware ESX VMDK, VMware ESX OVA, Microsoft Hyper-V VHD or Citrix Xen VHD file formats.

---

[10] Among others: Solution Manager Diagnostics and Wily Introscope and other tools.
[11] SAP Note 1656250 – SAP on AWS: Supported instance types.
[12] AWS refers to tools like "Tsunami USP" or "Aspera".

SAP production systems on AWS require having either a "Gold" or "Platinum" AWS Premium Support contract in place.

In order to receive *support from SAP and Amazon* for the operation of SAP production systems on AWS particular guidelines need to be followed.[13]

7.3.8 AWS Service Levels

AWS Service levels can be found on Amazon's website[14] in which Amazon provides details on how SLAs are calculated, SLA commitments and SLA exclusions. Amazon provides service levels on availability of its infrastructure components within EC2. We should keep in mind that this does not include the middleware (i.e. NetWeaver), SAP applications or the entire service.

SAP systems on top of EC2 might be managed by the internal IT department or by another external service provider.

Amazon commits to 99.95 %[15] availability however does not guarantee a specific RTO on EC2. Since Amazon provides only the backup infrastructure and does not execute backups, an RPO cannot be guaranteed. Amazon specifies the actual backup media (S3 storage) with 99.99 % of availability which is pretty solid.

If service levels are breached, Amazon compensates with service credits. Details on when and how service credits are granted can be found on Amazon's website.

7.4 Outlook: Public Clouds and SAP

Given the dynamic in the IT industry, it is always awkward to make a prediction. Obviously, there is not one direction or technology that will evolve but multiple parallel streams with different aspects and focus areas. Large and small organizations all over the globe develop cloud technology such as infrastructure and platforms. At the same time, the software ecosystem for cloud applications is growing fast since more and more PaaS offerings and corresponding development platforms become broadly available.

▶ *So what's next?*

Today, more than two billion people connect through the internet[16] using computers or mobile devices. The increasing appetite for digital content, social media and e-commerce over the internet is expanding at exponential rates. Worldwide e-commerce sales will reach an estimated $963.0 billion by 2013.[17]

---

[13] SAP note 1588667.

[14] http://aws.amazon.com/ec2-sla/.

[15] 99.95 % translates into 4.38 h per year, 21.56 min per month or 5.04 min per week of unavailability.

[16] Internet World Stats, http://www.internetworldstats.com.

[17] Source: Imran Khan, Goldman Sachs, 2011.

7.4 Outlook: Public Clouds and SAP   133

As an example, Amazon adds *each day* the equivalent server capacity to AWS as Amazon required when it was a global company in the year 2000.[18] It is obvious that today's infrastructure will hardly cope with the requirements of tomorrow given the fact that we face soaring numbers of servers, storage, and network devices today.

In that context, we would like to introduce initiatives around future virtualization technology and IT infrastructure. Furthermore, we will examine current programs by SAP's in the cloud space.

7.4.1 Beyond the Physical Boundaries

With today's cloud technology, a virtual machine can't exceed the size of the physical server building block (scale-up limitation). The easy answer would be: use a bigger server, but this would kill the "economy of scale using commodity x86 standard servers" and make cloud computing as expensive as any traditional hosting model.

In February 2012, SAP presented new concepts currently developed within SAP research labs in Ireland and Israel: *project Hecatonchires*. The basic idea behind this project is the aggregation of resources in the cloud by decoupling CPU, memory and IO from the boundaries of a physical node.

▶ *Project Hecatonchires*

Virtual machines will be no longer limited to the size of the physical host since resources are aggregated from multiple physical servers. The enabler for this technology is the commoditization of high-end interconnect-technology with very high bandwidth and very low latency (we briefly discussed similar technology in Chap. 8). Resource aggregation is not a new concept but it is relatively new to x86 commodity hardware.

In a first step, SAP plans to aggregate memory from multiple physical servers to a single RAIM (Redundant Array of Inexpensive Memory).

SAP calls the second step Lego-cloud which basically adds CPU aggregation under a flexible resource management. The intension is clear: virtual machines in a cloud will be no longer limited to grow beyond the underlying physical infrastructure and memory and CPU can be added with fewer restrictions than today. Potentially entire VMs can be swapped into a RAIM "memory cloud".

Current ×86 infrastructure is optimal for applications like SAP because high amounts of computational power is required. Other, *cloud enabled* applications such as web-services however show a very different workload profile. Large infrastructure providers such as Intel and Hewlett-Packard work on servers particularly optimized for content delivery, video services, distributed memory caching

---

[18] Source: Amazon, SAP v-Days, February 2012.

and search. These applications require "light scale-out," where fetching and delivering data is more important than computational power.

▶ **Project Moonshot**

In 2011, Hewlett-Packard kicked off project Moonshot with the goal to develop a high-density, low-power microserver platform that uses Intel Atom processors (although project moonshot is planned to be processor agnostic). In contrast to large, power-hungry, purpose-built server processors, microservers use a high number of small chips commonly found in commodity notebooks or mobile devices like tablets and mobile phones. CPUs are stored in a so called "server-cartridge". The aim of Moonshot is to significantly reduce server complexity, energy use and costs by increasing density and sharing components. A single rack can come with thousands of processors. Other hardware manufactures run similar programs (Advanced Micro Devices). Although traditional on-premise SAP applications are not supported by this platform, it is an interesting concept for the hosting of future true-cloud applications.

7.4.2 SAP NetWeaver Cloud

Although the PaaS market is still in evolution, Gartner[19] expects PaaS to become a significant technology driver in the near future.

SAP started its own Platform as a Service including an own programming language/environment called "project River". The primary focus was the development of a modular PaaS based on open standards.

After further development of SAP River was discontinued with the exception of SAP Carbon Impact, NetWeaver Neo became the new PaaS offering to complement SAP's SaaS such as Business By Design and Sales On Demand.

At SAP TechEd in 2011 NetWeaver Neo has been renamed into "SAP NetWeaver Cloud". SAP customers and partners can subscribe to the service and receive access to web servers, databases (Sybase ASE, MaxDB and HANA), development tools and a runtime environment where applications can be deployed.

▶ **NetWeaver on Demand, JPaaS, Neo, Project River, Edge Platform**

The development environment for SAP NetWeaver cloud is based on the Eclipse framework and applications will compile to the Java EE 6 web profile. SAP is currently offering a free trial version in order to create a new ecosystem of apps which can be consumed by clients.

The NetWeaver cloud offering targets two groups:

---

[19] http://www.gartner.com/technology/research/cloud-computing/report/paas-cloud.jsp.

7.4 Outlook: Public Clouds and SAP

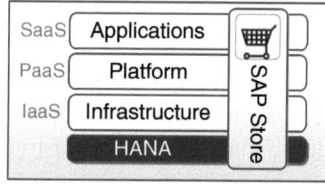

Fig. 7.4 SAP NetWeaver cloud high-level overview (Source: SAP NetWeaver Cloud Developer Center)

- SAP customers who want to use NetWeaver cloud as a PaaS in order to create new enterprise applications or extend existing functionality of their backend systems (hybrid solution).
- SAP partners who use NetWeaver cloud as a SaaS platform in order to build and provide applications or content to their clients (Fig. 7.4).

The NetWeaver cloud infrastructure runs within SAPs own data centers in Europe in a public cloud setup (there are no plans for a client dedicated infrastructure).

Similar to other PaaS offerings, the pricing is based on the usage of resources such as compute, storage, transaction and bandwidth (utility model). There are plans that partners will also have the option to sell apps on the SAP shop.

Basically, NetWeaver Cloud applications can integrate to other on-demand services such as Business by Design and Sales on Demand but also to on-premise software which is available on the web via a REST interface.

7.4.3 Project Titanium

When SAP customers start a project to implement new functionality, a significant amount of time and effort goes into the setup of the necessary development infrastructure (i.e. installation and configuration of the required SAP components).

Project Titanium has started as a SAP internal project with the scope to provide SAP employees on-demand access to pre-configured, instant-available SAP applications based on cloud infrastructure.

SAP considers making this service available for their customers also in order to reduce TCO and provide a new and faster way to provision sandbox, test and development environments.

▶ *Virtual appliance factory*

Because the machine images could be called virtual appliances the service is also referred as Virtual appliance Factory (VAF) and. The Titanium web front-end might be included in the SAP web shop.

Basically, a SAP customer can pick and choose from a library of machine images which contains hundreds of different SAP software components containing support packages or combinations of specific configurations. SAP provides and manages the actual content of the offering whereas the infrastructure for this service is planned to be placed in public clouds (IaaS).

▶ **LVM connector**

In April 2012, SAP released information about an SAP Landscape Virtualization Management (LVM) connector which can connect the on-premise cloud with a public cloud offering in order to manage cloud infrastructure resources in a unified and transparent way.

For SAP, the sweet spot of the VAF is on one side the reduction of the notorious high implementation and prototype costs, on the other side, customers can get provided with a 'try-and-buy' offering.

7.5 Summary

- SAP spent a significant amount of time and money over the last 10 years to transform itself from a purely on-premise software company to the new paradigm of software on demand.
- Today, public clouds offer a large variety on services for organizations and consumers. Enterprise critical SAP solutions are rather new to public clouds but will move into a commoditized service in the future.
- Public clouds can be proprietary or follow a specific (open) standard. A cloud offering which follows a widely used standard will be in most cases transitioned to a new provider or on-premise in a faster and simpler way.
- Cloud APIs are the interface into a cloud. Services and content are provided or consumed through the cloud API.
- Companies which intend to change their current way of hosting SAP applications will go through a decision process that needs to reflect a balanced view on all available options – public clouds should be just one of them.
- Although AWS falls short some aspects of high-availability and scalability, it provides a solid hosting option for small to medium SAP customers with moderate availability requirements.
- The next generation of cloud platforms will overcome some of today's limitations. New infrastructure might be required to cope with the workload of tomorrow's cloud-enabled web-applications.
- Whether public clouds will be able to meet every demand of enterprise critical applications has not been decided yet. As usual, market analysts and IT vendors have their 'own views of the world' depending on the individual background or agenda.

Private Cloud Infrastructures for SAP

8

> There are still good reasons why companies prefer to keep their mission critical SAP systems and sensitive data on their own premises. But they can still benefit from the cloud concept by adopting a private one. This chapter deals with the necessary infrastructure, discusses new developments like lossless Ethernet and converged networks as well as unified computing.

As described in Chap. 1, a private cloud is literally the deployment of cloud computing principles on your own premises and infrastructure. This is similar to use utility technologies but on your own power plant.

Like a utility consumer does not care much about the technology of the boilers, turbines and generators necessary to produce electrical power, a public cloud consumer does not need to care much about the computers and storage to generate the computing power he is consuming. However you should know something about the underlying technologies no matter you build and operate a private power plant or a private cloud datacenter.

▶ **What is the best platform for SAP?**

Since the inception of information technology, there has been discussion about which platforms and approaches represented the "best technology". Forty years ago the mainframe enabled the development of SAP R/2; 30 years ago, UNIX enabled the development of R/3. Since then, Windows and Linux have also proven themselves as capable SAP platforms. If we define "maturity" as the sum of scalability, stability, availability, and other architecture attributes, every platform essentially follows a similar development or maturity path (Fig. 8.1)

All SAP platforms initially scaled to only a few hundred users, with little to no HA, scalability or virtualization features. However, each one evolved over time to support thousands of users and all the features you can wish for – and always customers moved to the newer, cheaper platform as soon as it was good enough for

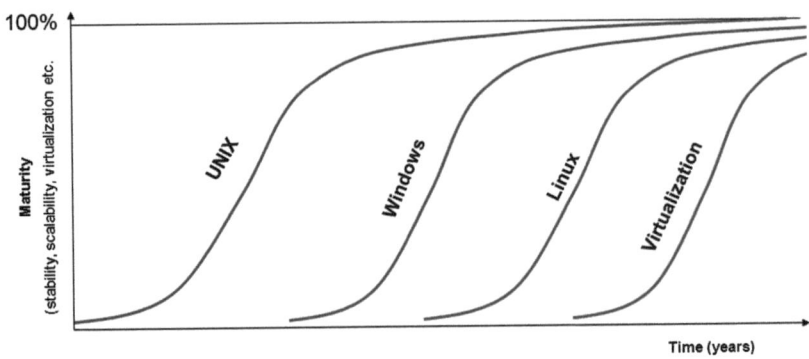

Fig. 8.1 Maturity of SAP operating system platforms over time

their purposes. So the question is not "what is the best platform for SAP?", but rather "is the platform good enough for SAP"?

Today the majority of all SAP installations worldwide run on so-called x86 architectures from Intel and AMD (representing approximately a 55 % Windows and 10 % Linux distribution). Many examples abound proving that the architecture is good enough for even the largest and most mission critical SAP systems. Also SAP code in general is developed on x86 only.

Due to its dominating role within the SAP market and public cloud market, we will focus in this chapter on x86 based servers for SAP private cloud infrastructures. After a short introduction to SAP system landscape architectures, we take a closer look at the effects of multi-core and hyper-threading processing, loss-less Ethernet and the "disc paradox" in regards to SAP systems.

Building on these fundamentals, the author introduce unified computing and stateless computing concepts and show how these concepts overcome many of the obstacles related to SAP on Cloud implementations.

8.1 SAP Landscapes

For obvious reasons, the focus of SAP system architectures and operation is on the productive systems which provide the business users with the necessary functionality to do their jobs. However SAP recommends the deployment of additional non-productive systems to ensure the stable operation of each mission critical business solution:
- A development system (DEV) for customizing, parameterization, andcustomer specific developments.
- A quality assurance system (QA) for validating customer developments, SAP updates, database and operating system patches before they are implemented in the production system.

Thus, only tested versions of operating system, database,and application code are executed on the production system to ensure a stable, reliable and optimal performing operation.

8.1 SAP Landscapes

Each of these systems has its own set of database and application instances; they are therefore entirely independent systems coupled via the *Transport Management System* (TMS).

> **Instances and Processes**
>
> In an SAP context, an instance is a self-contained unit, which comprises its own processes and memory, profiles, and executables. Instances write their own trace file, and can be started and stopped autonomously. A single SAP system with multiple instances can run distributed over several computers. However, you can also easily install and execute several instances of one or more SAP systems on a single server.

Larger enterprises deploy additional installations for training, integration, staging, pre-production purposes, or so-called *sandbox systems* for testing new processes.

Most of these systems are relatively small because the number of users and transactions is usually very limited. The QA system, however, should be the same size as the production system to enable meaningful stress tests.[1] With the stateless computing architecture and service profiles described later the same resources can be easily also used as technical sandbox and also serve the purpose of a fail-over infrastructure for production if required.

Due to the fact that Training and Sandbox systems do not store sensitive data they can be easily deployed in public clouds, even if QA and production systems will be hosted in the private cloud. Special configuration is necessary for the case where development systems are deployed in a public cloud to connect the SAP transport management system over Wide Area Network (WAN) connections.[2]

8.1.1 SAP System Architecture

The system architecture of most SAP solutions is organized in at least three logical layers or tiers:

- The presentation layer, where users interact with the system either via a SAP GUI installed locally on the user's PC or any web browser. Alternatively SAP solutions can be also accessed through mobile devices via Sybase Unwired Platform (SUP).
- The application layer, where the SAP business logic resides. As it is possible to implement several SAP WebAS instances on multiple physical computers, this

---

[1] *mySAPToolbag for Performance Tuning and Stress Testing*, George Anderson, Prentice Hall, ISBN 0-13-144852-8.

[2] The SAP on AWE Operations Guide v1.5, (http://aws.amazon.com/sap) describes at page 21 the configuration of a hybrid TMS.

layer fits well with multi-tenant cloud architectures. SAP Users communicate only with the application layer, never directly with the database.
- The database layer, which makes all business data persistent and store the code of the individual SAP applications. SAP has certified relational database systems like Oracle, Microsoft SQL Server, IBM DB2, MaxDB, and Sybase ASE. Distributed databases like Oracle RAC, Sybase ASE Cluster and IBM DB2 Purescale are quite rare in SAP implementations. With the fast proliferation of SAP HANA enabling a scale out configuration distributed over multiple blades, standard x86 servers will become the standard platform for the SAP database layer even for large SAP implementations.

8.1.2 2-tier versus 3-tier

Because of the huge, time critical data traffic between application and database both layers must be kept in the same high throughput, low latency network. A split of application and database layer between different data centers result in prohibitive high response times.

There are two choices for implementing SAP infrastructures:
- 2-tier: presentation tier on client, application and database tier sharing the same server and operation system.
- 3-tier: presentation tier on client, application and database tier on separate servers (but in the same datacenter network).

This leads to the question as to which one is the most cost-effective. In the past there was not much choice for larger systems: due to the fact that a single server couldn't provide sufficient resources the system had to be distributed physically over a database server and several application servers.

▶ *Central versus distributed*

Thanks to the tremendous performance enhancements, however, this issue has become more and more irrelevant – today a single blade server can easily provide enough power to execute the application and database layer together for more than 4,000 SAP users on a so called central system. Consultants who still claim that dedicated database servers are mandatory only demonstrating that they are not quite up-to-date.

However, there is still one reason for a dedicated database server which is more "financial" in nature than technical: In cases where the database licenses are acquired from the database vendor, the number of sockets or cores is relevant for license fees.

▶ *Be aware of database license schemes*

Most database vendors do not distinguish between sockets and cores utilized for the database or for other applications. So they will charge not only for the cores used for the database in a 2-tier setup, but also for the cores used for the SAP application layer, which usually accounts for 60–80 % of the total number of cores in a SAP system.

In this case, it makes sense to run the database of a SAP system landscape on a dedicated server so that only the cores on this server are counted for database licenses. Depending on the server's scalability and each system's workload characteristics, it makes even more sense to run *multiple* databases on this single server. Doing so allows the customer to benefit from the leveraging effects associated with shared cores.

If the database licenses are acquired as part of the SAP license, the number of cores the system utilizes doesn't affect costing. SAP licenses are mostly bound to user numbers, sometimes to memory, – but rarely to CPUs.

8.2 Server Architectures: Nifty Details?

Processor, memory, and the Input/Output (IO) subsystem are the three most important server subsystems from a performance perspective. In general, the tremendous improvements in SAP performance were mostly related to increased CPU clock frequency.

▶ *High clock speed – high performance?*

However, Fig. 8.2 demonstrates that improvements in processor and IO architecture can compensate for higher clock speeds. Current mass market x86 CPUs can provide the same or better SAPS per thread – as highly clocked proprietary RISC CPUs.

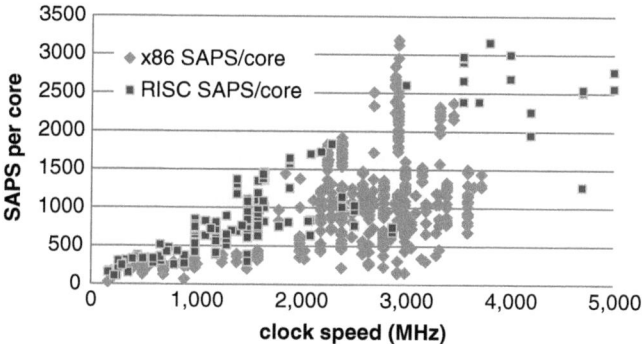

Fig. 8.2 SAPS per core in relation to the clock speed

Also, not only the fastest CPUs can be used for SAP implementations as the "benchmark race" might indicate. In most cases, somewhat slower "bread and butter" CPUs are sufficient from a performance perspective but much better from a price/performance ratio standpoint.

8.2.1 Multi-core and Multi-thread

Due to an electric phenomenon known as *parasitic capacitances*, higher clock speeds invariably generate more heat than slower clock speeds.[3] To circumvent this limitation while further increasing per-processor socket performance, the basic CPU (aka "core") is replicated multiple times on the same die. Multi-core CPUs are now the norm on the x86 space; mass-market processors – at the time of the latest review of this book – contain up to 16 cores. The newest generation of high-performance x86 CPU features already 50 cores, and as many as 80 cores per processor are expected in the next several years.

▶ *More cores – more performance?*

To better understand the implications of multi-core architecture, let us consider how programs are executed. A server runs a kernel and multiple processes. Each process can be further subdivided into "threads". Threads are minimum units of work allocated to cores. Each core comprises multiple execution units capable of working in parallel. Hyper-threading allows multiple threads on the same core at the same time.

A process that is single threaded utilizes only one core at a time and is limited by the performance of that core. A multi-threaded process can execute on multiple cores in parallel.

▶ *More threads – more performance?*

As discussed in Chap. 2; SAP HANA makes extensive use of Hyper-Threading. The SAP Web-Application server processes are single-threaded; however a SAP WebAS can invoke several hundred processes (best practice is not to exceed 99 because some internal functions in the core/kernel still have this limitation), so each user benefits from the performance of a full core as his request is executed. This approach serves well thousands of users working in parallel.

As opposed to online user workloads, batch workloads are a different story. These workloads are rarely coded to run multiple processes in parallel. The total run time of such a single-threaded batch job is therefore restricted by the performance of the single core on which it is executed, even if all other cores in a SAP landscape are idling. You have to setup parallel processing for batch, where the single

---

[3] The internal connections inside a CPU are isolated from each other by SiO_2 layers of only a few μm, which results in a "parasitic capacitance". With every clock impulse, electrons are moved to charge and discharge this capacitance, resulting in an energy proportional to $C \times U^2$ flowing into the device. This flow multiplied by the clock speed is the power dissipation which results in an equivalent heat dissipation.

threaded job execution becomes kind of a dispatcher, spawning off work to multiple work processes to circumvent this.

> **Intel® Turbo Boost Technology**
> To make optimal use of the available "thermal budget", Intel Turbo Boost Technology dynamically adjusts the clock speed to the number of cores active. For example a Intel Xeon 10-core processor rated for 2.4 GHz can run at 2.67 GHz with six cores active and 2.8 GHz with only four cores active. When the other cores are activated again the processor frequency is adjusted accordingly. The processor automatically reduces the core frequency also if temperature exceeds factory limits.[4]
>
> In the SAP context, Turbo Boost can speed up a single process by reducing the total number of SAPS.

Hyper-threading is a proven way to increase utilization; while one thread is waiting for data, another thread can be executed. However, this approach to increasing utilization comes at a price as it also often makes system load measurement quite difficult.

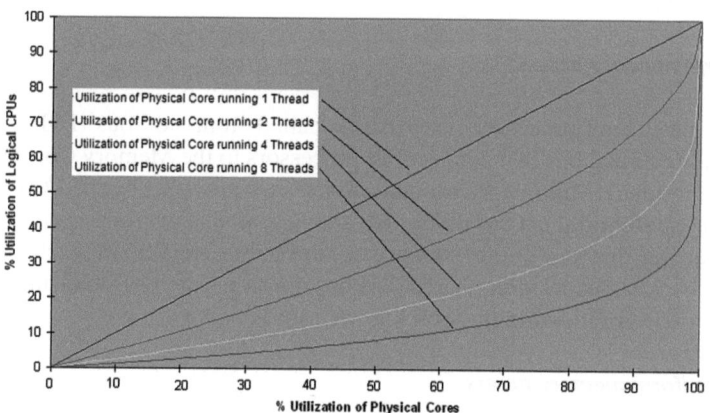

Fig. 8.3 Physical CPU (*cores*) versus logical CPU (*threads*) utilization

As Fig. 8.3 demonstrates, the utilization appears even lower for low to medium system workloads. Therefore, you might incorrectly assume that there is still plenty of CPU headroom available. However, for peak loads the whole Hyper-threading effect vanishes because utilization still cannot exceed 100 %. Therefore, Hyper-Threading can prove useful but will never serve as a replacement for real cores.

---

[4] http://www.intel.com/technology/turboboost/

> **SAP Platform Certification**
> SAP provides support only for installations on certified platforms. For proprietary UNIX systems, only the operating system has to be certified, not the individual server types. For Windows servers each vendor has to publish a SD benchmark result of at least the largest available server of each CPU family.[5] For Linux the server has to survive the SD benchmark, the publication of the result is voluntary. In general SAP does not certify storage or network devices.
>
> Public Cloud providers like Amazon have to certify their "instance types" (virtual machines) instead of their hardware. Like for Linux the cloud provider has to run a SD benchmark, but the publication of the result is voluntary.[6]

8.2.2 Inter Core Communication and Access to Main Memory

With multi-sockets, multi-cores, and in-memory technologies it is important to understand how communication between the cores works and how they access the main memory.

▶ *Uniform memory access*

In the past, Intel processors used the so called front-side bus (FSB), a single, shared bidirectional bus that connects all processors to the Memory Controller Hub (aka Northbridge). Multiple PCIe connections were provided by the I/O Controller Hub (aka Southbridge). One of the advantages of this *uniform memory access* architecture is that the entire memory is accessible equally by each processor. The drawback is that a single shared data bus doesn't scale well with an increasing number of CPUs following the well known 'Amdahls Law'.

▶ *Non-uniform memory access*

The Intel QuickPath Interconnect (QPI) and AMD HyperTransport architecture utilizes a separate memory controller local to each processor, multiple high-speed point-to-point links and an internal crossbar router interconnecting the processors and the chipset. In such a *non-uniform memory access* (NUMA) design, a CPU has direct access only to the segment of the main memory it is connected over its own

---

[5] Published on http://www.saponwin.com
[6] Amazon didn't publish the benchmark results, however the SAPS numbers for sizing can be found in SAP Note 1588667

8.2 Server Architectures: Nifty Details?

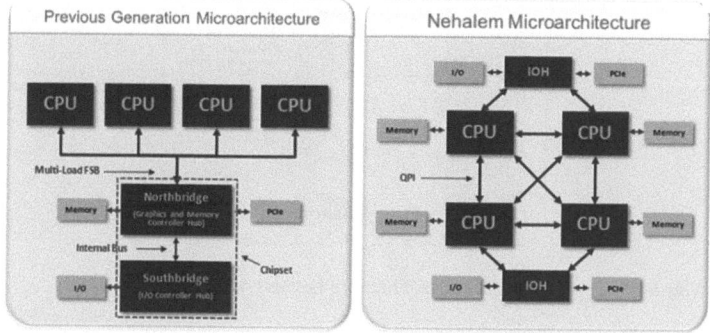

Fig. 8.4 *Uniform* versus *non-uniform memory access* architecture

controller (*local memory*), all other segments must be accessed over a QPI link through another processor (*remote memory*).

I/O can be also local to a processor or remote through another one. Because local memory can be accessed orders of magnitude faster compared to remote memory, vendors take care that in a benchmark the system is configured in a way that only local memory is used for any process (aka pinning). However in general SAP applications are not NUMA aware[7] because the SAP ABAP server isn't. SAP HANA however is NUMA-aware and thus benefits from pinning to local memory.

▶ *2-sockets and 4-sockets x86 – sweet spot for SAP*

In fact, the linear memory access capability via the Intel QPI architecture on multi-socket systems is granted up to 4-sockets servers where a full mesh of QPI links delivers a non-oversubscribed memory access between sockets/CPUs (see Fig. 8.4). Intel machines with 8-sockets and beyond would typically lead to a sub-optimal QPI-based memory implementation (as depicted on Fig. 8.5) given that memory access between nodes would be oversubscribed and latency would be driven by the slower common denominator QPI path.

Another more expensive option would be to add an external and proprietary memory controller. This factor, altogether with the lower price and high performance capacity of the new Intel CPUs have made 2-sockets and 4-sockets x86 machines as the new sweet spot for SAP implementations, both on premises and mainly for cloud.

> **Intel CPU Roadmap**
> The Intel road map distinguishes between "tick" and "tock" CPU families. A tick implements a new manufacturing technology that shrinks an existing processor, while tock is a new architecture done in the previous technology. Nehalem was the 45 nm tock, Westmere the 32 nm tick. Sandy Bridge again a new architecture on 32 nm.

---

[7] SAPNote 1612283 - Hardware Configuration Standards and Guidance.

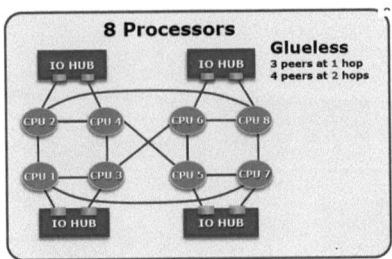

Fig. 8.5 *Non-uniform memory access* architecture beyond 4 sockets

8.2.3 Scale-up Versus Scale-out

Scale-up indicates a strategy using larger servers to maximize the leveraging effects of system consolidation. Because in the past you needed "big iron" anyway to run the database of larger SAP systems, it had made sense to run the application servers on the same server type to get a uniform system landscape.

However, the hardware for scale-up comes at a higher price because the servers are produced in low numbers. As Fig. 8.6 demonstrates, the SAPS ratings of commodity 4-socket servers today exceed the performance numbers of much larger servers a few years ago. Therefore the technical need for scale-up has simply become obsolete for most SAP implementations.

Scale-out concepts also known as horizontal scalability distributes the system landscape over relatively small commodity servers. In principle smaller servers would limit the size of the application; however given the dramatic increase of CPU power, even small blades can support relatively large systems nowadays and benefit from the same leveraging effects as scale-up servers. In addition the performance per thread is higher as Fig. 8.7 demonstrates.

As already mentioned typical SAP applications are scale-out friendly due to the 3-tier architecture. The SAP application code which counts for 60–80 % of the resource consumption of a SAP system can distribute easily over multiple small servers. And even the databases of larger SAP systems fit well to the commodity servers available today. With the proliferation of HANA as horizontal scalable database for all SAP solutions, the need for "big iron" even for very large SAP systems vanishes completely.

8.2.4 Rack Mount Versus Blade

With a few exceptions, the size of servers has shrunken to a degree that allows installing plenty of them in a 19″ rack. Rack mount servers still have their own power supplies, fans, and IO cards. The result is thick strands of cables for redundant power, LAN, SAN and system management. The often mentioned benefit of having local discs is rather meaningless in a cloud environment.

8.2 Server Architectures: Nifty Details?

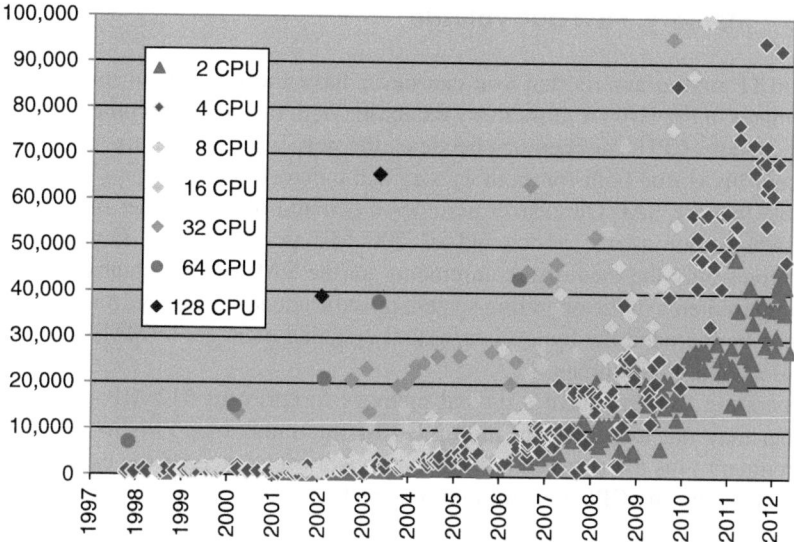

Fig. 8.6 Development of SAPS performance per server

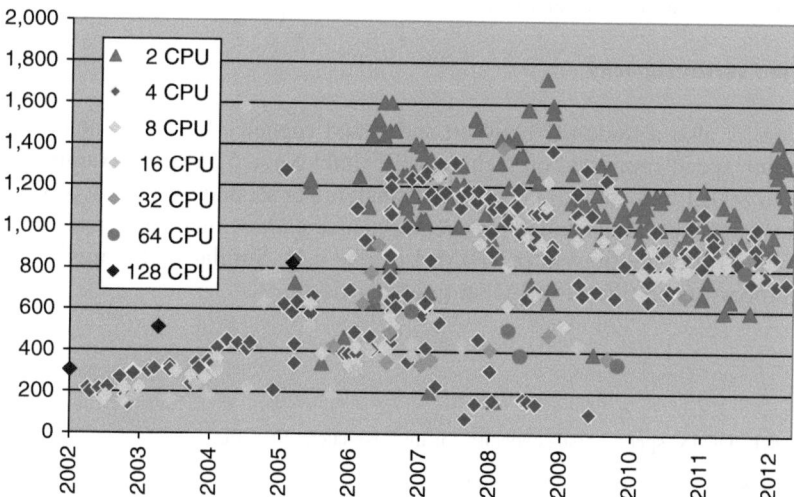

Fig. 8.7 Development of SAPS performance per thread

Blades servers were introduced to improve efficiency by sharing power supplies and cooling fans and reduce the number of cables. The biggest drawback in classic blade architectures is the sprawl of network connectivity switches (for both LAN and SAN) as well as management/controller modules, because each blade chassis needs at least two times each of these elements for redundancy.

Fortunately the fabric extender concept described in Sect. 9 completely removes the need for Fibre Channel (FC) and Ethernet switches as well as management modules in blade chassis.

8.2.5 Memory: Fast but Volatile

An old IT saying asserts that you can never have too much main memory. This culminates in the HANA in-memory database. With the growing computing capacity of modern CPU, the memory becomes the new frontier limiting server performance. This is true both for memory size and memory speed.

Note that the SAP Quicksizer assumes a demand of 10 MB per user, practical experience demonstrate a demand of 100 MB per user. The Quicksizer also determines only the memory requirements for the SAP and the database software. The requirements of the operating system must be added for each virtual machine as so must be included the hypervisor/virtual machine manager (VMM) itself on the pre-allocation of resources.

Operating Systems have a typical memory footprint of 512 MB–16 GB. This number may not look big, but multiplied by the number of VMs in a virtualized environment plus the overhead of the hypervisor often exceeds the capacity of the memory before the CPU becomes a bottleneck.

The number of Dual In-Line Memory Modules (DIMM) in a server is limited by electrical issues and the processors pinout. Each DIMM adds parasitic capacitance and further loads the memory bus. Three DIMMs directly attached on the bus is currently the practical upper limit.

▶ *Speed versus capacity*

There is also a trade-off between speed and capacity for main memory. The maximum speed supported on Nehalem-EP (Intel Xeon 5,500) for example varies between 800, 1,066 and 1,333 Million Transfers per second (MTps) depending on how many sockets are installed per memory channel, how many are populated, and how many ranks are present per DIMM (Table 8.1). Similar tables apply to other Intel processors certified for SAP at time of writing.

Table 8.1 DIMM speed versus capacity for intel Nehalem-EP CPU

DIMS slots per channel	DIMM populated per channel	Ranks per DIMM	Million transfers per second
2	1	Single, double	1,333
		Quad	1,066
	2	Single, double	1,066
		Quad	800
3	1	Single, double	1,333
		Quad	1,066
	2	Single, double	1,066
		Quad	800
	3	Single, double	800

▶ *Capacity versus costs*

Another important consideration is the cost of the DIMM per GB. This cost does not grow linearly, while the there is not much difference between 4 GB or 8 GB DIMMs, 16 GB and 32 GB DIMMs come at a substantial premium.

8.3 Storage: Hard and Other Disks

Almost all applications need to store data at some stage. This applies in particular to SAP applications, which – depending on the type and scope of business processes – can generate enormous amounts of data that must be accessed at a minimum of latency time. Response time lost with the storage system cannot be compensated by the server. Therefore, a storage subsystem with an insufficient IO performance adversely affects the performance of the SAP system and thus the users' productivity in public and private clouds.

▶ *The IO challenge*

In the past one of the biggest cost drivers was the demand for disk space for the database of a SAP system. Due to the relative small capacity of the individual disks, plenty of "spindles" were necessary to fulfill the demand of disk space even for moderate SAP systems. The many spindles working in parallel granted the necessary throughput implicitly.

▶ *The disk paradox*

During the past years, disk capacity has developed almost in parallel to Moore's Law for CPUs. Unfortunately, there was no such improvement with disk throughput for random IO, because the physical IO of a disk is restricted by mechanical parameters which cannot be further increased like rotation speed and positioning time of the write/read arm.

Ironically the development of advanced compression technologies has made the databases shrink dramatically, but the IO demand hasn't shrunk by the same rate. This result in the paradox situation, that today a disk subsystem needs much more disk drives to grant the necessary throughput than it would need for the necessary capacity.

8.3.1 Sizing for Throughput

As with the SAPS and Memory there is no exact formula to determine the necessary IO throughput measured in Input/Output operations per second (IOPS). Early

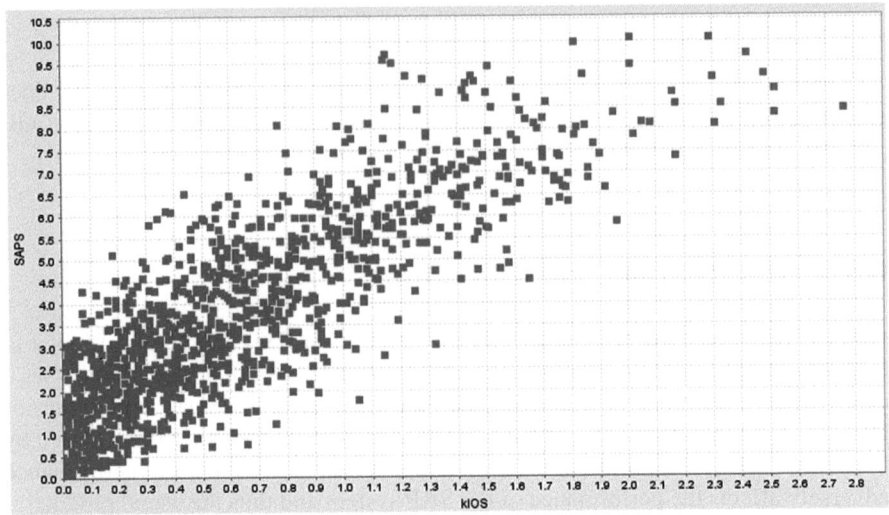

Fig. 8.8 SAPS consumed in relation to IO generated

studies initiated by one of the authors[8] result in some rules of thumb that are adopted in Quicksizer by SAP:
- IOPS = SAPS × 0.7 for SAP BW
- IOPS = SAPS × 0.4 for all other SAP solutions

Database Compression technologies offered by most DBMS vendors and SAP HANA as well as x86 servers with large amounts of physical RAM now make approximations between SAPS and IOPS even less applicable.

A common 300 GB or 600 GB disk with 15 k rpm has a throughput of only 180 IOPS. With a SAPS rating of more than 40,000 for a common 2-way server at time of writing you would need around 90 disks for a ECC system with this number of SAPS and 160 disks for a BW even if you do not need the resulting capacity of 27 or 48 TB.

As with any rule of thumb, there is no guarantee. The early studies had only a relatively small set of measurements available with extremely high scatter. More recent studies at the Hasso Plattner Institute analyzed approximately three million measurements on a multitude of SAP systems over several months to find possible correlations between the SAPS and the IO consumed of SAP systems.[9]

In a few cases the SAPS-meter correlation diagrams show a correlation between the IO generated in relation to SAPS consumed (Fig. 8.8).

---

[8] Statistical Analysis of Storage Subsystems in SAP Environments and development of a Application to determine the optimal size of such systems. Christoph Schelling, Master Thesis 2006.

[9] Analysis of resource consumption in virtual systems – Exemplified by the IO load of business applications; Robert Wierschke, Master Thesis 2009.

8.3 Storage: Hard and Other Disks

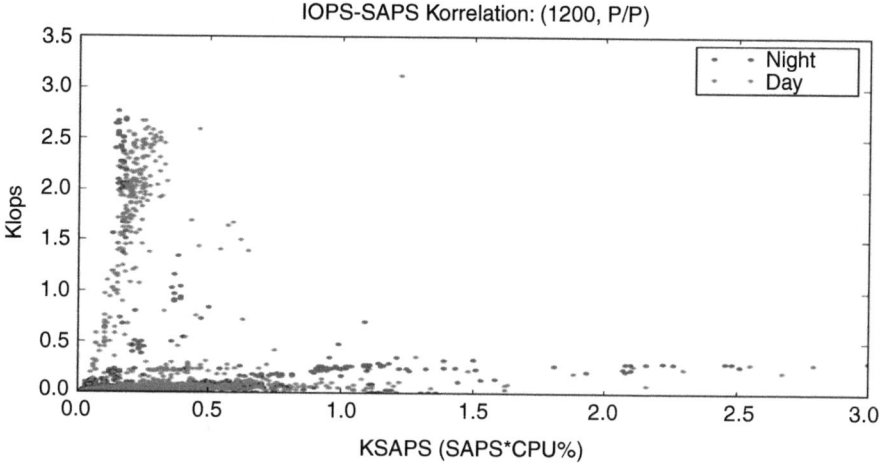

Fig. 8.9 V-shaped relation between IO generated and SAPS consumed

In most cases however the measurements result in different patterns that are neither related to specific usage phases nor associated with specific SAP Solutions (ECC, BI, CRM, XI etc.). Figure 8.9 shows a V-shape observed at some installations.

In general the relation is different for every customer installation – if there is a relation at all. High IO loads also do not correlate with high SAPS loads. As a result a prediction of IO requirements from SAPS capacity of a system is not possible due to high amount of statistical spread of the measurements.

As a result we recommend measurements using operating system tools, for example *perfmon* for Windows or *iostat* for Linux and UNIX. The output files of these tools can be transformed into a valid architecture by the experts of the storage vendors.

▶ **The in-memory paradox**

Ironically the SAP in-memory appliances BWA and HANA generate the highest IO demand to the storage subsystem. As described in Chap. 2 HANA by default flushes the whole memory to the persistency layer every 5 min. SAP specified a throughput of 100,000 IOPS for the Log Volume and 800 MB per second for the Data Volume in T-shirt sized appliances to avoid that users become aware of the necessary "freezing" of the HANA database.

Such a throughput is a challenge even for solid state drives (SSD) with an average throughput of 4,000 IOPS. Therefore, you need either several of them and carefully optimized controller configuration or PCIe-Flash cards to cope up with the demand. In both cases, however, data is still stored only inside the server, which is not the best option for any availability and cloud concept.

▶ *Storage controller – the new bottleneck?*

Taking benefit from the scale-out architecture of HANA and ensuring some availability demands external storage in most cases. To grant the necessary throughput you have to consider that typical "storage controller front end point" has a throughput of 6,000–8,000 IOPS.

8.3.2 The Disk Is Dead: But Is SSD Already King?

Solid-state drives (SSD) use non-volatile flash memory which is made from floating-gate transistors, named after a second "floating" gate (FG) below the standard control gate (CG) of a field effect transistor. Because the FG is electrically isolated all around by an insulating oxide layer, electrons placed there are trapped and will not discharge for many years under normal conditions. The trapped electrons partially cancel the electric field from the CG, so more voltage has to be applied to make the channel conductive. The current flow through the channel represents the stored data. This way the state (and thus data) is persistent like on traditional disk without power being connected.

Solid-state storage (SSD) technology has significant advantages compared to electromechanical, hard-drive disks (HDD):
- In HDD the data transfer is sequential. The mechanical nature of hard disks introduces seek time. Transfer rate can be influenced by file system fragmentation and the layout of the files.
- In SSD the data transfer is random access. There is consistent read performance because the physical location of data is irrelevant. SSDs have no read/write heads and thus no delays due to head motion (seeking).

Most essential however, SSD has a significant higher IO performance
- HDD: Small reads – 180 IOPS, Small writes – 280 IOPS
- Flash SSD: Small reads – 1,075 IOPS, Small writes – 2,100 IOPS
- DRAM SSD: Small reads – 4,091 IOPS, Small writes – 4,184 IOPS

After all this benefits there is also a drawback: – surprise – a significant difference in price. At the time of writing, SSD cost about US$ 0.90–2.00 per GB compared to US$ 0.05–$0.10 per GB for traditional hard drives. Due to patents on some key manufacturing processes the further decline in cost will be modest.

▶ *Consumer versus enterprise class SSD*

There is also a difference between consumer and enterprise class SSD both in price as in write lifetime. Commercial SSD typically grant a total write endurance of 900 TB for 8 k writes. This number may look impressive, but is a necessity when SSD is used for log files.

So the throughput of up to 300,000 IOPS per single PCI adaptor comes at a price that restricts flash based SSD to applications like SAP HANA, which depend on SSD to make the log entry persistent.

8.4 Network

The whole cloud paradigm is based on networks, even the word stems from the cloud symbol drawn on whiteboards and slides whenever it comes to the network, with the internet as the biggest clouds of all.

Any SAP on cloud implementation depends on fast and reliable network connections. The "best" software, server or storage technology is of no use, if the connections are slow and unreliable. Latency added by unnecessary "hops"[10] and re-transmission can't be compensated by higher CPU clock speeds. And because any chain is only as strong as its weakest link, the availability of a SAP solution depends on the connections between the cloud and user.

8.4.1 User Network

Since the proliferation of fully switched Ethernet the *local area network (LAN)* will always provide sufficient bandwidth for the end user connection. As public cloud services are by definition delivered over the Internet and even in private clouds many users will access SAP solutions over WAN links, determining the required bandwidth for clients remains a challenge.

▶ *Connecting the clients*

Again there are only rules of thumb for the required bandwidth per user:

▶ *Bandwidth*

- 10–12 kbps for OLTP solutions and local installed GUI
- 50–60 kbps for OLAP solutions and local installed GUI
- 50–90 kbps in general for Browser access

Also printing should not be forgotten – a laser printer that can print 32 pages per minute requires a network bandwidth of approx. 30 Kbps. Again measurements on comparable SAP installations are recommended.

▶ *Latency*

Particularly in WAN connections, not only bandwidth but also latency times are crucial. With very long package-transfer times, work processes become tedious for the user, even though the available bandwidth would be sufficient.

In general, not only the SAP traffic but also emails, print data, file transfers, and other forms of data exchange will use the connections. To enable users to access the

---

[10] Every active device on the path from source to destination is counted as a "hop".

SAP system at maximum speed, the relevant application packages must be assigned a higher priority than the other traffic. Sophisticated routers featuring embedded Quality of Service (QoS) and WAN acceleration and optimization technologies can meet this requirement.

▶ *Security*

For obvious reasons the connections between the users and the SAP application server must be secure. Any intruder who made his way into this server has also full access to the entire database, even if the database server is behind the firewall. This raises the question how to implement client access from the Internet to the SAP system behind the firewall.

For SSL connections, you need to decide at which device the connection will be terminated. The recommended configuration is to terminate the SSL connection on a SAP Web Dispatcher in a demilitarized zone. Alternatively the Web Dispatcher forwards the packages to an application server without terminating the SSL connection.

This scenario is subject to some restrictions because the Web Dispatcher cannot analyze session cookies to determine the application server to which the data is to be sent. The Web Dispatcher therefore can only analyze the client IP address and always forwards all requests from this IP address to the same application server. SSL connections require a server-side certificate.

If the SAP Web Dispatcher terminates the SSL connection, it must have an appropriate certificate that is accepted as valid by the clients. Modern firewall products like *Cisco Adaptive Security Appliance (ASA)* have the possibility of setting up several demilitarized zones. The advantage is that the permitted data traffic can be specified precisely for every DMZ.

▶ *Load balancing*

The main task of the SAP Web Dispatcher is to dispatch the user requests to the SAP Web Applications Servers (WAS) of an application (in case the solution is big enough to demand more than a single SAP WAS instance).

However this task can also be fulfilled by network based server load balancers like *Cisco Application Control Engine (ACE)*[11] providing some additional features and benefits worthwhile to consider their deployment:

▶ *Optimized application server selection*

Because of its proprietary link to the SAP message service, the Web Dispatcher can optimize the load distribution based on the performance rating and actual load of each server.

---

[11] http://www.cisco.com/en/US/solutions/ns340/ns414/ns742/ns743/ns751/landing_sap.html

Out of the box, a network load balancer relies on more generic server selection processes such as weighted round robin and least connections. XML scripts can be customized to influence server selection based on other variables such as the number of dialog processes available in a WAS.

However in systems like SAP, where the application keeps a user context, load balancing is nothing more than selecting the WAS instance with the lowest load in the moment a user logs on to the SAP system. Even if this server gets massive load the next moment, the user will be connected to this WAS till he log off.

▶ **High performance SSL**

SAP Web Dispatcher offers SSL offload, but as a software-based solution, the performance achieved is gated by the server platform that is running Web Dispatcher.

Network load balancer devices like Cisco ACE perform this function in hardware, providing much higher SSL connections per second. By terminating SSL on the network load balancer, the user traffic can be passed inside the cloud as clear so that security mechanisms such as intrusion detection/prevention and web application security can be employed before delivery to the server. After these security services have been applied, Cisco ACE can re-encrypt the traffic and forward it to the server, if needed or required by regulations.

▶ **TCP reuse**

Instead of setting up a new TCP connection for every flow destined to a server, Cisco ACE can multiplex multiple flows across a single connection. This reduces the processing load on the server, allowing it to support more simultaneous connections and increasing the amount of SAP users per server.

▶ **Resilient user connectivity**

Because Cisco ACE maintains the state of each connection and a sticky entry in the standby context, failover is seamless and connections remain intact. This means that service is not impacted during maintenance or failures in the network.

▶ **Load balancing consolidation**

While a pair of SAP web dispatchers must be dedicated to each SAP application, all these functions can be combined onto a single pair of Cisco ACEs.

▶ **WAN acceleration**

In high latency WAN environments, response time for web transactions can be unacceptably slow. Network load-balancers provide a scalable way to transparently move server-destined transactions to acceleration devices such as Cisco Wide Area

Application Services (WAAS)[12] to optimize the session before forwarding traffic to the real servers. This results in better session response time for clients while providing high availability and scalability for the optimization engines themselves.

8.4.2 Server Network

As discussed in Sect. 8.1.2, 3-tier architectures are deployed to avoid unnecessary database license costs. In such architecture any data needed for a business process by the SAP application server has to be requested and received from the database server over the network. In the past physically separated "server networks" where implemented utilizing early high speed technologies due to the fact that this "Server traffic" is approx. 10 times bigger than the "user traffic" in a typical SAP solution.

▶ *No need for dedicated server networks*

With today's fully wire-speed switched 10 and 40 G Ethernet featuring quality-of-service, there is no need for such dedicated physical networks from a bandwidth perspective. However it still makes sense to minimize the network hops with Fabric Interconnect concepts and eliminate re-transmissions with loss-less Ethernet.

General purpose firewalls between SAP database and application servers should be avoided, they add latency while not add any meaningful security since an intruder accessing the SAP application server has access to the SAP database also. There are network-based application firewalls being able to place themselves on this app-db interface, as so does some IPS, and both can indeed add some security value on this environment.

8.4.3 Storage Network

For many years a Fibre Channel (FC) based *Storage Area Network (SAN)* was the technology of choice for connecting database servers and storage because of its low latency, high bandwidth, deterministic behavior and availability.

▶ *Are storage area networks dead?*

However, FC switches and host bus adapters (HBA) are expensive because the manufactured quantities are considerably smaller than those of the ubiquitous Ethernet. In a cloud infrastructure where any server should be capable to take over any role it would be prohibitively expensive to equip any server with redundant FC connections. In addition, Fibre Channel demands a separate network for

---

[12] http://www.cisco.com/en/US/solutions/ns340/ns414/ns742/ns743/ns751/landing_sap.html

storage access as oppose to the cloud trend of consolidation and automation where a consolidated and unified IO approach "on top of" lossless Ethernet LAN would be more efficient, from a cabling spraw reduction up to a bandwidth per cloud tenant allocation standpoint.

Network Attached Storage (NAS) is often seen as the opponent of SAN technology, however other than the name suggests, it is not a technology for connecting server and storage, but a storage system that can be directly connected to an Ethernet LAN. So from a technical standpoint the *network* based *file system (NFS)* and iSCSI are the opponents of SAN and not NAS. Like FC, all these technologies use the SCSI protocol at some point, only the transport media are different.

With the availability of high bandwidth, low latency and especially "lossless" Ethernet technologies from vendors like Cisco, the implementation and operation of dedicated storage networks become obsolete. So it is foreseeable that in spite of all the undisputed benefits of SAN, dedicated storage networks will share the fate of UNIX being replaced by technologies "good enough" and cheaper.

8.4.4 Fibre Channel over Ethernet (FCoE)

The concept behind FCoE sounds simple – just encapsulate FC frames inside Ethernet ones. The overhead for the encapsulation is minimal and done in hardware. Thanks to the improved encoding efficiencies of FCoE on 10 GE Ethernet, this technology has a better performance than native 8 G FC.

> **How Much Bandwidth Provide FC and Ethernet Really?**
> The question then becomes: if a FC link would be of 8 G, how much do we actually get to use for data? The answer is not the obvious 80 % here. FC link speeds are a bit tricky as they are actually faster than the stated link speed would suggest. Original 1 G FC is actually 1.0625 Gb/s, and each generation – up to 8 G FC – has kept this standard and multiplied it. From this rational, 8 G FC would be 8 × 1.0625, or actual nominal bandwidth of 8.5Gb/s. Putting back the encoding factor, the end result would be 8.5* 80 % = 6.8 G FC of usable bandwidth on an 8 G FC link.
>
> On the Ethernet world, it works a bit different. 10 G Ethernet uses 64b/66b encoding. This means that for every 64 bits of data, only 2 bits are needed for integrity checks. With that, a 10GE link would then have 96.9 % of the nominal bandwidth available for user data, hence a sustainable 9.7Gb/s of throughput.
>
> This means that one would have around 50 % extra bandwidth headroom to run FCoE on a single 10GE adapter as oppose to using two server PCI slots for the same purpose (one Ethernet NIC and the 8 G FC HBA).

Standard 802.3 Ethernet had to be enhanced by a mechanism that prevents packets being dropped to enable FCoE. Ethernet is a non-deterministic destination-based flow control media where dropping packets is the default response to network congestion while Fibre Channel is the opposite (source-based flow control deterministic network) and can't tolerate packet drops.

FCoE has the advantage of being completely part of the Fibre Channel architecture, allowing the reuse of existing SAN infrastructure management tools and multipathing software. FCoE switches provide the unmodified zoning functionality ensuring that storage allocation and security mechanisms are unaffected.

An FCoE implementation into the Linux kernel exists as an open-source project.[13] However hardware is still necessary to encapsulate the FC packets and hand it over to the Ethernet NIC driver. As this book is written there is no Software-only FCoE stack that can be used with virtual machines.

> **"Lossy" and "Loss-Less" Ethernet**
> In the classical Ethernet architecture data frames are sent without any guarantee that the target and all of the network switches and routers on their path are capable to digest them. If one of the nodes en route is congested (e.g. buffer overflow); the packet is simply dropped and higher level protocols have to re-transmit them again.
>
> Such behavior with the intention to handle congestion works pretty well, but has a tendency to flood the network with re-transmits when utilization is already high which causes even more congestion and re-transmits. In many server networks an increasing part of the available bandwidth is consumed by re-transmits like Spam is said to consume half of the bandwidth of the Internet. Increasing the size of the input buffers however will increase the latency.
>
> In a loss-less Ethernet a signaling mechanism keeps track of buffer availability at the other end of each link. This allows a frame to be only sent out if a buffer is available at the receiving end.[14] This way no bandwidth is wasted by re-transmission avalanches and response times will not suffer from re-transmission of dropped data frames.
>
> In addition the enhanced data center bridging (DCB) standard for loss-less Ethernet allows a 10GE link to be seen as for example eight distinct lanes with customer defined bandwidth per lane as well as which lane(s) should be considered loss-less lanes.
>
> This allows for a single 10GE CNA (FCoE converged network adapter) per server to seamless handle loss-less traffic (like FCoE) and other type of traffic that are not sensible to data loss (like HTTP, FTP, etc.)

---

[13] www.Open-FCoE.org

[14] In this sense the term loss-less does not consider that data can still be lost to transmission errors which is quite rare within a data center infrastructure.

8.4.5 iSCSI

With *SCSI over IP*, the standard Ethernet infrastructure can be used to connect external storage systems as if they were connected locally via SCSI. This enables a block-level access and thus a database operation. iSCSI shows higher throughput over 10 GB Ethernet than 4 GB FC setups.

Virtual machines can access storage devices directly using TCP/IP as a transport. FCoE in comparison can only be used to connect the LUN's to the virtualization host, so raw-device-mapping must be used to connect the virtual machines at the hypervisor layer.

Especially the Sybase ASE database can benefit from iSCSI because the asynchronous direct IO data writer architecture finds a more direct access to the data files than with NFS.

There are several facts which show that a guest direct mapping over TCP/IP is a preferable setup over a virtual disk image:

▶ *iSCSI versus NFS*

- More overhead in writing to virtual disk image due to the virtualization layers in the I/O path
- Snapshot solutions like Netapp Snapcreator for SAP cannot process virtual disk images. They require direct access to the volumes where the Sybase data files are located.
- SAP Landscape Virtualization Management (LVM) is not able to work with virtual disk images.
- Virtual to Physical migrations (V2P) are not possible with virtual disk images (Fig. 8.10).

Cabling for 10 Gigabit

Fiber continues the media of choice for longer distances and inter-rack horizontal cabling, but copper is deployed in the datacenter to reduce costs. Due to the complexity of encoding and decoding 10GE traffic over 10 GBase-T twisted pair an enormous number of transistors are required. This translates to a significant power requirement of approx 4 W per line and additional latency of approx 2.5 μs.

A more practical solution is to use Copper Twinax cable as defined in Annex of SFF-8431 where a single SFP (twin-ax uses SFP interfaces) port consumes approx 0.1 W and generates a latency of 0.1 μs.

Training for 10 Gigabit

Practical experience demonstrates that the differences between the transmission and switching protocols of 1 and 10 G (cut through switching) demand some training of the network administrators.

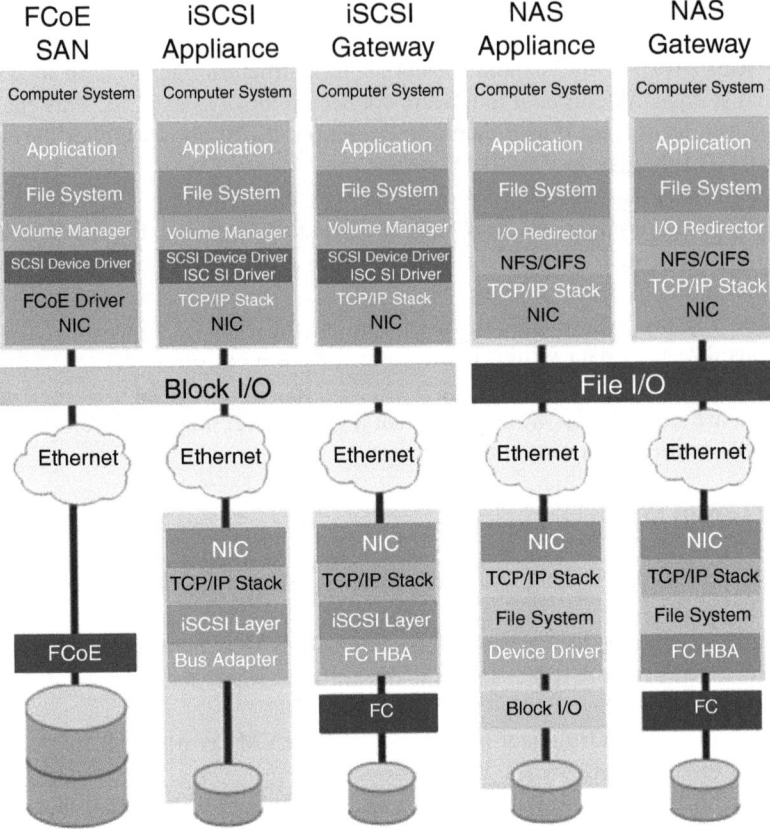

Fig. 8.10 Comparison of network stacks for server – storage connectivity

8.5 Unified Computing

In a *Unified Computing System (UCS)* SAN and LAN infrastructures are merged using *converged network adapters (CNA)*, which act simultaneously as both Fibre Channel HBA and Ethernet NIC and match unified switches. This way any server can be deployed as database with FC storage server at any time.

▶ *What's not there can't fail and doesn't generate heat*

A straightforward benefit of unified computing is the reduction in cabling and network components – by half, at least. Instead of redundant pairs of NICs and FC HBAs, only a pair of CNAs is necessary. A less than obvious benefit is that fewer components generate less heat. Also any component you do not have will not fail and does not have to be managed.

8.5 Unified Computing

However network unification is not as easy as it sounds. A unified network must be capable to carry quite different types of traffic with different characteristics and requirements over the same physical infrastructure without creating interferences where one type of traffic starves another.

▶ **Merging SAN and LAN**

Ethernet traffic is characterized by a large number of flows. In a SAP infrastructure this traffic becomes more and more sensitive to latency. An increasing number of applications also become sensitive to latency jitter.

Storage traffic must follow the FC model even in case of NAS technology, since SCSI is extremely sensitive to packet drops, losing frames is not an option.

QoS and per priority flow control is part of the lossless Ethernet standard (DCB); it guarantees a configurable minimal bandwidth for FC, and also allows bursting, if other bandwidth is not used (in contrast to rate limiting).

Inter processor Communication (IPC) used by VMware Vmotion, clustered file systems, distributed databases (Oracle RAC) and high availability solutions (Veritas, VCS, MSCS) is typically latency sensitive and require adapters providing zero-copy mechanisms (i.e. not making intermediate copies of packages). Cisco UCS is capable to properly handle IPC traffic between nodes while concurrently dealing with the regular Ethernet and storage based flows.

8.5.1 Converged Network Adapters

CNAs still need distinct device drivers for Ethernet and Fibre Channel. This allows the implementation to be transparent to OS and application. Several vendors manufacture CNAs, including Brocade, Cisco, Emulex, and QLogic.

The Cisco UCS VIC (Virtual Interface Card) uses a single chip ASIC that supports up 256 vNICs, each of them can be either an Ethernet NIC or FC HBA and dual 10 GE or a dual port channel of 40 GE ports (4 × 10 GE).

In addition, the ASIC provides hardware support for virtualization by an internal low latency switch. In this architecture the IO operations can be configured to bypass the hypervisor. This way the latency caused by the hypervisor soft-switch as well as the need for the network administrator to manage the soft-switch is no longer present.

Figures 8.11 and 8.12 show a comparison of the IO performance measured with IOzone during a Proof of Concept (PoC) at a customer.

Using Linux Netperf with 1,500 bytes MTU, the single 10 GE port throughput is measured 9.4 Gb/s (10 Gb/s minus the overhead of the headers).

The hardware latency is around 2 μs for sending and 1 μs for receiving. The application latency measured with Linux Net NetPIPE is 9.8 μs.

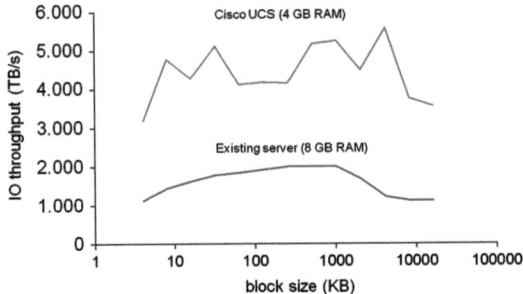

Fig. 8.11 Read performance on bare metal measured with IOzone

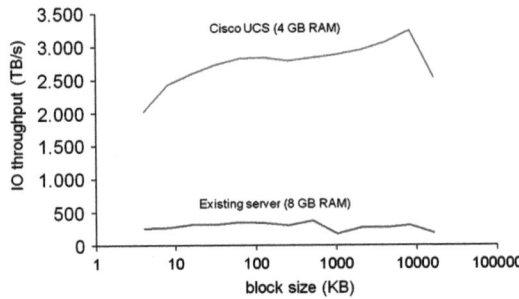

Fig. 8.12 Read performance on VMware measured with IOzone

8.5.2 Port Extenders

Port Extender (PE) provides additional MAC ports to an Ethernet Switch (Downlink Interfaces). When port extenders are combined with virtualization software, they allow the delegation of complex switching functions of the hypervisor softswitch to external physical Ethernet switches.

The port extender approach, standardized as IEEE 802.1BR, moves the IO interfaces from the Virtual Machines to an external Ethernet switch and makes them virtual. This way the Ethernet switch gets an expanded number of ports, one for each connected vNIC. These virtual Ethernet ports (vEth) are operated by the Ethernet switch like physical ones. Port extenders can be cascaded and allow consistent policy enforcement for all traffic for both physical and virtual network scenarios.

8.5.3 Fabric Extender

The port extender implemented in Cisco UCS is called a Fabric extender. It increases the number of ports without increasing the number of management points. This way a datacenter switch like the Cisco Nexus 5,000 family can be extended to support beyond 1,000 ports. Multiple uplinks of the fabric extender can be connected to different switches to grant redundant paths.

Typically deployed in active-active redundant pairs, the UCS fabric extender connects the UCS blade enclosure with the central fabric. The extender features an integrated chassis management controller for the enclosure physical components like power supplies, fans and temperature sensors.

8.5.4 Fabric Interconnects

Obviously converged network adapters depend on matching converged or unified switches. The Cisco UCS fabric interconnects feature the same low-latency, lossless 10 Gigabit Ethernet switching technology as the Cisco Nexus 5,000 Series. With the embedded UCS manager they unite up to 20 chassis with 160 blades into a centrally managed cloud infrastructure.

8.5.5 Unification and Virtualization

VMware ESXi/vSphere, Linux XEN and KVM as well as Microsoft Hyper-V are well-known solutions based on hypervisor architecture enabling multiple operating systems running in isolated virtual machines (VM). In such an environment SAP still runs on the certified operating systems for x86 servers like Windows; SuSE and RedHat rather than on VMware, XEN, KVM or Hyper-V.

▶ *Does SAP support virtualization?*

SAP has always taken a neutral stance in regards to virtualization: it is supported as long as it's transparent to the SAP system and does not cause significant performance issues. In case a customer runs into issues with a virtualized SAP environment he must demonstrate that the same trouble happens on bare metal. In this case SAP support will take action to identify the root cause. If the trouble is gone on bare metal: this will be the solution!

▶ *Virtualization challenges*

Another challenge with hypervisors is the implementation of network policies like Access Control Lists (ACL), traffic management, authentication, encryption etc. Because all VMs on the same hypervisor share the same policies, MAC Addresses used by the VMs are assigned by the virtualization software and may change over time. Using source MAC addresses would open the system to MAC address spoofing attacks. Moving VMs between different physical servers make the management of network policies even more challenging.

Classic Ethernet switches do not support the forwarding of frames where the source and destination MAC addresses are on the same physical port which is necessary to enable communication between two VMs on the same server. Also Port and Fabric Extenders require a new Ethernet tagging scheme between the NIC and the Ethernet switch to indicate the vNIC (virtual NIC) associated with the frame.

For these reasons, solutions have been created to avoid using software switching inside the hypervisor, but still allowing VM to VM communication. The virtual network tag (E-Tag) technology developed by Cisco solves this and other issues by creating a virtual Ethernet interface per each VM.

The E-Tag binds a vNIC to a vEth port and vice versa. This way vNIC and the vEth ports move with the associated policies when a VM moves from one server to another. This guarantees feature and policy consistency independently of the actual location of the VM.

E-Tag can be implemented either in hardware (for example the Cisco VIC) or in software (for example Cisco Nexus 1000v). This technology is recently standardized by IEEE in the 802.1BR specification.

8.5.6 Software Based Fabric Extender

VMware and Cisco collaborated to develop the Distributed Virtual Switch (DVS) API to address the issues of virtualization-aware networking. A fabric extender (FEX) delivers network-wide VM visibility and mobility along with consistent policy management. The first implementation is Cisco Nexus 1000v, a software switch embedded into the VMware vSphere/ESX hypervisor and Microsoft Windows Server 2012 Hyper-V 3.0.

Cisco has embraced a Nexus 1000v multi-hypervisor strategy and will also bring its VM networking functionalities to Linux based hypervisors KVM and Xen in the future.

VM Policy enforcement is applied to and migrated with the VM when a VMotion or DRS (Distributed Resource Scheduler) move a VM. Not only are the policies moved with the VM, but also all the statistical counters; the Netflow status and ERSPAN (Encapsulated Remote SPAN) sessions to allow traffic mirroring to an external sniffer even during a VM migration.

Network Policies are called "port profiles" and are created on the Nexus 1000v Virtual Supervisor Module by the Network Administrator. The Port profiles are automatically populated inside VMware Virtual Center (VC) and are visible inside VMware Virtual Infrastructure Clients as "port groups". The Server Administrator can assign them to vNICs and therefore ultimately to VMs.

Together with VEths, Port Profiles are the basic building blocks to enable automated VM connectivity and mobility of policies; i.e., to allow the interface configuration, interface state, and interface statistics to move with a virtual machine from server to server, as VMotion or DRS occurs. This also guarantees that security and connectivity policies are persistent.

8.5.7 Hardware Based Fabric Extender

An alternative approach is to replace the switch inside the hypervisor with a fabric extender like Cisco VM-FEX. The features are similar; however they are performed completely in hardware at wire speed. This approach is clearly superior from the performance perspective, since it does not consume CPU resources and enable hypervisor bypass for higher performance. Measurements on RedHat Linux reported that additional 400 SAP users can be supported on a standard Intel 2-socket server with VM-FEX compared to the KVM native Paravirtualisation IO pass-through. With the same number of SAP users (3,600) the database response time for SAP dialog processes improved by 39 %, the response time for DB Update by 27 % (Table 8.2)[15].

Table 8.2 User numbers and response times on a 2 socket blade

	User	Response time	
		Dialog processes	Update process
KVM pass-through	3,600	20.75	27.09
Cisco VN-Link	3,600	14.89	21.31
Cisco VN-Link	4,000	20.52	25.75

8.6 Summary

For the operation of mission critical SAP systems in private clouds, numerous requirements have to be considered. This starts with the selection and dimensioning of server systems and the storage architecture. The network however plays a much stronger role in cloud architectures than in traditional setups. Innovative concepts like unified computing are developed for that purpose.
- The majority of all SAP installations worldwide run on so called x86 architectures from Intel and AMD (approx 55 % Windows and 10 % Linux). Also SAP code in general is developed on x86 only.
- Besides the production system, the SAP system landscape usually consists also of systems for Quality Assurance, Development, Training, etc. Consider to run Development and Training in public, production and quality assurance with sensitive data in private clouds.
- SAP is scale-out friendly due to the 3-tier architecture. Scale-out concepts based on commodity servers can support extremely large numbers of users transactions and database sizes.
- Even large SAP systems can be implemented nowadays with database and application layer on the same server (aka 2-tier). In case the database licenses

---

[15] http://www.cisco.com/en/US/solutions/collateral/ns340/ns517/ns224/ns944/whitepaper_c11_703103.pdf

are acquired from the database vendor it make sense to run the databases on a dedicated server (aka 3-tier) so only the cores on this server are counted for database licenses.
- Multi-Core and Multi-Thread drive the single CPU performance beyond the clock speed limits. However Hyper-treading increases the throughput at low and medium utilizations only, it cannot increase the maximum throughput per thread.
- SAP HANA makes extensive use of Hyper-Threading to parallelize processing. The SAP Web-Application server processes are single-threaded, which restrict the performance especially for batches.
- Memory has become the new frontier limiting server performance. Practical experience demonstrate a demand of 100 MB per user and the requirements of the operating system must be added for each virtual machine. Memory extenders help to fully utilize the available CPU resources.
- In the past the many disks needed for capacity granted also the necessary IO throughput. Advanced compression shrinks the databases size dramatically, but not the IO demand. Therefore today storage must be sized for throughput rater than capacity. Ironically SAP in-memory databases like HANA are the most demanding in disk IO throughput.
- With lossless 10 GB Ethernet there is no need for a dedicated server network.
- With lossless unified networks there is no need for a dedicated Storage Network. Converged Network Adaptors and matching fabric switches enableany blade in a cloud infrastructure to be a potential database server.

Stateless Computing 9

> *Innovative concepts like unified and stateless computing and service profiles enable full flexibility for SAP on public and private Cloud implementations. This chapter deals with the details of stateless computing and how it influences the organizational structure of SAP operations. We take also a look at containerized datacenters and block and pod concepts and close with the discussion about how "green" clouds can be.*

▶ **Server personality**

In a traditional deployment model the identity of a server depends on its hardware. Servers are unambiguously identified by addresses such as Media Access Control (MAC), Universally Unique Identifier (UUID), World Wide Node Names (WWNN), World Wide Port Names (WWPN), etc. defining together the "personality" of this server. Some of these elements can't be changed. This makes it difficult to re-assign servers to other tasks in a cloud environment.

▶ **SAP license keys are hardware bound**

In addition there are still many applications never meant to be moved to other servers – SAP is one of the most prominent one. Such applications code some properties of the server they are installed on into the license key. If you boot SAP applications on another server the key does not fit. In this case the system assumes to be an evaluation copy which works for exactly 30 days and freezes after that time. Similar conditions apply to Microsoft License keys for the Windows operating system. This makes it difficult to move a solution to another server in a cloud environment.[1]

---

[1] In case of SAP systems a new license key can be generated on-line at any time. Alternatively a SAP license server can be deployed. At Amazon the SAP license key is bound to Amazon's Instance ID.

▶ **Application mobility on bare metal**

In a stateless computing architecture like Cisco UCS all elements which define the personality of a server are defined by a service profile. A service profile is a self-contained logical representation (object) of a server type and identity. The service profile defines hardware independent server features including firmware, boot information, fabric connectivity, policies, external management, and high availability configuration. By association with a service profile, the server adopts the personality from the service profile. This way any server in a cloud can take over every role within a few minutes.

A server associated with a service profile is similar to a traditional bare metal server in the way that it is ready to be used for production and to run business software. Once de-associated from the service profile, the server will be reinitialized (erased from any state) and returned to the pool (depending on current pool policies).

Servers and service profiles have a one-to-one-relationship. Each server can be associated with only one service profile at a given time. Each individual service profile can be associated with exactly one server at a time. However a service profile can be modified, cloned, or used to instantiate from a template.

> **The Mobile Phone Analogy**
> Mobile phones with their SIM cards are a excellent analogy of Cisco stateless computing model with service profiles. The SIM card carries the identity of the mobile line and associated subscription. The phone is actually stateless on that regards.
>
> You can use the same SIM cards on distinct types of cell phones – once at a time – and your mobile line and number would be always the same, so reachability is granted. You can even roam with your same SIM card between distinct carriers and countries.
>
> This same concept applies to Cisco UCS where the server is stateless but the service profile defining the identity of a SAP server. Like you can move your SIM card to a new cell phone the identity of a SAP server can "roam" to another UCS system on a remote datacenter, while seamless reachability for SAP users is granted.

Like SAP separates the business logic written in ABAP or Java from the physical hardware by the Web Application server, the Cisco UCS uses policies and service profiles to abstract state and configuration information for all the components that define a server. This is one of the key features that make UCS a stateless computing system. It allows separation of an operational state and service from the server hardware and physical connectivity.

For example, a service profile can be moved from one server to a different one. With stateless computing the new server becomes literally the old one by acquiring its identity. This way, even the SAP license key will always fit into the correct "license lock".

The personality can be even moved between different server generations or from physical to virtual or vice versa as long as the IO adapter is the same. Obviously this greatly simplifies adapting resources to demand in a private cloud environment. The uniform IO connectivity based on unified fabric model makes this operation straightforward. It should be mentioned that stateless computing requires boot from network (FC, FCoE, iSCSI, PXE, etc.).

▶ *DR for HANA and BWA*

One practical example of the advantages of the of stateless computing concept and service profiles isa fail-over between two data centers for SAP HANA and BWA in a disaster recovery scenario. Both solutions have static IP addresses and virtualization is not supported at the time of writing.

Actually it's the OS who has to take care for IP addresses. If you replicate not only the HANA data, but also all binaries, the OS and the Service Profiles to the DR site, the remote site will become an exact replica of the source site in case of a fail-over.

However the question is what would happen to the MAC und WWN Addresses in this case? As soon the OS recognizes a NIC with an unknown MAC address, a new eth device would be generated. This way the original eth0 would become for example eth3 which doesn't fit to the IP configuration.

This "minor glitch" will prevent the system to operate must usually circumvented by tons of scripting. Practical experience has proven that this workaround is a cumbersome and error prone process which has a tendency that the "fail-" will work, but not the "-over".

With stateless computing the MAC and WWN Addresses are part of the service profiles. So associating the service profiles of the servers in a going down data center with a new server in the second datacenter will grant also the "-over" for a HANA system.

9.1 Service Profile Definition

As discussed in the chapter about SLA, the business service dictates the required qualities and quantities for the infrastructure. SAP applications are typical examples of business-critical applications that need high availability and high performance. They also need to be able to scale quickly in case of load peaks. A SAP administrator understands the behavior of the application well, but has to cooperate with the infrastructure administrators to define a service profile that accommodates all the requirements.

The server administrator makes sure that the system in question is configured with sufficient CPU power and memory, redundant network connections and power supplies. The storage administrator assigns a fault tolerant storage array with sufficient IO performance and the proper RAID configurations. Even though the network load requirements are average, given the sensitivity of SAP users to response times the network administrator has to make sure that the SAP applications have high priorities. Service profiles make the work of all of them and the cooperation easier.

▶ **Upfront definition of policies**

Within the stateless computing model the definition of the policies can be done upfront and once for all SAP solutions in a complete landscape. Templates are used for instantiation of multiple service profiles. A server administrator can create specific templates for SAP database and applications servers to be used by a cloud administrator with limited expertise of the requirements to create a large number of service profiles. With policies predefined by experts for each topic the day-to-day administration of a cloud infrastructure based on the stateless computing model is minimal, since the critical configurations are already defined.

Benefits of "Bare Metal" Virtualization
In regards to application mobility, stateless computing can be thought of as a "bare metal" virtualization. Without any doubt hypervisor-based virtualization has great benefits – but it comes at a price – both in computing power and latency. In addition, commercial solutions generate license costs in the range of half of the hardware costs. Even if bare metal virtualization has not all the features, it has a unique feature: virtualize what can't be virtualized like the hard coded IP addresses of BWA and HANA and enable to boot a SAP solution on any server within a cloud without invalidating the license key. And best of all: no license fee for a hypervisor neither the associated management platforms!

▶ **Unified computing landscape management**

The Cisco UCS manager (UCSM) software (located in each Fabric Interconnect) is used to prepare the service profiles and to orchestrate the hardware. Any configuration and status change of a managed object (MO) is replicated to the secondary UCSM instance in the default HA configuration by a transaction service. This service also verifies that the changes are permanently stored ("persistified") in the embedded storage.

▶ **Auto discovery**

The UCSM always scans for changes to the hardware configuration like insertion and removal of servers, chassis and even cables. The discovery process is typically triggered by a presence sensor or by a link state change on a port. If, for example, a new chassis is discovered, it is assigned a chassis ID and all the slots, power supplies, fabric extenders, fans etc. are inventoried.

Next, the UCSM will continue to discover if servers are present in each slot, in which case it scans for model number, serial number, BIOS, memory, CPU, and adapters installed etc. A deep discovery via a UCS Utility OS runs on the server prior to boot, to discover local disk info, vendor specific adapter information and performs diagnostics, reports inventory or configures the firmware state of the server.[2]

Hardware can even be retired by a "remove command" which will remove the components from the internal database. However UCSM does maintain a list of decommissioned serial numbers just in case the administrator mistakenly reinserts a removed component.

▶ *Firmware management*

Even with only a few types of firmware, it would still be a challenge to manage hundreds or thousands of servers in a cloud environment. With stateless computing; the firmware follows the service profile and the blade is updated with the version specified by the firmware policy.

A host firmware pack contains host firmware images, like BIOS, adapters and local storage controller. A service profile that uses this policy will load all the applicable firmware into the different components of the server associated with that profile.

UCS Platform Emulator

UCSM uses a model driven framework approach. One of the benefits is the ability to develop the system configuration independently from the platform implementation. So the complete config can be simulated without the hardware already in place. The UCSemulator is built from the very same source code of the real system and emulates the entire set of UCS devices like Fabric interconnects, blades, IO adaptors, VMware virtual center (VM port policies) the UCS Utility OS etc. so all calls made to the emulator are identical to calls made to a UCS manager in a real system.

A complimentary version of the emulator (UCSPE Lite) can be downloaded from the Cisco Developer Network at http://developer.cisco.com/web/unifiedcomputing.

9.1.1 Unified Computing and VMware's vCenter

With the proliferation of VMware, methods to manage the virtualized switching layer became necessary. With the Cisco VM-FEX technology, the virtualized switching layer can be eliminated completely, while retaining the benefits and supported technologies (Vmotion, DRS, HA, etc.) within the data center infrastructure.

---

[2] http://www.cisco.com/en/US/prod/collateral/ps10265/ps10281/white_paper_c11-590518.html

Integration with VMware is embedded in the service profiles, which allows dynamic Virtual Interface (VIF) definition and policy consumption. Multiple dynamic vNIC connection policies can be created and each of the policies defines a number of dynamic vNICs. For Cisco VICs physical adapters, these vNICs are the pre-provisioned (stateless) uplink ports; the VM-NICs (Virtual Machine Network Interface Cards) are associated with these uplinks one-to-one dynamically as VM interfaces are created by vCenter.

To establish communication between UCSM and vCenter, an XML sheet is exported from UCSM as a plug-in for the vCenter administrator. When the administrator assigns a vNIC and a port-group to a given VM, meta-data such as adapter type, MAC address, port-group etc. are written into the .vmx file that describes the virtual machine.

When a given VM is powered on or migrated onto a host, the ESX kernel interacts with UCSM via the kernel modules to assign these identifiers to the dynamic adapters on the UCS server. During a live-migration event, these identifiers are moved to the target server, activated as part of the appropriate final steps in a VM move, and de-activated on the source server to be utilized by other VMs.

One of the benefits of the integration is that in contrast to the traditional vCenter management the roles of server and network administrators are separated. The network administrator can define the port-profile and other network related configurations. These port profiles are visible and available to the server administrator of vCenter as port-groups, where she/he can choose from these profiles while defining a VM or adding ESX hypervisor host in a "Data Center" (vCenter terminology for grouping and resource management of VM's).

▶ *vNIC template*

A port profile is also auto-created through vNIC template in UCSM. When a vNIC template with fail-over property is created, a corresponding port-profile is auto-created. After that, any property changes in the vNIC template (like addition or deletion of VLANs) are reflected to the auto-generated port profile as well.

Once the port policies are pushed to the vCenter and the service profile for the ESX host is associated with a physical UCS server, the server administrator can start managing that ESX host in the vCenter and creating virtual machines on the ESX host. The VMs use VMware's softswitch implementation by default, but in the case of a UCS server with Cisco VIC adapter VMs, Service Console, and VMkernel can be "migrated" to use the VM-FEX implementation (aka. VN-Link in hardware).

▶ *Runtime policy for dynamic VIFs*

At that point, the server administrator chooses the port-profile for a given vNIC. When the VM is instantiated (or powered up) on the server, the switch software of the Fabric Interconnect receives a "VIF Create" request. This request contains port-profile name (or alias), identity of VM, hypervisor host, DVS, and DVport.[3]

---

[3] http://www.youtube.com/watch?v=3A1BWyVltJU

9.2 Cloud Operation with Stateless Computing

In our book "SAP System operation[4]" we described the many different roles and tasks necessary to operate a SAP system landscape. When the book was published in 2004, SAP landscapes where already complex, but still relatively static. Only 1 year later our book "adaptive SAP infrastructure[5]" already described how to implement SAP in a more flexible and agile way in traditional data center structures. Today, stateless computing enables SAP to become fully dynamic on cloud infrastructures, but roles and tasks to operate a SAP system have not become obsolete but even more complex.

Policy-driven device managers like UCSM allow IT-Organizations to cope with the complexity and to implement their best practices as UCS policies. As described above, UCSM allows subject matter experts like networking, storage and server administrators to predefine policies within their area of expertise, which can later be selected by a cloud administrator when a certain business service is requested.

Policies control how a server or other components of the UCS will act or be affected in specific circumstances. The UCSM has a large number of different policies. These policies describe and control all aspects of the UCS such as network, storage, server configuration and system behavior.

Global policies are defined for the whole UCS, local policies are per organizational level. The majority of the policies are used to describe the configurations of the different components of the system. Figure 9.1 show a screenshot of the UCS configuration policies further explained in Table 9.1.

9.2.1 IDPools

Identity Pools are containers for resources and ID definitions. They make a system easier to manage and maintain for administrators by omitting boring repetitive tasks.

▶ *Identity pools*

One of the key components of stateless computing are identity pools since a stateless server gets his personality by assigning an ID from a pool. There are four types of identity pools: MAC addresses; WWPN addresses; WWNN; and UUID Suffixes. Figure 9.2 explains how they would interact with policies and isolation

---

[4] ISBN 1-59229-025-8
[5] ISBN 1-59229-035-3

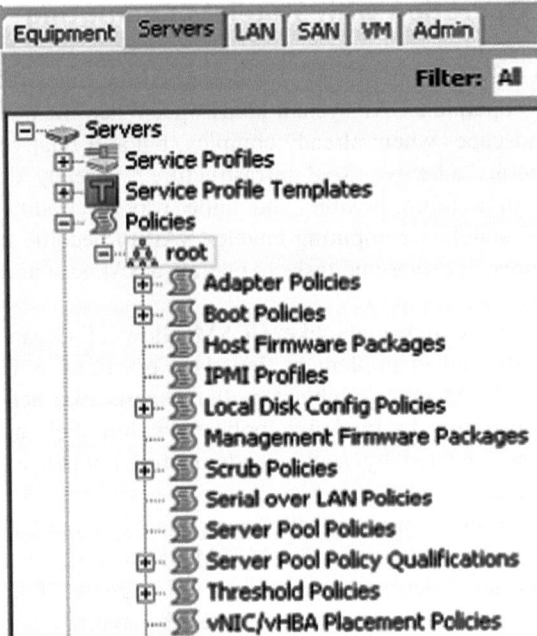

Fig. 9.1 Configuration policies of a Cisco UCS

functionalities in order to create templates to be used for service profiles associations.

▶ *MAC pools*

A Media Access Control (MAC) address is a hardware address that uniquely identifies each node of a LAN. With the UCSM the network administrator allocates blocks of sequential MAC addresses by defining a start address and a the size of the block; for example the command "From: 00:25:B5:00:00:01 Size: 15" will allocate addresses up to 00:25:B5:00:00:15.

▶ *UUID suffix pools*

A Universally Unique Identifier (UUID) uniquely identifies servers. Again the UUID pool is populated by assigning a start address and the size of the block. Assuming the prefix is 1FFFFFFF-2FFF-3FFF the command "From: 1000-0A0B0C0D01 Size: 15" will allocate a UUID suffixes from 1FFFFFFF-2FFF-3FFF-1000-0A0B0C0D01 to -0A0B0C0D15.

▶ *World Wide Port Names*

World Wide Port Names (WWNN) uniquely identifies a node and World Wide port names (WWPN) a port on a node in a SAN similar to MAC addresses in a

9.2 Cloud Operation with Stateless Computing

Table 9.1 Example of the configuration policies of a Cisco UCS

Policy	Description
Boot	Determines from which a server boot (SAN, LAN, local Disk, or virtual Media)
Host firmware pack	Determines set of firmware versions applied to servers
Management firmware	Determines firmware version that will be applied to the Cisco Integrated Management Controller (CIMC) on the server
Dynamic connection	Determines numbers and properties of dynamic adapters utilized by Virtual Machines (such as queue depth, performance, etc.)
QoS definition	Determines traffic quality of service for vNIC and vHBA (class, burst and rate)
Chassis discovery	Determines system reaction when a new blade chassis is discovered
Server discovery	Determines system reaction when a new server is discovered
Server pool	Determines pool memberships of servers that match a specific qualification
Server qualification	Qualifies servers based on inventory rules like # CPU's, amount of memory

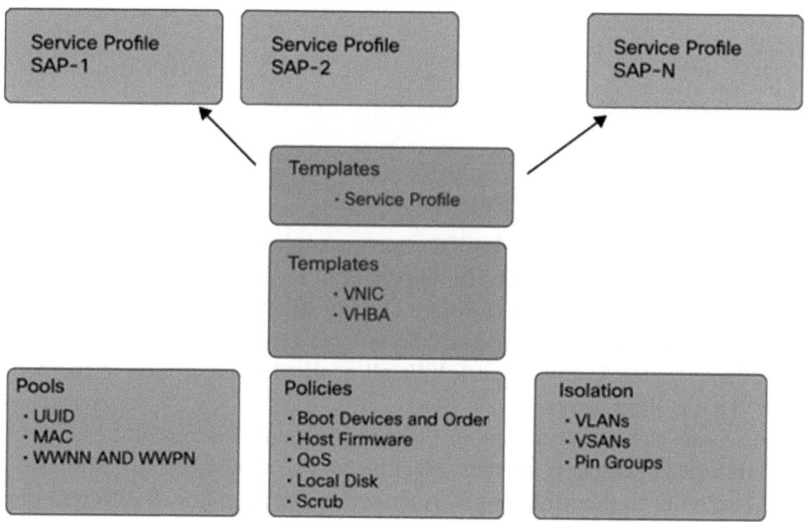

Fig. 9.2 Identity pools, policies, templates and service profiles

LAN. Again the command "From 20:00:00:25:B5:00:00:01 Size 15" will allocate a pool up to 20:00:00:25:B5:00:00:15. See screenshot on Fig. 9.3 for reference.

▶ **WWNN and WWPN pools**

See screenshot on Fig. 9.3 for reference.

9.2.2 Server Pools

A server pool contains a set of servers idle (unassociated) or in use (associated). The pool can either have statically or dynamically allocated servers. The latter can be

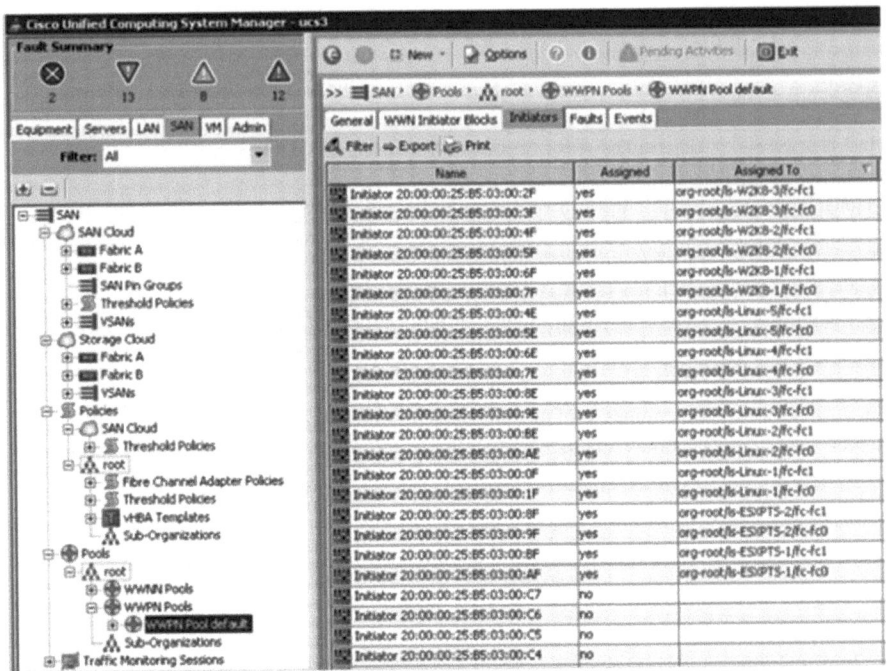

Fig. 9.3 WWPN pool elements and service profile mapping

automatically populated via policies. There are two policies that decide to which pool a server should become a member of: "Server Pool Policy" and "Server Pool Policy Qualifications". The "Server Pool Policy Qualifications" policy describes the hardware qualification criteria for servers, like number of processors, amount of RAM, type of adapters, etc. A server that fulfills all of the defined criteria in the policy is considered a qualified server.

Because the same server can meet multiple qualifications the "Server Pool Policy" describes which Pool the server becomes a member of. Multiple Pool Policies can point to the same pools. A server can be member of different pools.

The UCSM also has default pools that are pre-defined, but not pre-populated. The default pools are used as a last resource when a regular pool has drained out in the local organization and there are no other resources available in parent or grandparent's organization.

9.2.3 Administrative Organization for SAP on Cloud

As described in the book "SAP system operation" there are many good reasons to have specialized administrators for server, storage and network in a SAP infrastructure.

Separation of administrators and their administrative tasks can be done by the use of organizations, Locales and *Role Based Access Control* (RBAC). This can be accomplished by dividing the large physical infrastructure into entities known as organizations. As a result, administrators can achieve a logical isolation between organizations without the need for a dedicated physical infrastructure for each organization.

Organizations may represent a division within the company, such as marketing, finance, engineering, human resources, or different customers in a multi-tenancy environment.

▶ *Hierarchies*

The "base" organization is root and the other organizations are hierarchical. All policies and other resources that reside in a root organization are system-wide and available to all organizations in the cloud.

However, any policies and resources created in other organizations are only available to organizations in the same hierarchy. For example if organizations "Finance" and "HR" are not in the same hierarchy, they can't share any policies.

In general, resources and policies are not strictly owned by any particular organization but instead are shared across all organizations in a sub-tree using a rule of "first-come, first-served". However, unique resources can still be assigned to each organization or tenant.

▶ *RBAC*

Role Based Access Control (RBAC) is a method of restricting or authorizing system access for users based on roles and locales. A role may contain one or more system privileges where each privilege defines an administrative right to a certain type of object (components) in a system. By assigning a user a role, the user inherits the capabilities of the privileges defines in that role. Customers can create custom specific roles.

▶ *Locales*

A locale[6] in UCSM reflects the position of an administrator in an organizational tree and where the privileges of a role can be exercised. By assigning an administrator a certain user role and a locale, administrators can exercise their privileges in a certain sub-organizations defined by the locale.

9.3 Cloud Data Center Facilities

In principle a cloud data center is not different from a "traditional" datacenter described in our books on SAP infrastructures. However containerized datacenters and computing blocks and pods have been developed as alternatives to traditional "data bunkers" poured in concrete.

---

[6] not to be confused with the internationalization of character sets

▶ **Containerized data centers**

A prominent example are the Google container data center[7] housing typically 45,000 servers in 45 water cooled intermodal shipping containers in a hangar for shelter and an external yard for cooling towers, transformers and a diesel generator farm. Consuming 10 MW some sites are selected to be near inexpensive hydroelectric power plants. As the servers, the containers are tailor made and Google filed a patent on the technology.[8]

Similar concepts are available as **modular data center** from Cisco, HP, IBM and Oracle/Sun. Like Google they use the intermodal shipping container format that can be placed anywhere data capacity is needed. The modules are delivered literally ready to run with servers, storage and networking equipment and their own power distribution and cooling systems. The Cisco Containerized Data Center takes additional advantage from converged infrastructure and stateless computing.

▶ **Blocks and pods**

For demands of less than 1,000 servers and transformation of existing datacenters into cloud architectures you can select from smaller solutions like VCE Vblock and FlexPod.

The Vblock Solutions for SAP integrates technologies from Cisco, EMC, and VMware into prefabricated standardized "Compute blocks".

SAP Applications built on FlexPod are pre-tested, and validated solutions which combine technologies from Cisco, NetApp, and VMware.

In addition to the benefits of converged networks and stateless computing both solutions feature storage technologies, which offer data protection, remote replication and snapshots, features that enhance and accelerate testing and development.

9.3.1 How Green Clouds Can Be?

Green is everywhere these days: in the news, politics, fashion, and technology; data centers are no exceptions. So if an enterprise invests in a private cloud infrastructure it should be as green as possible. In trying to save energy, it should be understood how power consumption can be influenced most effectively.

Despite all the green marketing and "energy star" certified power supplies, the enormous increased CPU performance come at the price of an corresponding rise in consumption of electricity. The average wattage per server grew about 9% per year, and the costs for electricity increased about 4% in the last years (mileage would vary on a per-country and/or city basis).

---

[7] http://www.youtube.com/watch?v=zRwPSFpLX8I&feature=related

[8] United States Patent 7,278,273 – however one of the authors installed a computer center in an intermodal container already 20 years ago at an ALCOA plant in Germany

9.3 Cloud Data Center Facilities

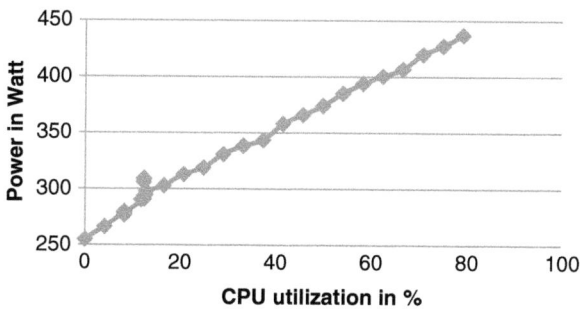

Fig. 9.4 Power consumption in relation to CPU utilization

Today cloud data centers have electricity consumption in the region of a small town. A view on the massive ductwork for the water cooling in a Google datacenter gives you an idea of the investment necessary to pump all this heat out into the air. Therefore savings in the energy consumption do not only save the environment but also the budget.

▶ **Water cooling is back**

The heat generated in a CPU is caused among others by parasitic capacities mentioned above and scale with the clock speed. So adapting the clock speed to the actual demand of computing power will reduce the demand of electrical power accordingly. Technologies like Intel "Speed Step" reduces the power consumed processorin sync with on the actual load as demonstrated at Fig. 9.4 measured for a bachelor thesis[9] under the supervision of one of the authors.

However the CPU counts only for less than 50% of the total power consumption of a server. A consumer of power often forgotten is the main memory. For good reasons this is called volatile memory, without refresh it will get amnesia. Figure 9.5 from the same study shows that the power consumption doesn't change at all with memory utilization.

Similar behavior was measured in the study for other components like the IO system. Because of this even a server which is not utilized at all consumes considerable power. Only a server which is switched off does not consume any power.

Without any doubts increasing the average utilization by virtualization increases efficiency, but due to the typical load curves described in Chap. 3 there will always be resources which will be only utilized during peak hours.

Therefore a green cloud data center is one where servers are temporarily switched off when there is no computing demand. With the stateless computing and service profiles in conjunction with the SAP virtual landscape manager (LVM) such a concept can be easily implemented with UCS.

---

[9] Extension of the SAPS-meter Web Service to provide the possibility of gauging the electric power consumption, Fabian Schneider, University of Cooperative Education Baden-Württemberg

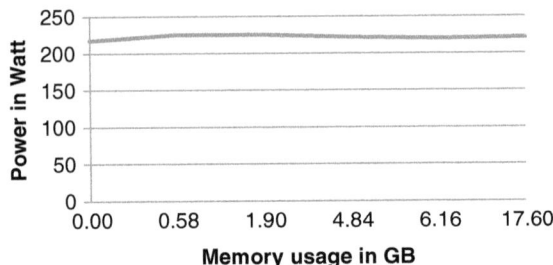

Fig. 9.5 Power consumption in relation of memory utilization

9.4 Summary

The traditional deployment model where the identity of a server is defined by its hardware makes it difficult to re-assign servers to other tasks in a cloud environment. Also many applications like SAP were never meant to be moved to other servers. One of the obstacles is license keys bound to the hardware they are installed on.

- The stateless computing model allows any server to be orchestrated for any role in a cloud. With service profiles, systems can be moved without invalidating the license keys of SAP (and Microsoft).
- Using UCS service profiles SAP systems can be deployed in minutes rather than hours or days.
- A cloud data center is not different from a "traditional" datacenter in regards of security. However in spite of power saving technologies, the extreme high density is a challenge for cooling. Containerized "pods" are alternatives to traditional "data bunkers" poured in concrete.
- The "greenest" cloud data center is the one where unused servers can be reassigned on demand to other applications through service profiles or completely switched off if there is no demand for the resources.

Economic and Legal Aspects of Cloud Computing   10

While the economics of the cloud ultimately promise disruptive business agility at lower apples-to-apples costs in the short term, the converse may also be true. No two organizations are alike, however, necessitating a thoughtful economic analysis informed by legal and other realities.

With regard to the economics of the cloud in the context of SAP's Business Suite applications and NetWeaver technical underpinnings, there is no single right answer for every customer or cloud hosting provider. Cloud computing affects and is just as greatly affected by a number of broad economic and legal factors.

Economic factors may ultimately yield either higher cost or more cost-effective computing, while legal factors will conversely always constrain and dilute any potential cost benefits. Factors spanning capital expenses, enterprise and solution architecture costs, technology costs, staffing and other organizational costs, operations and management expenses, and so on, create a complex cost model.

▶ **Business before technology**

But the economics can't be evaluated on costs alone. The cloud changes the game, finally giving organizations the ability to drive both top-line revenue *and* bottom-line cost metrics. Both the hype and a reasonable amount of the reality surrounding the cloud promises to one day transform how businesses conduct business, including how they might more effectively reach new customers, react to new market demands, better service customer relationships, and so on. To make sense of these two different focus areas – those that essentially affect revenue and those that essentially affect costs – a framework that emphasizes "business before technology" is in order.

Only to the unimaginative or uninformed is the cloud about new technology. Instead, it's about disrupting the competition by accelerating the business's capabilities to adapt to a changing marketplace. How? By failing faster and cheaper.

10.1 Trial and Error-Fast and Cheap

If you walk away remembering only a single theme from this chapter, remember this: use the favorable economics of the cloud to disrupt your competition. In history, all progress has been made through trial and error.

The cloud allows you to go through trial and error cycles much faster and at lower costs until you finally succeed. Utilizing the cloud, that day of success will arrive more quickly, accelerating return on your investment earlier while the competition still wait for approval of the necessary resources.

Cloud computing reduces the barriers to entry for business innovation by enabling new ideas to take hold quickly in an organization and then scale as demand increases.[1] For forward-thinking SAP IT shops, the cloud gives IT the ability to deliver business value more quickly than traditional computing platforms can. The cloud allows IT to scramble and give the business the ability to try new SAP business functionality, pilot new applications and components, test new socially-informed CRM and sales techniques, kick the tires on new methods of closing the accounting books more quickly, or definitively confirm that a system is ready for production loads.

▶ *Try and fail while the competition waits for approval*

In these ways, the cloud provides the business with more velocity and more chances at making a difference in the marketplace. Use the cloud to go after new business as well as to incrementally improve existing customer relationships.

And remember that lower costs, greater convenience, and equivalent functionality are important, but that these attributes alone cannot fundamentally change the way a business competes. Instead, the ability to try and fail fast, try again, fail perhaps yet again, and finally succeed – all at low cost and great velocity – is what makes the cloud a disrupter and a game changer.

10.1.1 Economic Risks and Other Considerations

The cloud holds the promise of being able to change the classic economics of business applications, especially how applications are hosted, how they are operated, and ultimately how they are paid for. As will be discussed, these economics will change over time.

---

[1] Anderson G (2011) Reference Architecture: Business View for SAP on a Private Cloud Infrastructure. Microsoft.

▶ **The cloud may drive costs up as well as down**

As many novelties do, cloud economics may even drive costs *up* (when poorly or inadequately implemented, or when net new services are introduced) just as easily as they may drive costs *down* (when appropriately implemented), increasing new business opportunities and challenges all around. Issues and opportunities related to achieving the appropriate level of technology infrastructure scaling, IT skills, and all around business unit and IT organizational readiness are detailed in this chapter.

10.1.2 Legal Implications

A discussion of cloud economics is incomplete without discussing the legal implications surrounding cloud business, technology, and people considerations. Together, these make the cloud for SAP either an appealing alternative or a horribly wrong choice depending on the specific company and its unique business capabilities and associated application software solutions.

▶ **Managing another level of constraints**

Legal implications represent *constraints* imposed by *Governance, Risk and Compliance* (GRC), sensitive data on intellectual properties, business processes, and people that together add complexity and cost to a cloud solution. In this way, legal factors actually layer another level of economic considerations atop our cloud discussions. Many of these constraining legal factors are also detailed in this chapter.

10.2 Economic Myths, Realities, and Other Observations

The popular press is filled with stories explaining how the cloud promises much, promises little, changes the world, and changes nothing.

With all the misconceptions surrounding the cloud, and a lack of context explaining these misconceptions, it's no wonder that so much confusion surrounds the cloud. Favorite economic myths include:
- Innovative cloud platforms naturally cost less
- Economies of scale are based on volume infrastructure and power discounts
- The cloud requires less power, thereby always facilitating 'green' IT
- Software licensing and payment models are less expensive for the cloud
- The CFO prefers operating expenditures to capital expenditures

A review of the actual truths often obscured within these myths, and the context of each myth, is covered next.

10.2.1 Innovative Cloud Platforms Do Not Necessarily Cost Less

For those customers already hosting their SAP systems on traditional platforms, the idea of adopting a 'new' innovative cloud platform isn't necessarily appealing. This is because, for the status quo, innovation rarely achieves both lower costs *and* greater value.

Those familiar with Clayton Christensen's book *The Innovator's Dilemma*[2] understand that this dilemma is quite normal. Clayton explains that new technologies, approaches, and other innovations initially and necessarily cost *more* (per unit of work, or horsepower, or capability) and actually offer *less* capability. The real benefit to such innovations is instead realized by new or very different customers – those with different needs and probably very different expectations of the new technologies.

▶ *The innovator's dilemma*

For the earliest cloud adopters, for example, trading the lower system availability and stability inherent to those nascent platforms was worth the significantly reduced cost per transaction (or SAPS, dialog steps/h, etc.). More importantly, early adopters recognized the cloud's ability for IT to help the business disrupt the competition and go after new markets, try new methods, fail fast, and ultimately deploy new solutions with greater velocity than previously possible.

As cloud platforms for SAP continue to mature, the trade-offs will certainly continue to shrink, to the point where those who choose to run their SAP systems on today's traditional platforms will be few and far between.

10.2.2 Volume Discounts Rarely Drive Economies of Scale

Large cloud service providers can indeed achieve incrementally superior economies of scale through volume discounts associated with all the bulk power, servers, storage, and network infrastructure they must purchase. With the exception of power, though, these purchases are one-time or somewhat infrequently realized savings.

Instead, *truly transformational* economies of scale come from aggregating inherently different workloads from many different customers representing vastly different industry solutions (IS) or verticals. It's the combination of all three that drive economies of scale, not just volume. As demonstrated in Chap. 3, SAP solutions like ERP, CRM, BW, SCM etc. reflect different kinds of workloads, each with different daily, weekly, and monthly peak loads. Even more so, SAP

---

[2] Christensen, CM (2003) The innovator's dilemma: the revolutionary book that will change the way you do business. Harper Paperbacks.

industry solutions (IS) drive very different peak workloads as well (again, in terms of the time of day, week, or month that the peak is observed).

▶ **Aggregating workloads drive incremental economics at best**

Because these workloads and industry solutions are naturally so different from one another, smart SAP cloud service providers are in luck. They can deploy SAP infrastructures in such a way as to combine their different customer workloads and industry solutions to realize higher infrastructure utilization and more efficient resource pooling at a lower cost per unit of measurement.

For such service providers, this means they can charge more billable kilo-SAPS-hours per infrastructure unit. In this intersection of workloads, solutions, and volume hardware discounts is found the cloud's true economies of scale. Volume discounts represent only a part of this mix.

10.2.3 The Cloud May Not Yield Greener IT for Some Time

As mentioned, intentionally standardized and effectively pooled cloud infrastructures that use energy purchased in bulk can result in a platform that may reduce overall power consumption and therefore an organization's carbon footprint. But this is true, in the short term at least, only for the largest cloud service providers who benefit from the economies of scale and well distributed workload attributes outlined previously.

▶ **Not necessarily greener in the short term**

For less efficiently utilized cloud infrastructures, and certainly for smaller SAP shops that must necessarily invest at scale to justify such a new business delivery platform, the cloud may consume more power and cooling – especially on non-unified infrastructures. Eventually, once a certain size and scale are achieved, the potential for greener IT becomes more realistic.

10.2.4 Cloud Software Licensing Models Remain Unchanged

For cloud IaaS and PaaS, licensing the software necessary to establish a usable platform for SAP remains relatively the same if not more expensive – contrary to the myth, it is certainly not *less* expensive.

Operating systems, hypervisors, databases, integration technologies, bolt-on applications, the SAP application itself, etc. still require run-time software licenses. Hypervisor licenses in particular can represent an enormous incremental expense in the wake fully virtualized server farms.

While pay-as-you-go infrastructure is germane to cloud infrastructure providers, pay-as-you-go licensing is actually quite uncommon. It is much more associated with SaaS or software delivered as a service. For internal IT organizations seeking to deploy a less expensive platform, it is more important than ever to realize that a new presumably less expensive OS or database will therefore actually *add* to the organization's costs. This occurs when the organization is forced to maintain both the old and new platforms during the transition from legacy/traditional platforms to the new cloud platform.

▶ *Pay-as-you-go licensing is still uncommon for IaaS and PaaS*

And the expense may be long-term, too, particularly if the old mainframe and UNIX-based platform must be maintained for a extended time as is often the case because of "political" reasons.

10.2.5 CapEx Versus OpEx May Myths

Avoiding a large capital expenditure may make a difference to new companies with little credit, dwindling first-round funding, or a pressing need for rapidly provisioned computing infrastructure. In these cases, taking on a month-to-month or pay-as-you-go operating expense is quite appealing.

But such a 'cash flow oriented' approach to finances is not always in order. In fact, for large companies investing in private cloud infrastructures for SAP and other mission-critical applications, capital expenses are just a part of doing business.

▶ *Capital expenditures may still be preferable*

In these cases, they simply need to show positive Return on Invested Capital (ROIC). Favorable tax treatment of such expenses can further encourage such investments. The real issue at hand is one of size and scale; at a certain scale, the purchasing power and tax benefits inherent to depreciating capital expenditures can far outweigh the benefits of OpEx-based financing models.

10.3 Business Economics of the Cloud for SAP

While it's fun to debunk myths and drill down into the fundamental truths that give rise to such myths, the "truth" can at times prove even more interesting.

▶ *Analyst predictions*

In 2009, a widely disseminated analyst report concluded that cloud computing economics would only pay off for small and medium businesses (SMBs), and would likely never be appropriate for larger companies and their similarly more sizable IT organizations.

Among other factors, the analyst's position was based on scale. In those early days of the cloud, it was believed that a cost-effective cloud platform absolutely mandated the tremendous scale associated exclusively with public cloud providers.

No other models seemed economically feasible; the capital investment could presumably never be recouped based on workload metrics alone. The analyst concluded that large IT shops interested in outsourcing their systems to cloud providers would pay double what they would pay if they just kept the systems in-house.

On the other hand, smaller organizations could "cloud-source" to their advantage, avoiding the overhead and people costs associated with building and operating an IT organization. The analyst asserted that the required investment in datacenter scale – servers, storage, network, and other infrastructure assets – meant that the cloud would be feasible only for very small companies.

The analyst went so far as to suggest that datacenter scale might never be achieved in certain countries or geographic regions, as the demand required to drive an adequate (and therefore cost effective) supply to make the cloud economically advantageous simply wouldn't exist. Said another way, the need for tremendous scale and the necessary underlying standardization and consistency would preclude big companies from investing in the cloud. Instead, large companies would need to remain on traditional technology and business infrastructures while their smaller counterparts moved their business systems to the cloud.

▶ *The cloud matured faster than the experts expected...*

The analysis was correct on several fronts but missed a few things too. First, it discounted the development of cost-effective private cloud platforms for SAP and other mission-critical business applications, basing their calculations on a popular public cloud provider's costing model. Second, it did not recognize how quickly public cloud pricing would drop in the face of widespread adoption and competition.

The analyst organization also discounted the effect that people-based savings would have on the cloud's economics. Finally, it failed to account for the fact that cloud service providers would mature quickly enough to provide the kind of Service Level Agreements (SLAs) necessary to support SAP and other business applications.

Of course, technology and people economics (both costs and skills) continue to change the cloud landscape (covered later in this chapter). However, the weight and emphasis of several business factors – including macroeconomics and other market drivers, risks, functionality, data sensitivity, role, and business innovation – have been dramatically changing the playing field. Each of these considerations is outlined next.

10.3.1 Macroeconomics and Other Market Drivers

Informal experience and formal studies alike are revealing a significant amount of activity intended to understand cloud economics. Cloud service providers (CSPs) are already beginning to consolidate, and the largest providers are growing faster than ever. The costs of compute and storage continue to drop, while self-contained standardized "data centers in a box" are growing more powerful, more reliable or resilient, and increasingly less expensive per megawatt.

The cost differential between public and private cloud is driving less-critical applications such as tax calculation and enterprise print solutions to the public cloud.

However, as significant as a cost delta may be, the potential risks and loss of business functionality may simply not be worth moving the mission critical components of an SAP system to the public cloud.

10.3.2 Business Risks, Functionality, Data Sensitivity, and Role

While a company may seek to increase its SAP business application agility and lower its infrastructure and operational costs through a cloud deployment model, three important factors need to be evaluated beyond the pure economics: how the cloud influence risks to the business, how the cloud may affect the business application's functionality, and finally the sensitivity of the data being hosted.

- **Risks**. Specific workloads and their data may need to be controlled at a more granular level than other workloads and data. Such workloads and their data warrant a "risk premium" which is essentially an extra cost allocated to the particular cloud model in use.
- **Functionality**. As described in Chaps. 2 and 3, some SAP solutions can be easily hosted on the cloud without affecting the business processes. Other applications are negatively affected (for example, in terms of performance, availability, integration requirements, or the need to provide access to real-time data). Understanding functional impact is paramount to determining which SAP applications are good candidates for the cloud.
- **Data Sensitivity**. Not all applications are a good fit for the cloud simply because of the data they host. Data scramblers, encryption techniques, and so on can certainly be employed to limit data exposure. But it's at a potentially significant cost to performance – as much as 50 % or greater for data-intensive transactions.

While some companies may wish to keep and protect their production SAP systems behind their internal firewalls and brick and mortar datacenter walls, most IT organizations admit that many non-production systems are ideal candidates for the cloud. In some countries however law's may not allow hosting sensitive HR data in the public cloud, even if that data resides on a non-production training, sandbox, or development server.

Besides the rare cases where data are so sensitive that they should never leave the companies premises, the systems used for training users, piloting new SAP components or business functionality, "proof of concept" tests or load testing are all excellent candidates for the cloud. In these cases, the cloud can dramatically increase a key organizational or business metric: time-to-value.

10.3 Business Economics of the Cloud for SAP

By way of example, most SAP IaaS providers can turn around an SAP functional team's request for the resources necessary to test new business capabilities in minutes to hours. Such fast turnaround not only appeases business leaders, but gives the organization the agility necessary to try new projects, pursue new initiatives, inexpensively "fail fast" and try again, and more. This kind of IT responsiveness helps paint the CIO and IT team in a positive light, too – as a partner to the business rather than simply a cost of doing business. IT organizations comfortable using the cloud for non-production SAP systems enable the business to deploy new capabilities faster, reduce its risks, and ultimately show greater and faster business value at less cost than historically possible.

▶ *Not all SAP applications are good candidates for the cloud*

But not all SAP applications or SAP landscape roles are good candidates for the cloud. Besides the HR systems mentioned above, multi-terabyte systems stuck in the middle of the SAP Transport Management System's promote-to-production process, network latency-sensitive applications distributed in hybrid cloud architecture across private and public clouds, or high-performance systems relying on the bursting capabilities of near-line application servers are poor candidates for the public cloud.

10.3.3 Developing Cloud Business Cases for SAP

Developing IT business cases is as much art as science. Historically, many IT projects have been overstated in terms of benefits, and understated in terms of costs. The danger in simply applying ROIC or other narrow or low rigor approaches to developing cloud business cases is multiplied, though, in that the expense and risks related to replatforming, retooling, retraining, and optimizing operations weighs heavily on even the most mature organizations.

The need to develop a cloud business case through the lens of a "real options analysis" (or a similar options valuation method) is instead called for. Real options analysis can address the holistic opportunity surrounding such a transformative business decision as adopting the cloud for SAP. Real options analysis takes into account the various steps and outcomes along the cloud adoption journey; each step is assessed and weighted in terms of financial as well as non-financial benefits.

▶ *Real options analysis circumvents traditional economics exercises*

Real options analysis also demands that each benefit, whether financial or otherwise, be quantifiable, measurable or at least observable. Herein is found the key to cloud business case development, as many cloud benefits are necessarily "soft": increased business agility, responsiveness to new market opportunities, the ability to test new features, the ability to rapidly validate production loads, and more.

Being able to ascribe some kind of value to these benefits helps an IT organization navigate a journey that might otherwise quickly stop once the hard costs associated with servers, network bandwidth, storage, developing and deploying new processes and tools, retraining staff, and so on are assembled. To learn more about real options analysis and valuation, turn to the works of John Ward, Elizabeth Daniels, and Joe Peppard.[3]

10.4 Technology Economics and Considerations

To the novice IT professional or uninformed business user, the cloud is tantamount to new technologies and processes related to taking advantage of those technologies. To the more astute, though, cloud technology considerations play only a supporting role in the overall cloud economics story as outlined next.

10.4.1 Demand, Supply, and the Buying Hierarchy

As described in Chap. 3, an effectively deployed cloud solution flattens the "resource demand" variations. This way, cloud services improves overall infrastructure utilization and increases server utilization rates[4] while lowering provider costing and consumer pricing in the process.

▶ *"Buying hierarchy"*

If the cloud is viewed as a "technology platform" product, then today's cloud platforms represent a natural evolution of a point in time on the technology platform lifecycle curve. This curve can be described as a *Buying Hierarchy*[5] comprised of four phases or stages:
- **Functionality** – The cloud, particularly for SAP, was a late entrant into the technology platform market. Once platforms were functionally adapted for SAP, the competitive platform market for SAP was changed.
- **Reliability** – In the next phase, cloud platform providers competed with one another and with traditional platform providers on reliability because no company would risk replatforming their SAP applications to the cloud in the absence of reasonable reliability and SLAs.
- **Convenience** – After functionality and reliability were established, cloud providers competed on convenience. The ability to easily support SAP applications and the ability to conveniently do business with a particular cloud

---

[3] Ward J, Daniels E, Peppard J (2008) Building better business cases for IT investments. MIS Quarterly Executive.
[4] Slater P (2012) Becoming an effective private cloud provider. Microsoft.
[5] Windmere Associates of San Francisco, California.

10.4 Technology Economics and Considerations

service provider, set it apart from the others. Interestingly, though, with its self-service portals, capacity on demand, automated workflows, and more, the cloud is inherently convenient. Thus, the basis of competition quickly transitioned to the final stage in the *Buying Hierarchy*: price.

- **Price** – Today's cloud service providers continue to leapfrog one another in terms of pricing. New features and capabilities are often brought to bear as well, with the idea that differentiation can help prop up higher relative prices. Such premiums for commodity SAP platforms are difficult to maintain in a market that may not require those specific features or capabilities, though.

The SAP technology platform providers will continue to compete on the basis of price and to a lesser extent on the other three phases of the *Buying Hierarchy*. This state is a natural outcome of a maturing lifecycle.

Only a transformational leap in technology or technical performance, combined with the ability to meet new functional requirements, will be powerful enough to change the market landscape and essentially restart the *Buying Hierarchy's* phases.

10.4.2 Technology Attributes and Challenges

While the concept of the cloud can be nebulous, a true cloud platform or solution will necessarily align to the five essential characteristics, three service models, and four deployment models outlined by the National Institute of Standards and Technology (NIST).[6]

Among other technologies, this includes fast wide-area networks, powerful and inexpensive commodity servers, and high-performance commodity virtualization (though virtualization is orthogonal to cloud implementation, and in some cases not even called for). It also includes specific technical capabilities or constructs such as the ability to pool resources, access resources via a self-service portal or other mechanism, scale out and back in on-demand, and abstract and measure services based on utilization.

The degree to which SAP can natively adhere to these attributes (as described in Chap. 2), versus the investment required by service providers and others to automate these capabilities, will drive each cloud service provider's unique set of cloud economics.

10.4.3 Public Cloud Opportunities and Challenges

NIST describes a public cloud as one in which "the cloud infrastructure is made available to the general public or a large industry group and is owned by an organization selling cloud services."[7] The public cloud is the least expensive of

---

[6] The public cloud is the least expensive of NIST (2011, January) National Institute of Standards and Technology Definition of Cloud Computing (Draft).

[7] NIST (2011, January) National Institute of Standards and Technology Definition of Cloud Computing (Draft).

the various cloud computing models, but it is also the most limiting in terms of infrastructure and platform customization – both of which may increase risks and thus dramatically affect economics. Public clouds are inherently the most scalable, however, in that they not only reflect denser infrastructures and support more customer systems, but reflect different types of workloads with different peak time-frames.

10.4.4 Private Cloud Opportunities and Challenges

While the public cloud's infrastructure can presumably be used most efficiently, it may not be the best choice. Interest in private cloud solutions has grown tremendously in the last several years. An IEC[8] study of projected public and private cloud adoption found that continued uncertainty regarding the potential risks of the public cloud will drive private cloud investment.

The private cloud delivery model justifies its premium by providing more control than the public cloud allows. Unlike the public cloud, a private cloud offers greater ability to customize and share infrastructure, albeit at a higher cost (ultimately, private cloud providers and consumers give up some of the cost benefits inherent to the public cloud; for reasons related to scale, automation capabilities, and people/organizational skills, it is simply not possible to provide private cloud services as inexpensively as public cloud services).

10.4.5 Hybrid Cloud Opportunities and Challenges

NIST views a hybrid as a combination of public and private clouds, but practical experience and the popular press include mixing in traditional platforms as well. For SAP, this more common perspective makes sense. Organizations might wish to maintain their critical SAP ERP system in their own datacenter atop a private cloud and deploy non-critical parts on a public cloud infrastructure.

Deploying non-production systems such as training, business sandboxes, and pilot systems (that do not hold sensitive data) on the public cloud could reduce ongoing infrastructure costs without incurring significant risks. Integrating these different systems into the transport management system add some complexity and administration effort. Assuming business functionality and risks are within acceptable limits, though, designing such a hybrid cloud solution for SAP could make drive significant cost reductions.

Finally, a hybrid SAP architecture could be deployed that seamlessly integrates internally hosted capacity (such as a system's SAP CRM web application servers) with other cloud-based application servers that can be quickly spun up and spun

---

[8] IEC (2011) The cloud computing shift: from custom-built to commodity hosting. The Corporate Executive Board Company.

back down. Such "cloud bursting" or "renting the peak" would reduce the system's fixed costs while enhancing its flexibility and ability to meet unknown peak demands.

▶ **Hybrids clouds for SAP web application servers**

Of course, the potential network latency and application performance implications are tremendous, necessitating thorough load testing to confirm that the bursting process indeed delivers at the necessary service levels. More realistically, a company might initially use such a bursting strategy to address batch workload or other asynchronous processing needs. Once the network and integration framework tying together private and public resources is proven in the real world, using it to deliver real-time computing would eventually become more realistic.

In all three cases, the potential to reduce overall SAP system landscape costs and increase business agility may outweigh the risks and other tradeoffs, making a hybrid cloud solution an ideal (albeit limited) interim state for SAP customers.

10.5 Organizational Economics and Considerations

From an economic perspective, the cloud introduces several organizational considerations. These range from end-user experinece to those affecting internal or external IT providers and their readiness and ability to change.

10.5.1 The Business End-User Community

If done properly, the fact that a once traditionally-hosted SAP system landscape has been relocated to the cloud should be invisible to the business. This inability to distinguish between the SAP infrastructures assumes that performance, availability, reliability, SLAs, and other attributes remain substantially the same.

In practice, though, something will change. It will be necessary to perform ridiculously thorough testing to identify these changes during integration and pre-production testing – well before the system is turned over to its business users.

On the other hand, the cloud should enable a new level of business agility and flexibility that, poorly communicated, could go unrealized. Be sure to let the business know that the new system can scale more quickly, that new resources can be provisioned more quickly, and that the system is ready for new demands. And take advantage of the fact that the cloud automates and streamlines many maintenance tasks, shrinking "application downtime windows" and therefore providing greater system availability and agility to its business users.

10.5.2 Reinventing the Internal SAP IT Organization

Despite the advances in cloud services, today's cloud solutions present a number of challenges for SAP IT organizations. These range from managing virtual machine image sprawl to creating effectively designed composite applications, connecting to legacy and off-premises applications, and connecting to third-party services and service providers.[9]

To stay focused on the business's most critical capabilities and most important applications delivering those capabilities, evaluate moving less-critical or non-differentiating systems to the cloud. Each business unit might make a strategic decision to focus exclusively on maintaining only their core or differentiating business systems in-house, and outsourcing or "cloud sourcing" the remaining non-core business systems. A forward-thinking incumbent IT organization can use that opportunity to compete with the cloud providers and traditional outsourcing providers by offering to:

▶ *Reinventing the SAP IT organization*

- Host the business's non-core systems on a private cloud platform.
- Manage a third party cloud hosting provider (which presumably might be leveraged by multiple business units).

10.5.3 Organizational Process Discipline or Hardening

The primary principle behind hardening an organization – increasing its robustness – relates to process discipline. How the SAP IT organization works to achieve its strategic goals and objectives, realizes its vision, and meets the needs of the business over time reflects its organizational process discipline or hardening.

Said another way, organizational hardening is related to the ability to execute, not organizational stagnation or calcification. This principle is enabled through process efficacy or process diligence. For example, the ability to consistently deploy an SAP instance is made possible through maintaining skills, establishing and automating processes, and maintaining those skills and processes.

▶ *Organizational hardening and process discipline*

The organization must seek out opportunities to maintain its skills, automate the repetitive, and carefully document the exceptions. Finally, take care to ensure that the SAP leadership team does not devolve into a mindset that focuses on

---

[9] Slater P (2012) Becoming an effective private cloud provider. Microsoft.

maintaining the status quo (including its own inevitable bureaucracy, which itself needs to be reviewed and refined regularly) at the expense of the business itself.

10.5.4 Cloud Service Providers and Hosters

External cloud service providers and traditional outsourcers alike are looking for new ways to add value for their customers. The private cloud model enables external cloud providers to build and offer a value-added "hosted private cloud" solution for specific industry solutions, industry verticals, or application providers such as SAP.

Hosted private clouds can be feasible when the pure economics related to achieving scale are simply not possible for a small organization or an organization without the necessary capital to deploy at scale.

In these cases, putting together a pay-as-you-go hosted private cloud contract with a cloud service provider yields a win-win for everyone. Companies can be confident that their SAP application provider is an expert in a particular or unique set of business applications and processes, requirements, regulations, and so on necessary to remain in business and hopefully grow the business.

Similarly, hosted private cloud providers can build a differentiating business model that brings in new customers as well as incremental revenue from existing customers. And because the cloud deployment model is presumably exercised at scale, both parties should benefit from the cost/revenue model.

10.5.5 Evaluating Organizational Readiness for Change

Before an organization can be asked to adopt a new method of working (whether a business unit or an IT department), the organization's readiness for change and staffing matters need to be considered in the same way that business and technology realities must be accounted for.

Most IT organizations are ill-prepared for the cloud. Improperly prepared IT organizations may simply reject new technologies, processes, and ways of working just as a human body may reject a new donor organ. In the wake of such a rejection, the IT organization could invest a tremendous amount of time and money and still remain mired in its status quo. Worse still, a fumbling IT organization could cause material business losses that affect the company's brand, hurt its customers, and alienate its partners and suppliers.

▶ **Readiness to change**

The key is to properly scope the breadth of organizational factors that will be affected, followed by putting together a plan that builds up each factor. Various change models can be useful in these situations. Effective models include factors, steps, cycles, or processes that, when followed, give an organization the framework and step-wise guidance necessary to make itself amenable to change.

10.5.6 An Effective Model for SAP IT Organizational Change

The popular Burke-Litwin Organization Change and Performance Model has been used time and again to help organizations evaluate their readiness and prepare for change.

▶ *The Burke-Litwin change model*

The model includes a number of factors that, combined, help describe an organization's ability to change. These factors are assembled in two groups: those that help the organization transform radically, and those that help it incrementally evolve. Burke and Litwin[10] adopted the idea of using transformational and transactional factors to help give focus to those change factors that affect discontinuous or transformational change against those more aligned towards enabling evolutionary or transactional change.

▶ *Transformational factors*

The five transformational factors are revolutionary change agents. These factors typically affect the very nature of the organization and are therefore powerfully impactful. The Burke-Litwin model's transformational factors include:
- **The external environment.** How the organization accounts for the specific elements of the external environment that will or could directly or indirectly affect the organization
- **Mission and strategy.** How the organization's employees perceive the organization's purpose
- **Leadership.** How employees view the organization's formal and informal role models
- **Organizational culture.** How an organization's values, rules, and customs unite to govern the organization's behavior
- **Performance (organizational).** How well the organization as a whole executes its fundamental business capabilities

Conversely, according to Burke and Litwin, IT leaders have at their disposal several organizational levers that can affect more incremental change. Less dangerous in the hands of novices, these transactional factors nonetheless must but be manipulated carefully as well. In the balance hang the keys to continuous improvement, effective performance, and individual satisfaction.

The Burke-Litwin change model's transactional factors and their effect on organizational change include:

---

[10] Burke WW, Litwin GH (1992) A causal model of organizational performance and change. J Manag 18(3):532–545.

- **Management practices.** How well managers deliver against the organization's strategy
- **Structure.** How control, responsibility, decisions, and authority are overtly and informally disseminated throughout the organization (more than just organizational hierarchy)
- **Systems and procedures.** How operational policies and procedures help or hinder the organization
- **Work-unit climate.** How employee relationships, thought patterns, and role perspectives combine to create the organization's unique collection of "work places" (work climate is deemed central to the model[11]; it is the "foreground" counterpart to an organization's "background" culture). Work climate includes capabilities, biases, self-efficacy, and so on.
- **Motivation.** How willing individuals are to work (and understanding the means of triggering such willingness) to achieve the organization's goals
- **Individual needs and values.** How employees view their roles in terms of job satisfaction and opportunities for job enrichment
- **Task and individual skills.** How well employee skills map to their specific roles
- **Performance (individual).** How well individuals execute their roles in support of the business

Interestingly, the "performance" factor is viewed as a single factor with both transformational and transactional aspects: one in terms of the organization, and one in terms of individuals.

By carefully considering and adjusting each factor, the Burke-Litwin model is ideal for managing IT teams responsible for high risk business and mission critical systems – especially teams that ultimately must transform themselves to stay relevant.

The many-to-many relationships between all of these factors helps put into context the degree of impact that changing one factor might have on several others. Review a figure of the Burke-Litwin change model at: http://wikiworldbook.com/global-address-book/Burke-Litwin to more clearly visualize each change factor and its relationships to other factors.

10.5.7 Organizational Skills and Staffing

Once an organization is positioned for successful change, it needs to be properly trained, retooled, and perhaps even restaffed (if the current personnel are unable to successfully bridge the transition).

Every traditional IT team will be affected as the organization seeks to transform itself into a vehicle for architecting, planning, building, deploying, managing,

---

[11] Burke WW (2002) Organization change: theory and practice. Sage, London.

operating and upgrading SAP in the form of a cloud service providers or internal Service Delivery Organization (SDO).

10.6 The Legal Landscape for SAP Cloud Computing

The legal landscape for SAP cloud computing introduces a number of constraints. These can be loosely grouped into Governance, Risk, Compliance, and geographic constraints, data considerations, and people considerations. This section examines each of these, and concludes with the need for developing a legally-informed cloud economics plan.

10.6.1 Governance, Risk, Compliance, and Geographic Constraints

In the context of legal considerations for SAP on the cloud, many constraints exist. Key to these is governance, risk, and compliance (GRC) constraints, which combined relate to risk management and corporate accountability. Further, geographic constraints – those related to specific countries or geographies – are becoming increasingly important to understand.

▶ *GRC and the U.S. Patriot Act*

Countries may pass laws and other regulations that impact the ability to effectively use their public cloud resources. For example, the U.S. Patriot Act can presumably be used to force U.S. cloud providers to disclose data to U.S. homeland security, even if the data is generated and stored outside of the United States.

Cloud providers operating their data centers on U.S. soil are subject to this as well. For example, if a Belgian SAP hosting provider were to place their customers' data under the control of a U.S. entity or subsidiary, they could presumably be held liable for any subsequent data release.

Thus, despite the 1967 U.S. Supreme Court decision in Katz v. United States (giving U.S. citizens the right to privacy), such rights can be quickly suspended in the name of preserving security.

Other countries have passed or are in the process of enacting similar laws and regulations as well, requiring data to stay within their national boundaries for example.

▶ *U.S. FDA validation requirements*

Further, certain industries within specific countries and geographies are also controlled more stringently than others. Government agencies and other entities, such as the U.S. Food and Drug Administration (FDA) have long required that pharmaceutical companies "validate their business systems" to ensure that the system, its infrastructure, and its data can be programmatically and systematically recreated or restored in the event of a system failure, corruption, or catastrophe.

Applying these principles to systems hosted on the cloud can incur a tremendous amount of complexity if the systems are not properly designed, deployed, tested, validated, and clearly documented.

10.6.2 Internal GRC Considerations

The previous section focused on GRC limitations primarily associated with company-external governance bodies and rules. But internal limitations established by the company or its IT organization's Legal/GRC department can weigh heavily on SAP cloud adoption, whether on an internal private cloud, hosted private cloud, public cloud, or hybrid.

The GRC department should have in place a set of filters or gates useful in evaluating an application or platform from various GRC dimensions (both for internal analysis and external uses).

▶ GRC filters, gates, and checklists

For example, one of our favorite customers utilizes a virtualization matrix that, among other dimensions, includes data security questions. At each gate, the application or platform is evaluated.

Poorer GRC alignment or compliance yields a higher score than higher alignment or compliance. Once a particular points threshold is exceeded, the application or platform "fails" and is therefore not allowed to be virtualized.

Another customer uses a checklist in a similar fashion, and adheres to the U.S. baseball analogy of "three strikes and you're out." These are examples of applying internal guidance that effectively limits the cloud choices an IT organization can pursue on behalf of its business stakeholders.

10.6.3 Data and Security Considerations

Data considerations include more than country-specific laws and regulations. Data can also be considered too sensitive to be hosted outside of the confines and control of an organization. If may be physically or logically difficult to access.

High quality or sufficient bandwidth may be unavailable in certain geographic locations. Finally, the amount of data or the monthly growth in data might preclude effectively hosting data in a location that's sensitive to network latency, impacting the ability to consistently or legally access the data in a timely manner.

Safeguarding corporate and customer data is only the tip of the iceberg. The growing number of legal compliance requirements, the ability to audit data trails, and safeguarding that data as it's moved between secured sites all conspire to create a complex web of challenges.

Data needs to be encrypted and protected as it enters the SAP system, as it's moved between database and application servers, as its cached in application servers and stored in a database, and as it's moved from the database server to backup resources (other disks, tapes, offsite locations, and so on).

Printed data needs to be physically safeguarded just as its electronic counterpart. Beyond encryption, companies may need to deploy Rights Management and Identity Management solutions to further protect their sensitive data.

Not surprising, security and compliance concerns are often cited as the greatest barriers to moving to the cloud, particularly the public cloud. An organization with special data-security needs or regulatory-compliance requirements spanning data encryption, user access, and incident response, may not be comfortable moving its critical SAP applications and workloads to the public cloud in the short term.

In these cases, a private cloud could prove useful, allowing an organization to control security and compliance and even simplify data recovery while delivering most of the benefits of cloud computing.[12]

10.6.4 People Considerations

Similar to other GRC concerns, organizations might be legally unable to employ people in certain countries. Beyond simple citizenship requirements, specific security classifications may be required as well, and so on.

▶ **ITAR: a classic people issue**

A long-time example can be found in the U.S. International Traffic in Arms Regulations (ITAR), which prohibits non-U.S. citizens from supporting systems related to national defense or the military. Thus, despite the fact that nearly every SAP ERP system supports general business processes such as marketing and engineering (which are not subject to ITAR), for companies using SAP to develop, manage, procure, or simply support business processes tied to national defense or the military, the entire SAP ERP system is off limits to all but U.S. citizens. For global defense contractors, this type of regulation significantly limits outsourcing and cloud hosting alternatives.

A similar example are German statutory health insurance funds ("gesetzliche Krankenkassen") forced by law that systems management has to be provided at least from a country of the European community.

---

[12] Anderson G (2011) Reference architecture: business view for SAP on a private cloud infrastructure. Microsoft.

10.6.5 Developing a Legally-Informed Cloud Economics Plan

Before a cloud strategy for SAP can be considered, develop a reasonable economic plan informed by the organization's GRC, geographic, data, people, and other legal realities.

Even a high-level financial plan – sometimes called a rough order of magnitude or ROM plan – can help an organization determine the general investment likely necessary to adopt a viable cloud strategy, including whether that investment is directionally aligned with the organization's investment appetite.

A reasonable plan should reflect the factors above and be framed in terms of the business, technical, and organizational matters outlined in this chapter.

Note that most of the major analysts agree that economics (both cost and revenue) represent one of the foundational pillars of business value, and that the key to cloud adoption resides in accelerating the time-to-business-value.

Only by understanding the cloud's underlying economic metrics can companies deploy a feasible business-enabling and agile cloud platform for their SAP business applications and components.

10.7 Summary

This chapter outlined several of the primary economic and legal factors germane to running SAP on the cloud. Spanning business, technology, and organizational matters, the opportunities for increased business agility and lower costs are weighed down in the short term by significant one-time and ongoing investments.

Further, the need to inform those economics through legal, GRC, geographic, data, and people considerations, and to take into account an organization's readiness and ability to change, complicates cloud economics further. The chapter concluded with a look at several cloud myths and the realities surrounding those myths.

Cloud computing reduces the barriers to entry for business innovation by enabling new ideas to take hold quickly in an organization and then scale as demand increases. The authors believe that in the next few years, companies with new ideas (to create new revenue streams, open new channels, create new products, and so on) will be able to test their ideas and get them out faster to the marketplace.

▶ **Conclusion**

The organization may respond to new business needs, and subsequently develop new business capabilities, in a fraction of the time needed to do so in a traditional environment. Worst case, they will "fail faster," another benefit in that less time and fewer resources are wasted on ideas that fail to pan out. Either way, a sound cloud strategy will increase a business organization's ability to try new ideas and essentially reinvent itself based on those ideas, markets, and opportunities that prove successful.

Ultimately, the cloud enables internal IT service providers who have deployed private clouds for their SAP systems to focus more on innovation and continuous improvement for the business. This elevates their role and value from mere IT professionals to business-enabling IT partners to the business. And by focusing on strategic innovation rather than more tactical operations, the internal IT organization becomes a place where both IT and business-oriented roles can flourish.

About the Authors

Dr.-Ing. Michael Missbach is the head of the SAP Cisco Competence Center in Walldorf, Germany. With 14 years of SAP experience, his work focuses currently on HANA, and unified and stateless computing infrastructures for mission critical applications in public and private cloud scenarios. As a senior consultant he was responsible for the development of adaptive SAP infrastructures and the SAPS-meter Web service. Earlier, he worked as IT Superintendent for ALCOA and implemented outsourcing and network projects for GE. He studied Mechanical Engineering at the University of Karlsruhe and received his doctorate in Materials Science at what has become now the Karlsruhe Institute of Technology (KIT). Besides this book where he acted as lead author, provided the concept and wrote Chaps. 2, 3, 8 and 9 he published also books on SAP hardware, SAP system operation, adaptive SAP infrastructures and SAP on Windows.

Josef Stelzel is a Senior Architect at REALTECH in Walldorf, Germany. In his job, he is regularly engaged in customer projects like IT optimization, migrations or upgrades around SAP infrastructures. These projects typically address the use cases of new technology as well as the operational aspects and in many cases also the risks associated with these technologies. His experience with SAP dates back to the early days of Release 2.2. As a consultant, he supported implementation of SAP systems and creation of operating concepts in large corporations and collaborated closely with SAP developers on infrastructure solutions. Over the past 10 years, he has published a number of books on SAP infrastructures and operation, for this book he wrote Chaps. 1 and 6.

Mark Tempes is a Senior Architect and leads the SAP NetWeaver consulting team at Hewlett-Packard Enterprise Services South Pacific. He has more than 11 years of experience in the SAP service market and his main focus is the management, delivery and sales of large scale SAP NetWeaver engagements. Mark has managed implementation teams in Europe, Asia and Australia primarily for enterprise customers of Hewlett-Packard. He has both governance and sales responsibility and manages the commercial aspects for initiatives on which his team is engaged. In his current role, he leads initiatives around SAP on Hewlett-Packard's  cloud and utility offerings including the transition, management and delivery of technical SAP projects from bid-phase through design and implementation, to go-live and support, he wrote Chap. 7.

Dr George W. Anderson serves as the managing architect and senior director for Microsoft's mission critical IP development team. He is an accomplished consulting professional with 15 years of SAP experience spanning business application architecture, deployment, organizational transformation, innovation and operational excellence initiatives, and more. A frequent speaker at conferences and industry events, George's perspectives on SAP implementation and support are considered by many to be the reference standard for SAP projects around the world. He has authored or co-authored numerous books, articles, and other papers relevant to how technology solutions may be used in conjunction with SAP to solve complex  business problems. George's aspirations are modest: To redefine what it means to architect, build, and operate the next generation of platforms underpinning mission-critical applications. He and his team are actively developing the architectural patterns and principles capable of enabling the kind of business agility and awareness that IT has been promising for years and business enterprises need more than ever. For this book he wrote Chaps. 5 and 10. You can reach him at george.anderson@microsoft.com.

Cameron Gardiner is a developer working for Microsoft SQL Server R&D team based in Tokyo Japan. His role is to run Microsoft's customer facing development programs such as "First Customer Shipment" of new releases of Windows, SQL Server and new technologies such as SQL Server 2012 Column Store, Hyper-V 3.0 and cloud deployments.

Prior to joining Microsoft he worked as a SAP Basis Consultant covering UNIX, Oracle and DB2 platforms. Cameron is a contributor to the popular SAP on SQL Server blog and has written numerous whitepapers on topics ranging from Hardware Technologies to Securing SAP systems on Microsoft platforms.

He is a regular speaker at events and is an instructor teaching a course on SAP on Microsoft platforms to several hundred students per year. His ambition is to transfer knowledge to allow customers to modernize their Business Critical Systems and benefit from modern high performance commodity platforms and cloud deployment options. For this book he wrote Chap. 4.

Index

A

ACC. *See* Adaptive computing controller (ACC)
Active directory domain (AD) service
  defined, 77
  factors, 76–77
  upload policy, SCW transform command, 79
  usage to windows, 78–79
Adaptive computing controller (ACC), 23–24
AD service. *See* Active directory domain (AD) service
Amazon Machine Images (AMI), 110–111
Amazon Web Services (AWS)
  Amazon Availability Zones, 111, 112
  Amazon EC2, 75
  AMI, 110–111
  AZs, 130–131
  backup/restore, 129
  CloudWatch, 131
  defined, 7–8
  description, 110
  Elastic Block Store (EBS) storage, 112
  Elastic Compute Cloud (EC2), 110
  ephemeral storage, 112
  monitoring, 131
  Network–Amazon VPC, 128
  physical access, datacenters, 74
  service levels, 132
  shared responsibility model, 73
  Simple Storage Server (S3) storage, 111
  storage
    Amazon EBS snapshots, 128
    Amazon S3, 128
    EBS storage, 127
  virtual instances, 74
  virtual machines, 131–132
AMI. *See* Amazon Machine Images (AMI)
Appliances, SAP
  Duet and Alloy, 29–30
  SAP Business Warehouse Accelerator, 30–31
  SAP High Performance Analytical Appliance, 31–37
Availability management, SAP
  downtimes, 62
  MTBF and MTTR, 62
  parallel components, 62–63
  planned downtimes, 63
  resources, disaster, 63–64
  serial components, 62
  stability, 64
Availability zones (AZs), 130–131
AWS. *See* Amazon Web Services (AWS)
AZs. *See* Availability zones (AZs)
Azure Storage
  accession, 108
  account settings, 109
  blobs, tables and queues, 109
  capacity, 108
  description, 108
  geographic replication, 109

B

BO. *See* Business objects (BO)
Business ByDesign (ByD), 29
Business economics, cloud computing
  analyst predictions, 186–187
  cost delta, 188
  IT business cases, 189
  macroeconomics, 187–188
  people-based savings, 187
  real options analysis, 189–190
  risks, functionality and data sensitivity, 188–189
  SAP applications/landscape roles, 189
Business objects (BO), 28

Business Suite, SAP
  SAP CPM, 22
  SAP CRM, 20
  SAP ERP/SAP ECC, 19
  SAP GRC, 23
  SAP NetWeaver, 24–27
  SAP PLM, 22
  SAP SCM, 20–21
  SAP Solution Manager (SSM), 23–24
  SAP SRM, 21–22
Business warehouse accelerator (BWA), 30–31
Buying Hierarchy
  convenience, 190–191
  description, 190
  functionality, 190
  price, 191
  reliability, 190
BWA. *See* Business warehouse accelerator (BWA)
ByD. *See* Business ByDesign (ByD)

C

Cache misses, 33
CCMS. *See* Change and configuration management system (CCMS)
Change and configuration management system (CCMS)
  business and IT lifecycle, 87
  business applications, 84
  cloud infrastructure, 84
  data types, 85
  elements, 84–85
  IT and business accountability and alignment, 87
  logical systems, 84
  organizational change (*see* Organizational management, CCMS)
  public cloud network latency, 86
  technological changes (*see* Technology management, CCMS)
CISC. *See* Complex instruction set computers (CISC)
Cisco Application Control Engine (ACE)
  high performance SSL, 155
  load balancing consolidation, 155
  optimized application server selection, 154–155
  resilient user connectivity, 155
  TCP reuse, 155
  WAN acceleration, 155–156
Cloud computing
  IaaS, 7–8
  internet area, 3

  iron, commodity
    dinosaur, stone age, 2
    settlements and agriculture, 2
  PaaS, 8
  performance and address space, 4
  private clouds, 10–12
  public cloud
    defined, 6–7
    SAP, 8–9
    SaaS, SAP, 9–10
  service orientation, IT, 6
  tailored service offerings, 9
  virtualization
    abstraction and pooling of resources, 5
    IT services, 5
Cloud data center
  blocks and pods, 177
  containerized data centers, 178
  data bunkers, 177
  energy star, 178
  green cloud data center, 179
  intel "Speed Step", 179
  power consumption, CPU, 179
  water cooling, 179
Cloud deployment models, 72
Cloud operation, stateless computing
  adaptive SAP infrastructure, 173
  Cisco UCS, configuration policies, 173, 174
  global policies, 173
  identity pools (IDPools), 173–174
  MAC pools, 174
  SAP system operation, 176
  server pools, 175–176
  UUID Suffix pools, 174
  WWNN, WWPN pools, 174–175, 176
Cloud services
  attributes, 101
  characteristics, 101–102
  IaaS, 102–103
  models, 102
  on-demand self-service, 102
  PaaS, 102
  SaaS, 102
Cloud standards
  physical move, infrastructure, 119
  virtualization, 119–120
  VMs, 120
COBIT. *See* Control objectives for information and related technology (COBIT)
Complex instruction set computers (CISC), 2
Composite applications, 17
Control objectives for information and related technology (COBIT), 71
Converged network adapters (CNAs), 161

Index

Corporate performance management (CPM), 22
CPM. *See* Corporate performance management (CPM)
CRM. *See* Customer relationship management (CRM)
Customer relationship management (CRM)
    call center, 20
    cloud, 20
    web-shop, 20
Cybercrime, 67

D
De-militarized zones (DMZ), 3
DMZ. *See* De-militarized zones (DMZ)
Dual In-Line Memory Modules (DIMM), 148

E
Economic and legal aspects, cloud computing
    business (*see* Business economics, cloud computing)
    business before technology, 181–182
    classic economics, business applications, 182
    constraints, 183
    costs, 183
    description, 181
    economic myths (*see* Economic myths, cloud computing)
    legal landscape (*see* Legal landscape, SAP cloud computing)
    organizational (*see* Organizational economics, cloud computing)
    technology (*see* Technology economics, cloud computing)
    trial and error cycles, 182
Economic myths, cloud computing
    CapEx *vs.* OpEx, 186
    description, 183
    greener IT, 185
    innovative cloud platforms, 184
    licensing models, 185–186
    pay-as-you-go licensing, 186
    volume discounts, 185–186
Enterprise core component (ECC). *See* Enterprise resource planning (ERP)
Enterprise portal (EP), 60–61
Enterprise resource planning (ERP)
    business processes, 19
    ECC, cloud, 19
    industry solutions, 19
EP. *See* Enterprise portal (EP)
ERP. *See* Enterprise resource planning (ERP)

F
Fabric controllers (FC)
    control and monitor, new node, 105
    running role, 106
    utility (UFC), 104
    Web and Worker roles, 106
    Windows Azure OS, 105
Fibre Channel over Ethernet (FCoE)
    advantage, 158
    bandwidth, 157
    description, 157
    implementation, 158
    "lossy" and "loss-less" Ethernet, 158

G
Government-risk-compliance (GRC)
    filters, gates, and checklists, 199
    and U.S. Patriot Act, 198
GRC. *See* Government-risk-compliance (GRC)
Greenfield projects, 48

H
HANA. *See* High performance ANalytical Appliance (HANA)
High performance ANalytical Appliance (HANA)
    cloud, 37
    compression, 35
    database, 34
    delivery, 36–37
    legal business report, 32
    main memory, 35
    memory, 32–33
    OLAP, 33–34
    OLTP, 33
    recognition reaction time, 31
    response times, 31
    restore, 36
    row *vs.* column orientation, 33
    savepoints and logs, 36
    volatile and persistent data storage, 35
Hypervisors security, 81

I
IaaS. *See* Infrastructure as a Service (IaaS)
Information security management system (ISMS), 71
Infrastructure as a Service (IaaS)
    AWS, 7–8, 110
    Azure Storage, 108
    description, 102

Intel® Turbo Boost Technology
  description, 143
  hyper-threading, 143
  physical *vs.* logical CPU utilization, 143
Internet Small Computer System Interface (iSCSI)
  description, 159
  10 Gigabit, 159
  NAS, 157
  vs. NFS, 159
  storage connectivity, 160
  Sybase ASE database, 159
Inter processor Communication (IPC), 161
iSCSI. *See* Internet Small Computer System Interface (iSCSI)
ISMS. *See* Information security management system (ISMS)
IT service management reference model, 41–42

K
Knowledge warehouse (KW), 26
KW. *See* Knowledge warehouse (KW)

L
Landscape & virtualization management (LVM), 23–24
Legal landscape, SAP cloud computing
  data and security considerations, 199
  GRC
    filters, gates, and checklists, 199
    and U.S. Patriot Act, 198
  legally-informed cloud economics plan, 201
  people considerations, 201
  U.S. FDA validation requirements, 199
LVM. *See* Landscape & virtualization management (LVM)

M
MAC. *See* Media access control (MAC)
Markov chain model, 46
Master-data management (MDM), 27
MDM. *See* Master-data management (MDM)
Mean time between failures (MTBF), 62
Mean time to repair (MTTR), 62
Media access control (MAC)
  identity pool, 173–174
  meta-data, 172
  SAN, 174
  service profile, 169
  UCSM, 170

MI. *See* Mobile infrastructure (MI)
Microsoft Private Cloud
  building blocks, 114, 115
  description, 114
  Microsoft System Center
    App Controller 2012, 115
    Operations Manager 2012, 115
    Orchestrator 2012, 115
    Service Manager 2012, 115
    Virtual Machine Manager 2012 (VMM), 115
Mobile infrastructure (MI), 27
MTBF. *See* Mean time between failures (MTBF)
MTTR. *See* Mean time to repair (MTTR)

N
NetWeaver
  BW, cloud, 25
  characterization, 24
  InfoCubes, 24–25
  portal, cloud, 25–26
  SOA, 17
  TREX, 26
Network attached storage (NAS), 157
Network file system (NFS), 157
Networks
  cloud implementation, 153
  description, 153
  FCoE (*see* Fibre Channel over Ethernet (FCoE))
  iSCSI (*see* Internet Small Computer System Interface (iSCSI))
  server, 153
  storage, 153
  user (*see* User network)
Non-uniform memory access (NUMA), 144

O
OLAP. *See* Online analytical processing system (OLAP)
OLTP. *See* Online transaction processing system (OLTP)
Online analytical processing system (OLAP), 34
Online transaction processing system (OLTP), 33
Organizational economics, cloud computing
  The Burke-Litwin change model, 196
  business end-user community, 193
  cloud service providers and hosters, 195
  organizational process discipline/hardening, 194–195
  organization's readiness for change and staffing matters, 195

Index

SAP IT organizations, 194
  skills and staffing, 197–198
  transactional factors, 197
  transformational factors, 196
Organizational management, CCMS
  help desk and operations, 97–98
  human involvement, minimization, 95–96
  IT's process discipline, 99–100
  organizational change processes, 96
  outsource and augment, 98
  real life experience, 98–99
  SAP
    service operations, 93–94
    staffing backup, 96–97
  staffing paradigms, 98
  technology perspectives, 94–95
  ultra-lean service operation organizations, 93

P

PaaS. *See* Platform as a Service (PaaS)
Performance management, SAP
  Queue theory, 46
  response time
    cloud provider, 44
    CPU load, 44–46
    database size, 52
    productivity, 43
    transactions, 52
    users, 45
Phishing, 70
PI. *See* Process integration (PI)
Platform as a Service (PaaS), 102, 103
  SAP, 8
  Windows Azure, 8
PLM. *See* Product lifecycle management (PLM)
Predicting the system load
  Greenfield sizing, 48
  Quicksizer, 50–51
  seasonal peak loads, 50
  transaction based sizing, 49–50
  users, 48–49
Private cloud infrastructures, SAP
  landscapes (*see* SAP landscapes)
  maturity, 137
  networks (*see* Networks)
  platforms, 137–138
  server architectures (*see* Server architectures)
  storage system (*see* Storage system, SAP)
  UCS (*see* Unified Computing System (UCS))
  utility consumer, 137

Private clouds
  assessment, 103
  benefits, 81
  vs. classic outsourcing, 11–12
  development, 113
  FlexPod, 81
  implementations, 113
  Microsoft Private Cloud, 114–115
  Off-premises operations, 10–11
  On-premises operations, 10
  and public (*see* Public clouds)
  resource requirements, 113
  tenant user access, 82
  vs. traditional IT processes, 113
  VMware vCloud, 115–116
Process integration (PI)
  and EP, 60–61
  SAP NetWeaver, 27
Product lifecycle management (PLM), 22
Public clouds
  AWS (*see* Amazon Web Services (AWS))
  cloud services (*see* Cloud services)
  defined, 6–7
  and private (*see* Private cloud)
  SAP
    Amazon virtual private cloud, network, 128
    application requirements, 123–124
    applications, 119
    AWS (*see* Amazon Web Services (AWS))
    AZs, 130–131
    cloud APIs, 121–122
    loud application programming interfaces, 121
    NetWeaver Cloud, 134–135
    office-like-apps/services, 117
    project hecatonchires, and moonshot, 133–134
    Project Titanium, 135–136
    service and infrastructure, 118
    VM, 120
  security
    Amazon AWS, 73–75
    automation and management, 75–81
    patches, 80
    protection, windows kernel and main memory, 79–80
    running system, 80
  technologies, 103
  and utility computing, 101
  Windows Azure (*see* Windows Azure)

Q
Queue theory, 46

R
RBAC. *See* Role based access control (RBAC)
Red Dog Frontend (RDFE), 106
"Red Hat Network Satellite", 76
"Red Hat Update Infrastructure", 76
Role based access control (RBAC)
  physical infrastructure, 176–177
  role, locales, 177
R/3 to HANA. *See also* High performance ANalytical Appliance (HANA)
  BO (*see* Business objects (BO))
  building, cloud infrastructure:, 38
  data analysis, 16–17
  database, 18

S
SaaS. *See* Software as a Service (SaaS)
SAP
  application requirements
    availability and performance, 124
    business criticality, 123–124
    integration and interfacing requirements, 124
    organizational and operational requirements, 124
  applications, 118–122, 169
  AWS (*see* Amazon Web Services (AWS))
  AZs, 130
  COBIT, 71
  compliance and corporate governance, 70–71
  customer control, IaaS, 72–73
  cybercrime, 67
  defined, 39
  early watch reports
    hardware configuration, 53
    performance indicators, 53
    resource consumption, 54
  EP and PI, 60–61
  external threats, 67–68
  founders, 15
  HANA (*see* High performance ANalytical Appliance (HANA))
  hypervisors, 81
  infrastructure, hardening, 72
  internal backend systems, 121
  internal threats, 68
  ISMS, 71
  IT service management reference model, 41–42

KW (*see* Knowledge warehouse (KW))
license keys, 167
load profiles
  analytical systems, 60
  SAP BW systems, 58, 60
  SCM system, 60
measurement, 39–40
monitoring function, 131
mule and bag, 47–48
mySAP.com, 17
NetWeaver Cloud, 134–135
non-technical threads, 70
PaaS/SaaS, 117
performance management, 43–46
prediction, 40
principles, 64
private cloud, 81–82
project hecatonchires, 133–134
public clouds (*see* Public clouds, security)
SAPS (*see* SAP Application Performance Standard (SAPS))
service level management, 42–43
sizing, measurement, 52–54
sourcing and hosting options, 122–123
sourcing options, 123
system operation
  locales, 177
  organisations, 176–177
  RBAC, 177
  resources and policies, 177
technical attacks, 69–70
types, 126–127
vendor-logins, 120
windows kernel and main memory, 79–80
SAP Application Performance Standard (SAPS)
  horsepower, SAP system, 47
  release-independent, 47
  SAPS-meter, 54–58
SAP central services (SCS), 89
SAP landscapes
  database licenses, 141–142
  description, 138
  instances and processes, 139
  special configuration, 139
  system architecture, 139–140
  systems, 138
  2-tier *vs.* 3-tier, 140–141
SAPS-Meter
  architecture, 56
  features, 54–55
  subscription based payment, 57
  web service, 56
SAP solution manager (SSM)
  ACC & LVM, 23–24
  defined, 23

Index

SAP solutions for small and medium companies
  SAP All-in-One, 28
  SAP Business ByDesign, 29
  SAP Business One, 28–29
SCM. *See* Supply chain management (SCM)
SCS. *See* SAP central services (SCS)
Security configuration wizard, 79
Server architectures
  batch workloads, 142
  high clock speeds, 141
  Intel CPU roadmap, 145
  Intel® Turbo Boost Technology, 143
  inter core communication and access
    NUMA, 144–145
    2-sockets and 4-sockets x86, 145
    uniform memory access, 144
  memory
    capacity *vs.* costs, 149
    DIMM, 148
    operating systems, 148
    size and speed, 148
    speed *vs.* capacity, 148
  multi-core, 142
  multi-thread, 142–143
  parasitic capacitances, 142
  platform certification, 144
  rack mount *vs.* blade servers, 146–147
  scale-up *vs.* scale-out, 146, 147
  subsystems, 141
Server network
  connection, 156
  firewalls, 154
  3-tier architectures, 165
"Server sprawl", 2
Service level agreement (SLA)
  performance management, 43
  quantity and quality, 42
  response times, 46
Service-oriented architecture (SOA), 17–18
Service profile
  auto discovery, 170–171
  bare metal virtualization, 170
  firmware management, 171
  policies, 170
  SAP applications, 169
  UCSM, 170
SLA. *See* Service level agreement (SLA)
SOA. *See* Service-oriented architecture (SOA)
Software as a Service (SaaS), 102
Solid-state drives (SSD)
  consumer *vs.* enterprise class SSD, 152
  cost, 152
  description, 152
  vs. hard-drive disks (HDD), 152
  IO performance, 161
SRM. *See* Supplier relationship management (SRM)
SSM. *See* SAP solution manager (SSM)
Stateless computing
  application mobility, bare metal, 168–169
  cloud data center, 177–180
  cloud operation (*see* Cloud operation, stateless computing)
  HANA and BWA, disaster recovery (DR) site, 169
  SAP license keys
    Cisco UCS, 168
    mobile phone analogy, 168
    servers and service profiles, 168
  server personality, 167
  and service profile (*see* Service profile)
Storage networks, 156–157
Storage system, SAP
  applications, 149
  disk paradox, 149
  in-memory paradox, 151
  input/output (IO) challenge, 149
  Input/Output operations per second (IOPS), 149–150
  operating system tools, 151
  SAPS-meter correlation, 150
  SSD (*see* Solid-state drives (SSD))
  V-shaped relation, 151
Supplier relationship management (SRM), 21–22
Supply chain management (SCM)
  cloud, 21
  defined, 20–21
  LiveCache, 21
  load profile, 60
  RFID, 21

T

Technology economics, cloud computing
  attributes and challenges, 191
  Buying Hierarchy, 190–191
  opportunities and challenges
    hybrid cloud, 192–193
    private cloud, 192
    public cloud, 191–192
  "resource demand" variations, 190
Technology management, CCMS
  baseline, 92
  cloud constructs, 87–88
  configuration management process, 88–89

Technology management (cont.)
  development system, 90–91
  load tests, 92
  modules, 89
  regular testing tools, 91
  SAP technology stack and tools, 91
  service templates and profiles, 89–90
  technical sandbox, 90
Titanium, 135–136
Trojan horses and rootkits, 69

U

UCS. *See* Unified Computing System (UCS)
UCSM. *See* Unified Computing System Management (UCSM)
Unified Computing System (UCS)
  CNAs, 161–162
  description, 161
  Ethernet traffic, 161
  fabric extender, 162–163
  fabric interconnects, 163
  hardware based fabric extender, 165
  IPC, 161
  port extender (PE), 162
  SAN and LAN, 161
  software based fabric extender, 164
  unification and virtualization, 163–164
Unified Computing System Management (UCSM)
  default pools, 176
  ESX kernel, 172
  hardware configuration, 170
  locales, 177
  MAC, 174
  platform emulator, 171
  policy-driven device managers, 173
  remove command, 171
  transaction service, 170
  utility OS runs, 171
  vNIC template, 172
User network
  bandwidth, 153
  connection, 153
  LAN, 153
  latency, 153–154
  load balancers, ACE (*see* Cisco Application Control Engine (ACE))
  security, 154

V

VAF. *See* Virtual appliance factory (VAF)
VDI. *See* Virtual desktop infrastructures (VDI)
Virtual appliance factory (VAF), 135
Virtual desktop infrastructures (VDI), 69
Virtual interface (VIF)
  runtime policy, 172
  VMware, 172
Virtual machines (VMs)
  export/import, 120
  lift and shift application data and configuration, 120
  online-transition, 120
Virtual private cloud (VPC), 128
VMs. *See* Virtual machines (VMs)
VMware's vCenter
  ESX kernel, 172
  runtime policy, VIF, 172
  vNIC connection policies, 172
  vNIC template, 172
VMware vCloud
  building blocks, 115, 116
  description, 115
  Resource Group, 115
  vCenter Chargeback, 115–116
  vCloud Director, 115
  vShield Manager, 115
  vSphere Management Assistant, 116
VPC. *See* Virtual private cloud (VPC)

W

Web service
  architecture and proliferation, SAPS-meter, 57–58
  features, 54–55
  simulation mode, 56
Windows Azure, 8
Windows Azure cloud fabric
  affinity groups, 106
  AWS, 103, 116
  Azure Storage, 108–109
  compute services, 104
  definition, 103
  deployment
    Azure OS, 105–106
    RDFE, 106
    service, 106
  fault and upgrade domains, 107–108
  FC (*see* Fabric controllers (FC))

Microsoft, 103
multi-instance service, 104
new node, control and monitor, 105
portal, 106
structure, 104
top-of-rack router (TOR), 104

Virtual Hard Disk (VHD) file, 107
web and. Net server, 107

Z
Zero-day exploits, 69

MIX
Papier aus verantwortungsvollen Quellen
Paper from responsible sources
FSC® C105338

If you have any concerns about our products,
you can contact us on
ProductSafety@springernature.com

In case Publisher is established outside the EU,
the EU authorized representative is:
**Springer Nature Customer Service Center GmbH
Europaplatz 3, 69115 Heidelberg, Germany**

Printed by Libri Plureos GmbH
in Hamburg, Germany